Oracle Solaris 11.2 System Administration Handbook

Harry Foxwell
Glynn Foster

New York   Chicago   San Francisco
Athens   London   Madrid   Mexico City
Milan   New Delhi   Singapore   Sydney   Toronto

Cataloging-in-Publication Data is on file with the Library of Congress

McGraw-Hill Education books are available at special quantity discounts to use as premiums and sales promotions, or for use in corporate training programs. To contact a representative, please visit the Contact Us pages at www.mhprofessional.com.

Oracle Solaris 11.2 System Administration Handbook

1 2 3 4 5 6 7 8 9 0   DOC/DOC   1 0 9 8 7 6 5

ISBN   978-0-07-184418-5
MHID   0-07-184418-X

Sponsoring Editor	**Copy Editor**	**Composition**
Brandi Shailer	Megha Saini,	Cenveo Publisher Services
	Cenveo Publisher Services	
Editorial Supervisor		**Illustration**
Donna Martone	**Proofreader**	Cenveo Publisher Services
	Cenveo Publisher Services	
Project Manager		**Art Director, Cover**
Kritika Kaushik,	**Indexer**	Jeff Weeks
Cenveo® Publisher Services	Jack Lewis	
Technical Editor	**Production Supervisor**	
Tom Plunkett	Lynn M. Messina	

To Eileen, for enduring all my endless hours at the computer.

Harry Foxwell

To Jayne, Isla, and Emerson for the tireless support
(and patience) as a work-at-home Dad.

Glynn Foster

About the Author

Harry J. Foxwell, PhD is a Principal Consultant for Oracle's Public Sector division based in Reston, Virginia, where he focuses on Operating Systems, Virtualization, and Cloud Computing for Oracle's Public Sector (U.S. Government) customers. He is a coauthor of *Oracle Solaris 11 System Administration: The Complete Reference* (Oracle Press, 2013), *Pro OpenSolaris* (Apress, 2009), and coauthor of several Oracle/Sun white papers, including *READ_ME_FIRST: What Do I Do with All of Those SPARC Threads?* (Oracle Technical White Paper, August 2013). He is also an Adjunct Professor of Computer Science for the Volgenau School of Engineering at George Mason University.

Glynn Foster is a Principal Product Manager for the Oracle Solaris core technologies engineering organization. Glynn is responsible for various Solaris technology areas such as OpenStack, deployment, and lifecycle technologies, including IPS, AI, Unified Archives, Puppet, and Remote Administration Daemon (RAD). Glynn is an active contributor to the Oracle Technology Network. Glynn lives in Wellington, New Zealand.

About the Technical Editor

Tom Plunkett is an active author and technical editor for a number of books on Oracle technology, most recently serving as lead author of *Oracle Big Data Handbook*. Tom is a Principal Consultant with Oracle and teaches Computer Science for Virginia Tech. Tom volunteers for AtrocityWatch, a non-profit organization which uses Big Data for early warning of atrocities and human rights violations. Tom is a frequent public speaker, having presented at over 50 conferences. Tom holds a B.A. and J.D. from George Mason University, an M.S. in Computer Science from Virginia Tech, and has completed graduate coursework in Management Science and Engineering from Stanford University.

Contents

Foreword

Welcome to the (next) Revolution!

If you've been around the industry for any length of time, you know that the world of system administration is changing, in ways that go way beyond simply bringing up a box and keeping it patched. As you'll learn in this book, Oracle Solaris is not just tracking that change, but leading the charge.

This shouldn't be a surprise; hindsight shows that the technologies in Oracle Solaris have more often than not been right at the front of the revolutionary curve. Even the birth of Solaris, via its predecessor SunOS, was a revolution, breaking open previously closed doors to innovation. Sure, we take open interfaces and interoperability for granted today, but the first shots in the platform services revolution were fired when the first mainframe sales rep warned their customer who was daring to look at Sun and UNIX: "Don't get locked into open systems!"

The sign of a good operating platform is that it's continuously sowing the seeds of revolution—before anyone knows what the next revolution is going to be. Just as one example: The Z file system (ZFS) broke countless dusty rules, assumptions, and paradigms, and wound up as a natural fit for flash and hybrid storage, even though it was designed during a time when spinning rust seemed set to rule the data center for decades to come. In Oracle Solaris 11, it becomes the underpinning for amazingly fast, efficient, and resilient provisioning technologies that are not just nice to have, but critical for today's data center transformation.

This brings us to the revolution du jour. Long before the phrase itself ever existed, the *ideas* behind cloud computing have been top of mind with the architects of Solaris. Here the example might be another of our core technologies, Oracle Solaris Zones. They're key to Oracle Solaris' built-in virtualization, and they came about not by the team looking backward at older ideas like mainframe virtual machines, but looking forward and asking the right questions. The big one: if we're deploying a bunch of applications, does each one really need its own operating system instance? Didn't we figure out how to isolate resources, security, and fault management a long time ago? Wasn't that, in short, what operating systems already did?

The result: by designing a virtualized system that leveraged the existing strengths of a robust operating system, the Solaris team built a lightweight, agile, secure container system that allowed developers to build and quickly deploy services that could be lit up, reconfigured, and torn down, without touching (or even needing access to) the underlying system. And you didn't have to change, or even recompile, your existing code. Revolution! This is now what the majority of Oracle Solaris customers are deploying, and some of the ways they're using it are pretty revolutionary, in turn. And this is where revolution morphs into continuous reinvention, as we work with customers to bring in yet more of their suggestions into production. (I could tell you all about these new features, but it turns out Harry and Glynn wrote a whole book about it… .)

The revolution continues, and like all worthwhile revolutions, the ideas spread and take hold elsewhere. Open systems went from being derided by older established companies to becoming key to almost every IT company's strategy. We see the same thing happening with many of the other concepts we've championed in Oracle Solaris over time. Zones were once scoffed at by certain of our competitors; the same ideas are now recognized as key to efficient, reliable micro services and DevOps. The week I'm writing this, the industry is bursting with news about the Open Container Project and Docker—and Oracle's involvement in these projects. This is exciting stuff, because it not only validates everything that's been going on with Oracle Solaris Zones for over a decade; part of the news is that it will be yet another way for people to get Oracle Solaris into their enterprise computing strategy, as the Oracle Solaris team has announced that Docker will be integrated with the technologies you'll be reading about in this very book.

And that takes us back to "continuously sowing the seeds" … as you'll learn in this book, there's a whole garden that's sprung up just between Oracle Solaris 11 and 11.2. But perhaps as big a story are the elements you may be familiar with from elsewhere, such as the integration of OpenStack and Puppet. If you're an experienced admin, but new to Oracle Solaris, you'll find it easier than ever to get to work with stellar new Oracle Solaris features such as Unified Archives and Elastic Virtual Switch, as well as old favorites like Zones and ZFS.

Harry and Glynn have deep experience with not just Oracle Solaris and its associated technologies, but the industry as a whole, and they've spent more time than you can imagine working with customers and communities who are putting these features to the test every day. I think you'll find that expertise shines through in this book. If you're going to join a revolution, this is the right team to have on your side.

Larry Wake
Pleasanton, California
August 2015

Preface

Oracle Solaris operating system is the premier implementation of UNIX, continually innovating and driving change in support of modern enterprise computing. Today's massively parallel servers, used for memory-resident databases, application consolidation, cloud computing, and data analytics ("Big Data"), require powerful and scalable operating systems. System administrators for such servers and operating systems need clear and detailed guidance to cope with the frequent updates and new features so that they can make optimal use of new technologies and methods. And while old, manual procedures are giving way to graphical administrative tools, there is still a requirement to understand the underlying programs and command options that are used to install, configure, customize, monitor, and troubleshoot large, complex IT infrastructures. This book provides that guidance, presenting specific examples and best practices for Solaris 11, including details on the 11.2 release. Oracle continues to support and advance Solaris and the servers it runs on; the chapter contents herein will help readers keep pace with the remarkable advances in operating system capabilities.

Acknowledgments

First, I want to recognize and thank the Solaris community of engineers and consultants at Oracle for their support and sharing of their knowledge of this complex and powerful operating system. I have learned much from them, and am happy to share it in this book. Additionally, our coauthor and contributor Glynn Foster and Joerg Moellenkamp, McGraw-Hill Education editor Brandi Shailer, and technical reviewer Tom Plunkett have all been invaluable in producing this important new reference on Solaris 11.

Harry Foxwell

I would like to thank the following people who have kindly taken time out of their busy schedules to review the chapters I have written in this book—Jesse Butler, Dan Krasinki, Girish Moodalbail, Ethan Quach, Michael Raskey, Cindy Swearingen, and Sean Wilcox. I would also like to thank my colleagues in the Oracle Solaris product management (Alex, Cindy, Duncan, Eve, Joost, Onder and Scott) for keeping things fun all these years. Thanks also to my coauthor, Harry Foxwell, the team at McGraw-Hill Education, contributor Joerg Moellenkamp and the many engineers who have spent many long hours to make Oracle Solaris and this book possible. I hope you enjoy it.

Glynn Foster

Introduction

Who Is This Book for?

We are excited to introduce this second Oracle Press title on Oracle Solaris. *Oracle Solaris 11 System Administration, the Complete Reference*, by Jang, Foxwell, Tran, and Formy-Duval (2011, Oracle Press) was the first book covering Solaris 11. That book introduced the OS to new Solaris users, Linux developers, and administrators of earlier Solaris releases by focusing on selected new Solaris 11 features and basic installation and configuration.

Oracle Solaris 11 System Administration Handbook is directed at current Solaris system administrators. This handbook covers a broad range of topics, including Solaris 11.2's new features like kernel zones, virtual networking, Puppet, and OpenStack. The authors cover major Solaris 11 system administration tasks and practices, including installation, configuration management, zones, networking, performance, and security, along with new Solaris-supported technologies such as Puppet and OpenStack, and presents several example deployment use cases. The book emphasizes the most commonly used system administrator commands usage and procedures and assumes prior knowledge of Solaris 10.

How to Use This Book

Each chapter covers basic Solaris 11 administration and configuration tasks, starting with installation and setup of the OS, network, and zones. Chapters can be read in any order, but may assume knowledge of a previous chapter. We provide examples of typical commands and their output to illustrate how to use and interpret them, including the very helpful and popular *Solaris 11.2 Cheatsheet* contributed by Joerg Mollenkamp. We recommend reading through the book first and trying the commands as you read in order to familiarize yourself with Solaris' new features and best practices. Then you can use this as a handy reminder and reference, especially using the included cheatsheets.

Contents of the Chapters

Chapter 1: Introduction to Solaris 11

Chapter 1 introduces Oracle Solaris 11, reviewing the 11.1 release and highlighting the new features of the 11.2 release. We remind Solaris administrators about the changes from Solaris 10, including the Image Packaging System, the ZFS File System, Automated Installation, Unified Archives, Oracle Solaris Kernel Zones, and new security features. We give an overview of the OS optimizations for Oracle software, and emphasize the Solaris features that support cloud computing. This chapter concludes with instructions for downloading the latest Solaris release.

Chapter 2: Basic Solaris 11 Installation

Chapter 2 begins the detailed examples that we provide in the book for the most common system administration tasks. This chapter covers the requirements for Solaris 11 installation on SPARC and x86 systems using the Live Media, Text Install, and Automated Installation methods. We also describe what to expect when you first log in to a Solaris 11 system, and introduce some basic configuration tasks such as mirroring your root disk, setting ZFS options, adding users, and setting up remote VNC (Virtual Network Computing) login.

Chapter 3: Solaris 11 Lifecycle Management

This chapter introduces some of the key lifecycle management technologies and how they can be used together through development, test, and production environments. We detail how to use boot environments, how to update your system using IPS repositories, how to deploy preconfigured OS/application environments using Unified Archives, and how to set up the Automated Installer service for hands-off multinode installation and deployment.

Chapter 4: Solaris 11 Zones

Chapter 4 reviews the important concepts of Solaris zones, and describes the various types—global, non-global, branded, and the new kernel zones. It describes how to create, configure, and manage these zones, as well as how to relocate a zone from one server to another. We also cover creating the highly secure Immutable Zones, and provide a reminder of how to restrict zone resources for performance or Oracle software licensing purposes. We conclude with a brief discussion of how to choose an Oracle virtualization method.

Chapter 5: Configuring Solaris 11 Networking

Networking in Solaris 11 is significantly different from that in Solaris 10, and in this chapter we cover the new network configuration commands for both physical and virtual interfaces. We provide a chart showing the differences between the two releases, and show how to create a virtual network infrastructure. We include a brief overview of the Solaris 11.2 Elastic Virtual Switch (EVS) feature that can be used with OpenStack (described in Chapter 10).

Chapter 6: Solaris 11 Performance and Observability

Chapter 6 covers the methods and tools for observing and troubleshooting Solaris 11 performance. We review the traditional programs for monitoring OS activity, and include how to use newer programs specific to Solaris 11 and virtualization, including a bit about DTrace. We describe how to monitor software and hardware errors, and show how to watch CPUs, memory, network, and I/O activity in the OS. We briefly discuss how to monitor and optimize ZFS performance, and how to observe zone resource usage.

Chapter 7: Secure Solaris 11 Deployment

This chapter covers Solaris 11 security features, including how to perform secure installation and configuration, verifying IPS software installation, and configuring user access privileges. We also present an overview of Solaris auditing, and review how to create secure zones. We include coverage of the new Solaris 11.2 Compliance tool, and conclude with a review of Solaris 11's certifications with published security standards.

Chapter 8: Installing Applications Using Templates and IPS

In this chapter, we cover the installation of Oracle Solaris 11 into Oracle virtual machine (VM) VirtualBox as a great way to easily evaluate the operating system on a different host platform. We will also take two traditional Oracle applications—Oracle WebLogic Server 12c and Oracle Database 12c—and install them into zones as a best practice for secure application deployment. Finally, we will take a look at the process for creating your own IPS packages and publishing them to a repository for deployment across multiple systems at scale.

Chapter 9: Solaris 11 Configuration Management

This chapter covers the basic and advanced techniques for service and configuration using the Service Management Facility (SMF), and demonstrate how administrators can write their own SMF manifests for applications they would like to keep running on an Solaris system. We also cover the open source utility Puppet that is used for configuration enforcement, how it is integrated into Solaris, and some best practices for starting to deploy a Puppet environment in your data center. Finally, we will touch on the Remote Administration Daemon (RAD), a technology that provides programmatic access to Solaris administration using C, Java, Python and REST based interfaces.

Chapter 10: OpenStack on Solaris 11

In the final chapter we cover OpenStack, an open source cloud platform that provides both Infrastructure as a Service (IaaS) and Platform as a Service (PaaS) capabilities. We discuss the integration points with Solaris technologies, demonstrate how an administrator can quickly install a single-node environment for evaluation and show how this can be used to architect a typical starter multinode cloud environment.

Appendix A: Solaris 11.2 Cheatsheets

This Appendix presents a handy, categorized summary of example command usage for typical administrative tasks, including General Administration, ZFS, Zones, SMF, and Networking.

Appendix B: Solaris 11.3 Preview

Oracle released a beta version of Solaris 11.3 in July 2015; the production release will be available later in 2015. In this Appendix, we preview some new key features of the 11.3 release.

Scope of This Book and Further Study

Oracle's SPARC Solaris servers implement several forms of virtualization: Physical Domains, Logical Domains, and Zones. In this book, we limit our coverage to Solaris Zones. Oracle's infrastructure management tools, such as *Oracle Enterprise Manager* and *Ops Center*, are likewise beyond the scope of this book.

   The authoritative documentation for Solaris is online at the *Oracle Solaris 11.2 Information Library*, **https://docs.oracle.com/cd/E36784_01/**. It comprises several thousand pages of detailed descriptions and examples of Solaris 11.2 features. Readers of this book should consult that reference for further elaboration of those features and for any topic not covered herein.

Typographical Conventions

Program commands and their output are printed in `Courier New` typeface; the system command line prompt will be a '#' character if the command is executed as the `root` user, '$' otherwise. The command and its parameters to be typed are printed in **bold** font, the remainder output is printed in standard font. For example:

```
# ping -a 192.168.1.216
192.168.1.216 (192.168.1.216) is alive
```

   For commands that require a parameter, if we have not provided an example, we have indicated the required parameter in brackets. For example:

```
# ping -a {hostname}
```

That is, the user/reader is expected to provide the required parameter.

CHAPTER
1

Introduction to
Oracle Solaris 11

S ince Oracle Solaris 11 was released in November 2011, there have been two major updates—the 11.1 release in October 2012 and the 11.2 release in July 2014. These updates added significant new technologies and enhancements to Solaris, already regarded as the premier enterprise UNIX operating system for scalability, stability, and security. As enterprise computing has recently evolved to exploit new virtualization capabilities and cloud computing features, these Solaris updates have led the way in delivering mission-critical IT infrastructure for Oracle's industry-leading SPARC servers as well as for servers based on modern Intel processors. In this chapter we present an overview of Oracle Solaris 11's major features, with an emphasis on the most recent 11.2 release. In subsequent chapters, we provide tips, techniques, and advice on how to take advantage of Solaris 11's numerous capabilities.

About Oracle Solaris 11 11/11

The initial Oracle Solaris 11 11/11 release (sometimes referred to as the "11.0 release") was a major change for Solaris system administrators familiar with earlier releases. While the changes required a bit of learning effort, the goal was to dramatically improve the manageability of modern Oracle Solaris servers, with a focus on scalability, virtualization, networking, security, and storage administration. The most dramatic changes from Solaris 10 and earlier versions included:

- **The Image Packaging System (IPS):** This system provides for network-based change management of operating system and application patching and updating. It is a framework for OS and system software lifecycle management that includes safe and verifiable installation and upgrading of software using network, local, or device-based repositories. A major feature of this system is automatic checking of dependencies—a request to install a new component will discover and install any other required components. Additionally, IPS exploits the snapshot and data integrity features of the Oracle ZFS File System to create new boot environments (BEs) even on production systems without interruption, thus minimizing planned downtime and enabling safe and quick reversion to earlier configurations if desired.

- **The ZFS File System (ZFS):** ZFS, first introduced as an option in Solaris 10, is now the default root and boot file system for Solaris 11. ZFS includes scalability features that eliminate the file size and directory size limitations of UNIX File System (UFS), provides data integrity assurance through check-summing of all data and metadata along with copy-on-write data update semantics, and is the foundation for Solaris 11's safe storage, OS, and IPS software management. ZFS is also leveraged to enable the creation and management of Solaris zones, and now includes full support for file system compression, encryption, and deduplication.

- **The Automated Installer (AI)**: Solaris 11 introduced a new framework for automating server installation and provisioning. It integrates with ZFS and IPS to provide network-based services for customized deployment of bootable Solaris OS images to both "bare metal" and virtualized (zones) destinations. AI replaces the Solaris 10 JumpStart utilities, and includes a conversion tool to assist in translating JumpStart profiles to AI manifests. Other installation methods delivered with Solaris 11 include a Live Media image for x86 systems for both learning purposes and for virtualized installation of the GNOME graphical desktop environment, and text-only installation images for both SPARC and x86 systems that lack graphical displays.

- **Solaris Zones**: Solaris 10 introduced an efficient form of OS virtualization that did not require a hypervisor—zones (also called *containers* in some contexts). Solaris 11 has expanded the integration and features of zones, including the ability to create and use a Solaris 10 zone within the Solaris 11 global zone. Additionally, tools are now provided to migrate Solaris environments currently running in zones or on bare metal to zones on different servers using "physical-to-virtual" (p2v) and "virtual-to-virtual" (v2v) utilities. The use of "sparse" and "full" root zones in Solaris 10 has gone away in Solaris 11 due to ZFS's data separation features, linking to IPS images, and the resulting ability to create "immutable" (read-only) zones. Other zone enhancements include the ability to deploy a Network File System (NFS) server within a zone, assigning a separate, full IP stack per zone, and a new performance observability tool, `zonestat`, for monitoring zone resources.

- **Role-Based Security**: By default, the privileged `root` user in Solaris 11 is now a role like any other user whose access rights can be limited. Instead of logging in directly as root, users now log in normally and assume the root role if authorized. The familiar `sudo` tool is included with Solaris 11 for managing privileged program execution.

■ **Networking**: Because Solaris now supports both bare-metal and virtual OS environments, it was necessary to review and enhance how both network hardware and virtualized network interfaces and IP stacks are created, configured, and managed. This work is based on Sun Microsystems' earlier Project Crossbow, which virtualized Solaris' network space allowing the creation of virtual NICs over a virtual switch. Much of the TCP network code had not been updated or optimized for many releases; new feature support and performance improvements were also needed. Solaris 11 introduces new system tools that improve system administrators' abilities to manage and observe real and virtualized network interfaces, allocate network bandwidth resources, and create virtual network topologies that improve system performance and reduce the need for external network hardware. Solaris zones can now have their own exclusive IP stack. Additionally, system administrators can customize server networking features for manual or automatic configuration, create customized names for network interfaces, and manage MAC addresses for virtualized environments.

The preceding text lists only a sample of the many changes from Solaris 10 to Solaris 11 11/11; the sections that follow and the references at the end of this chapter contain additional and more detailed descriptions of those changes and new OS features. Subsequent chapters in this book cover how to use many of the new Solaris capabilities.

NOTE
Unfortunately, there is no magic procedure to simply convert or upgrade a Solaris 10 system to Solaris 11; you must do a new install of the operating system (new Oracle servers come with Solaris 11 preinstalled). This is primarily due to the significant differences created by Solaris 11's dependence on ZFS and IPS for the root/boot file system. Chapter 2 will suggest one method for converting your UFS-based data to ZFS if you are not already using ZFS on Solaris 10 for your user data file systems. Upgrades from Solaris 11 11/11 and beyond are supported using IPS.

The Oracle Solaris 11.1 Update

Oracle Solaris 11.1 was the first update to the operating system, released in November 2011. Many of the changes in this update were simply improvements or enhancements to existing features, or provided new tools to help administer them. Some of the more prominent updates included:

- **AI (Automated Installer) Enhancements**: Added new subcommands to the `installadm` command to improve administration of installation services; added role-based delegation of AI tasks.

- **SMF Manifest Creation Tool**: Added the `svcbundle` utility to ease the creation of SMF manifests; editing of XML files is reduced.

- **Editing of configuration files**: Added the `pfedit` utility allowing delegation of editing permissions for administrative files such as `syslog`.

- **Zones on Shared Storage**: Updated the `zonecfg` command to allow specification of shared (SAN) storage components.

- **Parallel Zone Updates**: Zones configured in Solaris 11 11/11 and Solaris 10 were updated serially, resulting in very long system update times for servers with many zones. Solaris 11.1 now supports updating zones in parallel for significant speedup.

- **Security Enhancements**: Solaris 11.1 supports OpenSCAP compliance reporting and now includes exploit prevention technologies such as address space randomization and prevention of non-privileged memory-based execution.

- **Security Evaluations**: Oracle Solaris 11.1 has been evaluated under the FIPS 140-2 Cryptographic Framework and Common Criteria EAL4+ Protection Profile; it also supports the FIPS 140-2 modes for `ssh` and `sshd`.

- **Network Configuration**: Solaris 11.1 now supports updates to virtual network interface cards (NICs) without interrupting network connectivity.

- **ZFS Enhancements**: ZFS properties can now be easily configured to share file systems using NFS or Common Internet File System (CIFS).

■ **Power Management**: Power for idle central processing units (CPUs) can now be automatically reduced for both x86 and SPARC systems.

■ **x86 Boot Loader**: GRUB2 is now the default boot loader for Intel-based systems.

■ **Observability**: The `mpstat` and `cpustat` tools have been updated to improve the output for systems having very large numbers of hardware threads (CPUs) to make it easier to spot utilization problems.

Solaris 11.1 included many other enhancements; we have reviewed those having the greatest impact on typical OS administration tasks; we provide examples of how to use these enhancements in later chapters.

The Solaris 11.2 Update

Oracle Solaris 11.2 was released in July 2014; it includes a significant number of new features and improvements and is the focus of Oracle's approach to providing an operating system that fully supports cloud computing infrastructures through scalability, OS and network virtualization, security, and ease of management. In this section, we provide brief descriptions of Solaris 11.2's additions and then show you how to use them in the remaining chapters.

■ **Provisioning with Unified Archives**: Because administrators now need to provision both virtual and bare-metal application and OS environments using both types of sources, a new archiving format and utility were needed and are now included with Solaris 11.2. This new capability supports the deployment of physical and virtual images that include both operating systems and applications. The included `archiveadm` utility can also be used to create full system recovery archives.

■ **Kernel Zones**: Earlier Solaris zone implementations were limited to "branded" Solaris 10 zones and to non-global zones that were the same kernel version as that of the underlying global zone. Solaris 11.2 now features full Solaris kernel virtualization within a new kind of zone—a "kernel zone," for both SPARC and x86 servers—that can run at a different kernel version than the global zone and can be independently updated. Kernel zones are created and managed like other Solaris zones using the familiar `zonecfg` and `zoneadm` commands.

- **Software-Defined Networking**: With the increasing focus on virtualized OS environments comes the need for accompanying virtualized network services. In addition to Solaris 11's support for virtual NICs and Ethernet devices, a major addition to Solaris 11.2 is the *Elastic Virtual Switch*, which supports sharing a virtual network across multiple physical nodes using a distributed switch, along with resource management of network bandwidth.

- **Immutable Zones**: Solaris 11.2 now includes the ability to configure both non-global and global zones with read-only root file systems for enhanced security of virtualized environments.

- **Open Source Configuration and Cloud Computing Software**: Solaris 11.2 includes support for Puppet provisioning and configuration software for managing complex infrastructures. Also included is a complete distribution of the OpenStack cloud management system for administration of virtualized compute, network, and storage services.

- **Compliance Checking and Reporting**: A new utility program— `compliance`—is provided to verify system updates and configuration files and monitor potential security compromises.

- **Image Packaging System (IPS) Updates**: IPS can now check and update required firmware versions for certain hardware devices; it also includes a new package for preparing a system for installation of Oracle Database 12c, checking that all dependencies are met for installing that product.

- **Preflight Application Checker**: This bundle of tools is used for checking the readiness of earlier Solaris applications, kernel modules, and device drivers for compliance with Solaris 11 and reports any problems and recommended changes for deployment on the updated OS version.

Solaris 11 End-of-Feature Notifications

As operating systems and hardware evolve, some features become obsolete or are replaced by newer and better components. Oracle Solaris system administrators and application developers should periodically review the published End-of-Feature (EOF) notices to ensure that they are using currently supported features and are aware of any potential removal of programs that they have been using. In particular, Solaris 11 has removed certain programs from the OS environment and has posted notifications that some currently supported programs will not be supported at some future date.

Commonly used programs and services that are no longer available in Solaris 11 include the following:

- `crypt`: Replaced by the `encrypt` command.

- `rdist`: Replaced by `rsync` and `scp` commands.

- **Adobe Flash Player:** No longer available for Solaris.

- **32-bit kernel:** Libraries for 32-bit applications are still supported.

- **LP print services:** Replaced by the Common UNIX Printing System (CUPS).

- **Solaris Management Console:** No longer available; replaced by command line utilities.

- **Application software:** Certain older versions of Web and database software are no longer included or supported, including Apache 1.3, MySQL 5.0, and PostgreSQL.

Some currently supported utilities of Solaris 11 may be removed in future releases, including the `appcert` ABI checker (use the new Preflight Checker instead), the old `pkgmanager` utilities (use IPS instead), and the `/usr/ucb` directory (use the programs in `/usr/bin` instead).

Solaris 11 Optimizations for Oracle Software

As a consequence of today's extraordinarily scalable servers with terabytes of main memory, hundreds or even thousands of processor cores and hardware threads, new types of virtualization technologies, and enterprise-scale applications that demand optimal performance and stability, operating systems like Solaris must continually evolve and scale along with advances in both SPARC and x86 processor and server hardware. Oracle has invested billions of dollars in R&D, optimizing their "hardware and software, engineered to work together," enabled by the fact that they own the intellectual property and engineering resources for the entire "stack" of applications, middleware, database, operating systems, virtualization technologies, SPARC and x86 server hardware, and storage systems. As a result of this ownership, Oracle has developed optimizations in Solaris 11 that benefit specific Oracle applications—like the Oracle database—and also benefit general purpose applications, third-party software, and administrative computing tasks. Some of these optimizations include:

- *A New Virtual Memory System*: Designed to handle large in-memory Oracle applications, predicting and optimizing assignment of memory resources, and supporting very large memory pages. This feature also improves the performance of all memory-intensive applications.

- *Optimized Shared Memory for the Oracle Database*: Allows for the dynamic resizing of the System Global Area (SGA) without restarting the database, and providing for faster database startup.

- *Database and JVM Observability*: Oracle Solaris DTrace probes have been added to the Oracle Database and to the Java VM to support detailed tracing of query and object performance and troubleshooting.

- *Oracle Solaris Studio IDE*: Includes code optimization, parallelization, memory checking, and performance analysis tools for developers deploying applications on Oracle systems. Includes support for Solaris on SPARC and x86 systems, as well as for Oracle Linux. Also supports gcc compiler compatibility.

Solaris 11 The Cloud Operating System

Oracle Solaris 11 has been promoted as the "First Cloud OS." What does this claim mean? "The Cloud" has many definitions and interpretations from various hardware and software vendors, industry analysts, and end users. But a good, objective definition comes from the US National Institute of Standards and Technology (NIST) that defines five key characteristics of cloud computing:

1. *On-Demand Self-Service*: The ability for cloud users and developers to provision compute, network, and storage resources without human intervention.

2. *Broad Network Access*: All cloud services are available from any network access device such as laptops, smartphones, tablets, or workstations.

3. *Resource Pooling*: The cloud infrastructure enables dynamic assignment and sharing of real and virtualized computing resources in order to safely and efficiently serve multiple tenants.

4. *Rapid Elasticity*: Resources for compute tasks are dynamically added or reduced as needed; no intervention is required to manage resource allocations of memory, number of CPUs, or network bandwidth.

5. *Measured Service*: Cloud resources are metered for the purpose of users paying only for the resources they use; this eliminates the need for owning and overprovisioning hardware and software and its associated acquisition and licensing costs.

Solaris 11 supports all five of these capabilities, including the key foundational virtualization technologies on both SPARC and x86 hardware which provide resource pooling and elasticity using dynamic hardware domains, hypervisors for both processor types and operating systems, and efficient non-hypervisor workload virtualization using zones. Additionally, Oracle's Enterprise Management software suite includes features for self-provisioning, automated resource allocation, secure multitenant environments, and pay-for-usage chargeback models. As a result of these features, Oracle now has the richest set of cloud computing infrastructure capabilities and services available from a single vendor.

Summary of Major Changes from Oracle Solaris 10 to Oracle Solaris 11.2

Table 1-1 summarizes the major changes from the Solaris 10 to the Solaris 11.2 release. In subsequent chapters, we detail many of these changes and provide examples that illustrate the most common administrative tasks.

Feature or Command	Oracle Solaris 10	Oracle Solaris 11.2
Installation		
x86 boot loader	GRUB Legacy	GRUB 2
GRUB configuration file	menu.lst	grub.cfg
x86 firmware	BIOS	BIOS and UEFI
GUI installation	CD or DVD	Live Media (x86 only)
Interactive installation	CD or DVD	Text Installer
Automated installation	JumpStart	Automated Installer (AI)
Automated installation configuration	JumpStart rules and profile	AI manifests, system configuration profiles, and client criteria
Disaster recovery/Archive	Flash Archive	Unified Archive
Software Lifecycle		
Software package management	SVR4 and patch commands	IPS pkg command
OS and application upgrades	Live Upgrade (lu)	IPS pkg command and BEs (beadm)

TABLE 1-1.   *Summary of Changes from Solaris 10 to Solaris 11* (continues)

Feature or Command	Oracle Solaris 10	Oracle Solaris 11.2
Storage		
OS root/boot	UFS or ZFS	ZFS
System Configuration		
System configuration	`sys-unconfig` Edit files in `/etc`	`sysconfig` and SMF profiles
Set hostname	Edit `/etc/nodename`	Use `hostname` command
Power management	Edit `/etc/power.cf`	Use `poweradm` command
Networking		
Network configuration	`ifconfig`	`dladm` and `ipadm`
Virtualization		
Zones	Oracle Solaris 10 zones, Oracle Solaris 8 and 9 Legacy Containers	Oracle Solaris 11 Zones, Oracle Solaris 11 Kernel Zones, Oracle Solaris 10 Zones
Security		
System security	Solaris Security Toolkit	Secure by Default `compliance`
User Environment		
Desktop environment	CDE or GNOME	GNOME
Java Environment	Java 6	Java 7 or 8
User Interactive Shell	`ksh`	`bash`
Root account	Full system privileges	`root` as a role
Printer configuration	LP print system	CUPS print system

TABLE 1-1.   *Summary of Changes from Solaris 10 to Solaris 11* (continued)

Oracle Solaris Future

As you can see from the updates and enhancements described earlier in this chapter, Oracle Solaris continues to evolve in order to support advances in processors and servers as well as new IT infrastructure models like cloud computing and Big Data. Oracle will continue to develop and release such innovations and enhancements for Solaris. The publicly available Oracle Solaris/SPARC Roadmap* highlights plans for future SPARC processors and the Solaris features designed to support them. Some of the most exciting developments expected in the next Solaris updates include support for greater processor scalability, and processor hardware accelerators—"Software in Silicon"—for database queries, decompression, data integrity, and Java applications. And Oracle continues to offer the Solaris Binary Compatibility Guarantee that ensures applications running on earlier versions of Solaris will run on future versions; this can eliminate the need to recertify applications when updating the Solaris operating system.

NOTE
*Oracle released a beta version of Solaris 11.3
in July 2015; we review some of its features
in Appendix 2.*

Obtaining Oracle Solaris 11 Software

The easiest way to get Oracle Solaris 11 is to download it from the Oracle Technology Network (OTN) at http://www.oracle.com/technetwork/server-storage/solaris11/downloads. This site contains a wealth of information about the various Solaris 11 installation options, including installs from DVD, USB, and network; it also includes a link to VM templates that make it easier to start using Solaris. We cover the use of these templates in Chapter 9.

NOTE
*Oracle no longer offers physical media for the
Solaris operating system; users should download
the DVD or USB image files and then create
physical media as needed.*

---

*http://www.oracle.com/us/products/servers-storage/servers/sparc/oracle-sparc/sparc-roadmap-slide-2076743.pdf

Summary

In this chapter, we have reviewed some of the major features of the three most recent Oracle Solaris 11 releases, how to obtain Solaris software, documentation, and support, and presented a brief glimpse of Oracle's future plans for the operating system. The remaining chapters will now focus on how to take advantage of the many special capabilities of Solaris 11.

References

What's New in Solaris 11

Oracle Solaris 11 11/11 What's New,
http://www.oracle.com/technetwork/server-storage/solaris11/documentation/
solaris11-whatsnew-201111-392603.pdf

Oracle Solaris 11.1 What's New,
http://www.oracle.com/technetwork/server-storage/solaris11/documentation/
solaris11-1-whatsnew-1732377.pdf

Oracle Solaris 11.2 What's New,
http://docs.oracle.com/cd/E36784_01/pdf/E52463.pdf

Oracle Solaris 11.2 Information Library,
http://docs.oracle.com/cd/E36784_01/

Transitioning from Oracle® Solaris 10 to Oracle Solaris 11.2,
http://docs.oracle.com/cd/E36784_01/html/E39134/index.html

Frequently Asked Questions (FAQs)

Oracle Solaris 11.2 Frequently Asked Questions,
http://www.oracle.com/technetwork/server-storage/solaris11/documentation/
solaris-11-2-faqs-2191871.pdf

Cloud Computing

The NIST Definition of Cloud Computing,
http://csrc.nist.gov/publications/nistpubs/800-145/SP800-145.pdf

Oracle Press Publications

Oracle Solaris 11 System Administration: The Complete Reference,
http://www.mhprofessional.com/product.php?isbn=007179042X

OCA Oracle Solaris 11 System Administration Exam Guide (Exam 1Z0-821),
http://www.mhprofessional.com/product.php?isbn=0071775749

Additional Resources

Oracle Technology Network,
http://www.oracle.com/technetwork/server-storage/solaris11/overview/index.html

Oracle Solaris Social Media

Blogs, https://blogs.oracle.com/

Facebook, http://facebook.com/solaris

LinkedIn, http://www.linkedin.com/groups/Oracle-Solaris-Insider-3951282

YouTube, http://www.youtube.com/oraclesolaris

Twitter, https://twitter.com/ORCL_Solaris

Oracle Solaris Training and Support

Training,
http://www.oracle.com/technetwork/server-storage/solaris11/training/index.html

Support,
http://support.oracle.com (Support subscription required)

For Users of Other UNIX Systems

Migrate to Oracle Solaris 11,
http://www.oracle.com/technetwork/server-storage/solaris11/overview/evaluate-1530234.html

Oracle Solaris 11 System Administration for Experienced UNIX/Linux Administrators course,
http://education.oracle.com/pls/web_prod-plq-dad/db_pages.getpage?page_id=609&get_params=dc:D82701

CHAPTER
2

Basic Installation
and Updates

Solaris 11 is available for both SPARC and x86 systems from Oracle, and for systems from other x86 hardware vendors. New systems purchased from Oracle include options to have Solaris 10 or 11 preinstalled. Installation options include interactive graphical methods and non-graphical methods using media-based or network-based OS boot images. System administrators can also create custom boot images that include specific software packages. In this chapter, we describe these various installation options and show you how to perform the most common installation and update tasks.

Installation Requirements

System hardware requirements for installing Solaris 11 vary according to the processor architecture and desired system deployment. The OS can be installed on x86 laptops and desktop workstations, as well as on both physical and virtual systems ranging from small, single-processor servers to large, enterprise-class, multiprocessor servers. Solaris 11.2 for x86 can be installed as a virtual machine guest on hypervisors such as Oracle VM, Oracle VM VirtualBox, and VMware. Minimal system memory needed for basic installation is 1.5 GB for x86 systems and 2.0 GB for SPARC systems, although you will likely want more memory available if you plan to use virtualization technologies or use large, memory-intensive applications. Disk space requirements also vary according to expected usage, from at least 6 GB for a minimal server install to at least 13 GB for an x86 desktop workstation that includes the GNOME graphical user interface (GUI). Again, you will want additional disk space for user data and applications.

Oracle Hardware Compatibility List

Solaris 11 is, of course, supported on servers sold by Oracle. If you plan to install Solaris 11 on non-Oracle systems, you should check the Oracle Hardware Compatibility List (HCL) for your system and devices:

- http://www.oracle.com/webfolder/technetwork/hcl/data/s11ga/index.html
- http://www.oracle.com/webfolder/technetwork/hcl/devicelist/index.html

Generally, Solaris 11 for x86 systems will install directly on many laptops and desktop workstations, although drivers for certain graphics processors or wireless network devices might not be available. Check NVIDIA's UNIX Driver Archive for potential Solaris graphics drivers at http://www.nvidia.com/object/unix.html. In the event that no suitable drivers are available, installation in a virtual environment such as VirtualBox might be a better alternative, as we have described in Chapter 8.

If you plan to use Kernel Zones (described in Chapter 4), there are additional processor and system requirements:

■ *for SPARC systems*: T4, T5, M5, or M6 servers with supported updated firmware

■ *for x86 systems*: Modern Intel or AMD processors that support hardware virtualization such as VT-x(Intel) or AMD-V (AMD) and Extended Page Tables (Intel Nehalem processors or later, and AMD Barcelona processors or later), and are enabled in the system's BIOS.

■ *memory*: a minimum of 8 GB of RAM

One important fact to remember is that since nearly all of the Solaris 11 source code is common to both SPARC and x86 systems (with the exception of some installation and device driver differences), OS features such as the ZFS File System (ZFS), configuration tools, Image Packaging System (IPS), DTrace, zones, and security capabilities are essentially identical on both processor platforms. This means that if you want to learn and experiment with Solaris 11, you can install it on an x86 laptop, desktop, or virtual machine (VM) and explore its features and then apply what you've learned to SPARC-based servers. We discuss any important differences between the two processor environments in this and remaining chapters.

Solaris 11 Installation on x86 Systems

Your choice of an OS installation method for Solaris 11 on x86 systems will depend on your purpose. Are you just testing it to learn and explore its features? In that case, you might use the Live Media installation for your laptop or workstation. If you are ready to deploy Solaris 11 on an Oracle x86 or on other vendor's server, then you would choose either the Text Install or Automated Installer (AI) method. Installation in a VM using VirtualBox is covered in Chapter 8.

GUI/Live Media Installation for x86 Systems

A "Live Media" installation is based on a loadable OS image that boots and runs in your system's memory without disturbing your currently installed OS and files. The purpose of this approach is to allow exploration of the OS features without actually installing the OS on your system's hard disk. This method is commonly used with many Linux distributions; it's also used to start up Solaris 11 instances on x86 laptops and workstations running Windows or other base operating systems. You can boot the Solaris 11 Live media from a DVD image or USB image.

You might need to alter your system's BIOS boot order parameters to allow booting from a DVD or USB memory device. See your system's hardware documentation for how to do this. Usually it involves hitting the F2 or F4 function key as the system is booting up, then using the BIOS or Unified Extensible Firmware Interface (UEFI) menu options to change the boot order to allow recognition of the DVD or USB device to be checked before trying to boot from the hard disk. Additionally, many Intel desktop systems now use the UEFI and Secure Boot parameter. This can prevent booting of OS images which are not digitally signed; typically it is only Microsoft operating systems that are signed in this manner, although Solaris will boot if the UEFI firmware is at least version 2.1. So, in order to boot a non-MS operating system such as Linux or Solaris on your x86 workstation or laptop, you might need to disable the Secure Boot parameter in the UEFI menu if your system has old UEFI firmware.

Booting from a Live Media DVD

As we wrote in Chapter 1, you can download Oracle Solaris 11 DVD boot images from http://www.oracle.com/technetwork/server-storage/solaris11/downloads/index.html. You must first read, understand, and accept the Oracle License Agreement for Solaris prior to installing and using the software. You may use Solaris for testing and learning purposes without a software support license; any production use requires an *Oracle Premier Support* license, or an *Oracle Solaris Premier Subscription for non-Oracle Hardware*. Note that servers purchased from Oracle include production use licenses, while non-Oracle systems require purchase of separate production-use license subscriptions.

To install Oracle Solaris 11.2 on an x86 laptop, workstation, or server using a DVD, download the `sol-11_2-live-x86.iso` image and use one of your other systems to create the DVD. Then boot your target system from that DVD, and you will see the Live Media startup menu screen shown in Figure 2-1.

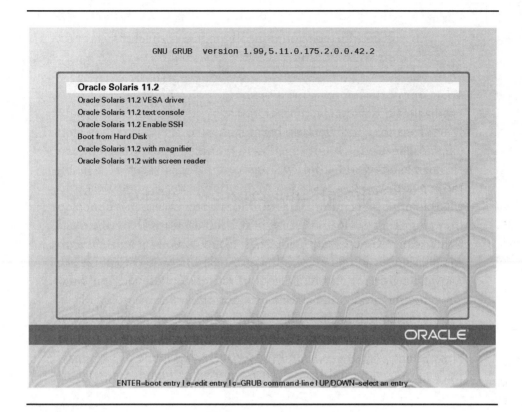

GNU GRUB version 1.99,5.11.0.175.2.0.0.42.2

Oracle Solaris 11.2
Oracle Solaris 11.2 VESA driver
Oracle Solaris 11.2 text console
Oracle Solaris 11.2 Enable SSH
Boot from Hard Disk
Oracle Solaris 11.2 with magnifier
Oracle Solaris 11.2 with screen reader

ORACLE

ENTER=boot entry I e=edit entry I c=GRUB command-line I UP/DOWN=select an entry

FIGURE 2-1. *The Live Media startup menu*

Choose the first option on that menu to boot the in-memory instance of
Solaris 11.2. If the graphical interface fails to display, you might try the second
option with the VESA driver. The boot process should start, display some
device initialization messages, and then ask you to select your keyboard
and preferred language. If all goes well, you should then see the Live Media
Solaris 11 Environment screen in Figure 2-2.

What you see here is a memory-based OS environment that you can use
to explore some of the basic features of Solaris 11. Note that there are options
available for partitioning your system disk using GParted and for checking
required device drivers; we discuss these later. But we are concerned here
now with direct installation on your system, assuming that is your intent.
Don't select the "Install Oracle Solaris" option if you do not want to replace
your previously installed OS such as Windows; in that case you should
consider installing Solaris as a VM using VirtualBox (see Chapter 8).

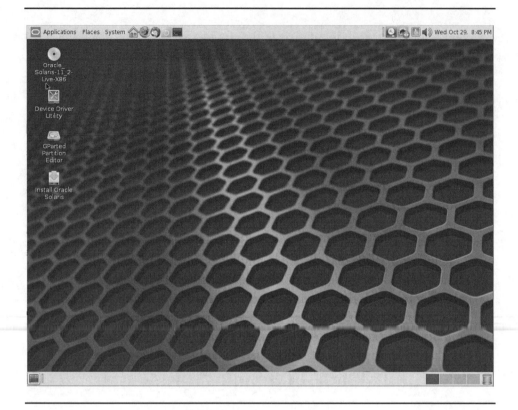

FIGURE 2-2. *The Live Media Solaris 11 environment*

If you do intend to install Solaris 11 *directly* on your system, double-click on the "Install Oracle Solaris" icon and follow the installation and configuration instructions on the subsequent screens. You will need to select your target disk, specify your date, time, and time zone, and choose a login name and password for the initial user. The initially defined user will have root-like system configuration privileges; the initial root password will be the same as for that user, and will require a change upon the first root login. The install process will start, copying Solaris system files to your system's disk. Reboot from the hard disk when this copying process is finished, then complete the installation by logging in and making any needed configuration changes. Note that by default, Solaris will use DHCP for assigning an initial network address; see Chapter 5 for additional details on configuring network services.

Booting from a Live Media USB Memory Device

In order to boot your x86 system from a USB memory device, first download the x86 Live Media image at http://download.oracle.com/otn/solaris/11.2/ sol-11_2-live-x86.usb to your Windows, OS X, Linux, or other system. Don't simply copy the file to the USB device; the file must be installed on the device as a bootable image. On UNIX-like systems such as OS X and Linux, this is typically accomplished using the dd program. After you insert the USB device into an available port on your system, you must identify its device name; on OS X and Linux, it will generally be something like /dev/disk3. Then copy the image to that device, for example:

 # **dd if=sol-11_2-live-x86.usb of=/dev/disk3 bs=16k**

You can now boot your x86 system from this image in the same way as we described previously for the DVD image, assuming you have set your system's boot order to check the USB device before the hard disk.

NOTE
Occasionally, the Live Media GUI installation fails on some laptops and desktops. In that case, you can try the Text Install method described in the following section and then add the desktop GUI components later using IPS.

The Interactive Text Installer Image

If you intend to install Solaris 11 on a server or on a system that has no suitable graphics hardware and driver, you can use one of the Interactive Text Installer images at:

http://www.oracle.com/technetwork/server-storage/solaris11/downloads/ index.html

and then proceed with your installation as described earlier. Note that the Text Installer images include software packages more appropriate for servers; they do *not* include the GNOME desktop package. However, after text-based installation, you can use IPS to add the desktop software using:

 # **pkg install group/system/solaris-desktop**

```
Welcome to the Oracle Solaris installation menu

          1  Install Oracle Solaris
          2  Install Additional Drivers
          3  Shell
          4  Terminal type (currently sun-color)
          5  Reboot

Please enter a number [1]: █
```

FIGURE 2-3. *The Text Installer main menu*

Text-based installation proceeds much like the GUI-based process. Select your preferred language and keyboard, then you'll see the Text Installer menu shown in Figure 2-3. Select the Install Oracle Solaris option.

At this selection, you will be presented with a text-based display like the Installation Screen shown in Figure 2-4 that is navigated using your keyboard's TAB and function keys.

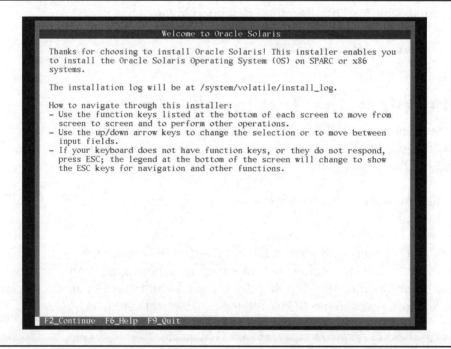

FIGURE 2-4. *The Solaris text-based installation screen*

The installation continues from this point, asking you to select your target boot disk. Generally, it is preferable to assign an *entire disk* to the ZFS root pool device.

Installation on SPARC Systems

You can install Solaris 11 on SPARC servers using the Text Installer; Live Media installation is *not* available for that platform. The installation process is similar to that for x86 systems, although the SPARC boot process and interface is different. Download and create DVD or USB boot media as described previously, only now selecting one of the SPARC images at:

■   http://www.oracle.com/technetwork/server-storage/solaris11/
    downloads/index.html

When a SPARC server without an installed OS powers up, the boot interface will simply display an "ok>" prompt. Not all SPARC servers have integrated DVD drives; external USB-based DVD drives can be attached so that you can boot from the DVD boot image. Alternatively, you can boot SPARC systems from a USB image and device. The show-disks command will list available internal and inserted/attached devices, including DVDs and USBs. Then, at the ok> prompt, boot the system from your prepared boot device's name, for example

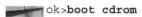ok>**boot cdrom**

or

ok>**boot /pci@400/pci@0/pci@9/pci@0/usb@0,2/hub@2/storage@2/disk**

System bootup and initial configuration will then proceed just as it did for the x86 systems we discussed earlier.

What You'll See When You Log In

After you have performed a basic installation, there are numerous additional observations, tasks, and customizations that you will need to or want to perform, such as configuring your ZFS data file systems, adding storage devices, creating zones and virtual network components, adding users, and implementing data protection and access policies. While much of the Solaris 11 environment may look familiar to Solaris 10 administrators and UNIX users, there are important differences to be aware of. Some of these initial postinstall issues are described next.

The Solaris 11 Login Environment

When you log in to your newly installed Solaris 11 system, you will notice many similarities to earlier Solaris versions, along with some notable differences. The initial user you created during installation has administrative privileges. By default, *and by design*, you cannot log in directly as `root`. The `root` user and its privileges are now role-based and fully configurable and *auditable*; no longer is `root` the all-powerful master of the system.

NOTE
Although it is now considered very poor security practice to allow remote and direct `root` *logins to a Solaris system, that older practice can still be enabled. However, we strongly recommend against it. But if you must, for some reason, implement remote or direct* `root` *logins, log in as the admin user (the first user created during installation),* `su` *to* `root` *or use the* `sudo` *program, and do the following:*

edit the `/etc/ssh/sshd_config` *file and set* `PermitRootLogin=yes`
edit the `/etc/default/login` *file and comment out the* `CONSOLE=/dev/login` *entry*
execute # **`rolemod -K type=normal root`**

Some Postinstallation Tasks

After your initial installation of the operating system, you should familiarize yourself with the differences and similarities between Solaris 10 and Solaris 11.

The top-level root directory looks familiar:

```
# cd /
# ls
bin        dev       home      mnt      platform   rpool     usr
boot       devices   kernel    net      proc       sbin      var
cdrom      etc       lib       nfs4     rmdisk     system
Desktop    export    media     opt      root       tmp
#
```

but it is based on ZFS. That is, all the traditional UNIX root directories are there but are now part of the `rpool` ZFS root pool:

```
# zpool list
NAME    SIZE   ALLOC   FREE   CAP   DEDUP   HEALTH   ALTROOT
rpool   928G   34.5G   893G   3%    1.00x   ONLINE   -
# zfs list
NAME                              USED    AVAIL   REFER   MOUNTPOINT
rpool                             34.7G   879G    4.96M   /rpool
rpool/ROOT                        14.1G   879G    31K     legacy
rpool/ROOT/solaris                16.3M   879G    7.50G   /
rpool/ROOT/solaris/var            5.13M   879G    352M    /var
rpool/VARSHARE                    156K    879G    62K     /var/share
rpool/VARSHARE/pkg                63K     879G    32K     /var/share/pkg
rpool/VARSHARE/pkg/repositories   31K     879G    31K     /var/share/pkg/repositories
rpool/VARSHARE/zones              31K     879G    31K     /system/zones
rpool/dump                        4.08G   879G    3.96G   -
rpool/export                      14.5G   879G    32K     /export
rpool/export/home                 14.5G   879G    32K     /export/home
rpool/export/home/hfoxwell        14.5G   879G    14.5G   /export/home/hfoxwell
rpool/swap                        2.06G   879G    2.00G   -
#
```

Also notice that your default login shell is `Bash`, which is a more modern shell that provides command-line editing and improved programming features:

```
# ps
  PID TTY         TIME CMD
 1977 pts/2       0:00 su
 2004 pts/2       0:00 ps
 1978 pts/2       0:00 bash
#
```

Displaying Your System Characteristics

Although you may be aware of what your system's hardware and software *should be*, it is good practice to observe and verify how the system is actually configured. For example, you can display the version of Solaris that is running in several ways:

```
# uname -a
SunOS narya 5.11 11.2 i86pc i386 i86pc
# cat /etc/release
                         Oracle Solaris 11.2 X86
Copyright (c) 1983, 2014, Oracle and/or its affiliates. All rights reserved
                         Assembled 23 June 2014
# pkg list entire
NAME (PUBLISHER)                               VERSION                   IFO
entire                                         0.5.11-0.175.2.1.0.2.1     i—
```

The latter method shown above using the IPS pkg command is important in that it shows the exact full OS release version you have installed and booted; you might need that information later for support and bug fix purposes.

The isainfo and psrinfo commands will display data about the x86 or SPARC processor installed on your system, including the number of hardware threads that Solaris has discovered.

```
# isainfo -v
64-bit amd64 applications
avxxsavepclmulqdqaesmovbe sse4.2 sse4.1 ssse3 amd_lzcntpopcnttscp
ahf cx16 sse3 sse2 ssefxsr mmx cmovamd_sysc cx8 tscfpuefs bmi2 avx2
        bmi1 f16c fmardrand
32-bit i386 applications
avxxsavepclmulqdqaesmovbe sse4.2 sse4.1 ssse3 amd_lzcntpopcnttscp
ahf cx16 sse3 sse2 ssefxsr mmx cmovsep cx8 tscfpuefs bmi2 avx2 bmi1
f16cfmardrand
# psrinfo -pv
The physical processor has 4 virtual processors (0-3)
x86 (GenuineIntel 306C3 family 6 model 60 step 3 clock 3193 MHz)
        Intel(r) Core(tm) i5-4460  CPU @ 3.20GHz
# psrinfo
0       on-line    since 11/10/2014 14:35:02
1       on-line    since 11/10/2014 14:35:05
2       on-line    since 11/10/2014 14:35:05
3       on-line    since 11/10/2014 14:35:05
```

The prtconf command will display detailed information about your hardware configuration; the first few lines of the output will include the amount of memory installed and active on your system.

```
# prtconf
System Configuration:  Oracle Corporation   i86pc
Memory size: 16301 Megabytes
System Peripherals (Software Nodes):
…(output truncated)…
```

Mirroring Your Boot Disk

One of the first tasks that should be performed on servers with multiple disk devices is to enable disk mirroring on the boot device. A quick way to observe the needed logical device names for candidate disk drives is to use the `format` command:

```
# format
Searching for disks...done
AVAILABLE DISK SELECTIONS:
       0. c3t0d0<ATA-HITACHI H7210CA3-A39D-931.51GB>
          /pci@0,0/pci1028,622@1f,2/disk@0,0
       1. c3t2d0<ATA-HITACHI H7210CA3-A39D-931.51GB>
          /pci@0,0/pci1028,622@1f,2/disk@2,0
Specify disk (enter its number):
```

In this example, we see two identical disks. The first, c3t0d0, is where Solaris was initially installed, and we happen to know that the second disk, c3t2d0, is currently unused so we can set it up as a root mirror:

```
# zpool attach rpool c3t0d0 c3t2d0
```

Note that these device names by default point to block devices in the /dev/dsk directory; you can change the default directory or you can explicitly indicate the full device path name.

You will probably want to add some users along with their home directories, but before you do, you might want to consider setting some ZFS parameters for their file systems, such as compression, encryption, or deduplication. For example, if you want to save disk space by using compression, create or set that option using the `zfs` command:

```
# zfs create -o compression=on rpool/{newfsname}
```

or

```
# zfs set compression=on rpool/{existingfsname}
```

Any *new* data stored on these file systems will be compressed. To encrypt data on a *new* file system, set that option as follows:

```
# zfs create -o encryption=on rpool/{newfsname}
```

You will be asked to supply a password/passphrase (remember it!). Any *new data* written to that file system will then be encrypted. ZFS on Solaris 11 now also supports deduplication (elimination of duplicate disk data blocks); this also can save significant disk space. To create or set that feature, use the following:

```
# zfs create -o dedup=on rpool/{newfsname}
# zfs set dedup=on rpool/{existingfsname}
```

New data written to these file systems will use deduplication.

To verify the setting of a ZFS dataset parameter use

```
# zfs list -o {option} rpool/{fsname}
```

So, before adding users, consider setting one or more of these options on the `rpool/export/home` file system.

Adding Users

There are two methods of adding users: the `useradd` command and a GUI utility. For servers without the desktop tools installed, you must use the former. The `useradd` command will assign default values for the user's home directory, login shell, and UID/GID numbers, although you can provide those values explicitly:

```
# useradd jsmith
# useradd -m -d /export/home/jdoe -u 200 -g 70 -s /bin/csh jdoe
```

and you can then display what has been added:

```
# tail /etc/passwd
...
jsmith:x:102:10::/export/home/jsmith:/usr/bin/bash
jdoe:x:200:70::/export/home/jdoe:/bin/csh
```

If you prefer to use the GNOME graphical interface tools to manage your system, and specifically for adding users and setting their permissions, select the *System->Administration->User_Manager* drop-down menu item and enter the desired values in the *User Manager GUI* as shown in Figures 2-5 and 2-6.

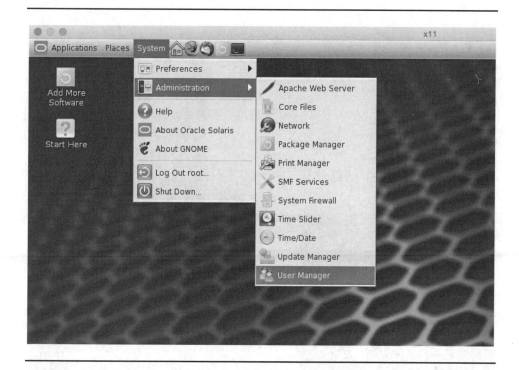

FIGURE 2-5.   *The System Administration User Manager Menu*

Setting Up the VNC Server Graphical Interface

The GNOME GUI environment provides a rich and easy-to-use interface for using your system and managing its features; if you've installed in on a desktop using the Live Media method, the GUI is of course directly available to you. But if you have installed the `solaris-desktop` group on your server and want to access the GUI remotely, then you need to set up a Virtual Network Computing (VNC) service. Fortunately, this is fairly simple. Edit the `/etc/gdm/custom.conf` file and add `DisallowTCP=false` under the `[security]` item, and `Enable=true` under the `[xdmcp]` item. Then configure the X-server property to allow for remote connections:

```
# svccfg -s application/x11/x11-server
svc:application/x11/x11-server> setprop options/tcp_listen = boolean: true
svc:application/x11/x11-server> end
```

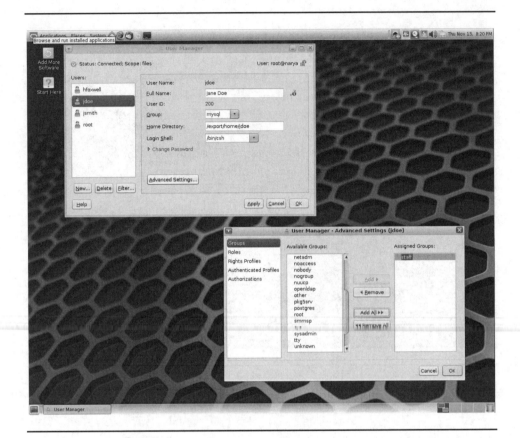

FIGURE 2-6.   *The Solaris 11 User Manager GUI*

Next, configure the VNC service startup property to include your desired screen resolution, for example:

```
# svccfg -s xvnc-inetd
svc:/application/x11/xvnc-inetd>setpropinetd_start/exec = astring: "/usr/bin/Xvnc
-geometry 1024x768 -inetd -query localhost -once securitytypes=none"
svc:/application/x11/xvnc-inetd>end
```

Finally, you must restart the gdm and xvnc-inetd services:

```
# svcadm restart gdm
# svcadm restart xvnc-inetd
```

After this VNC setup procedure, you should be able to use VNC client software from another system on your network to connect to and display the Solaris graphical login screen.

NOTE
*This VNC setup method also works for setting
up GUI desktop access to non-global zones
on your system.*

Automated Installation

The Solaris 11 Automated Installer (AI) framework includes configuration
tools and methods for "hands-free" installation of individual or multiple
Solaris OS images using network-based repositories. Typical setup requires
an "install server" which can be an x86 or SPARC system; it can host both
x86 and SPARC OS images. In this section we describe a basic AI setup.

The AI Server

Any Solaris 11 system with sufficient memory and disk space can be an AI
server, including x86 laptops and servers, SPARC systems, and virtual OS
instances such as zones. Performance and efficiency of an AI server will of
course depend on its compute and I/O capabilities, the speed of your local
network, and how many different client servers will boot from it. Each client
OS and architecture will need its own set of images, which are typically
around 400 MB.

AI uses the `installadm` program. Verify that it is installed, and if not, use
IPS to install it:

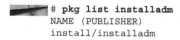
```
# pkg list installadm
NAME (PUBLISHER)                              VERSION                 IFO
install/installadm                            0.5.11-0.175.2.0.0.42.2  i--
```

Alternatively, if it is not already installed:

```
# pkg install install/installadm
```

The AI server will present Solaris OS images to clients. For example,
you can make the image available by starting the service and pointing to
its disk location:

```
# installadm create-service -s /root/Downloads/sol-11_2-ai-x86.iso
```

You must inform the AI service of the MAC address for clients that will boot from the server, for example:

```
# installadm create-client -n solaris11_2-i386 -e {clientMACaddr}
```

or

```
# installadm create-client -n solaris11_2-sparc -e {clientMACaddr}
```

Booting an x86 client using this method might require a change in the client's BIOS boot order specification; for SPARC systems, at the OK prompt, specify:

```
ok> boot net:dhcp - install
```

Your text-based OS installation will proceed as we showed in the previous section. We will cover more about AI setup in Chapter 3.

Updating Your Operating System

There is no direct way to upgrade a Solaris 10 system to Solaris 11, this is due to Solaris 11's dependence on ZFS boot and IPS requirements. So, you must do a fresh install of Solaris 11. You'll need to archive your user data and applications from your Solaris 10 system then reinstall them on the Solaris 11 system. If your data is already on a different Solaris 10 ZFS, transferring your data is quite easy—use the zfs send command from the source system and accept the data using zfs receive on the destination system. For example:

```
# zfs send rpool/{sourcefilesysname} | ssh {remote sys name} zfs
receive rpool/{destfilesysname}
```

If your data is on a UNIX File System (UFS), first save it using the ufsdump command:

```
# ufsdump {ufsfilesysname} -f {dumpfilename}
```

Then create a ZFS on the target system and restore the data to that file system:

```
# zfs create rpool/{newfsname}
# cd /rpool/{newfsname}
# ufsrestore rvf {dumpfilename}
```

A convenient way to migrate data from a Solaris 10 UFS on one server to a new Solaris 11 ZFS on a new server is to use a ZFS feature called *shadow migration*. This method creates a new ZFS file system on the destination server and streams data to as it is accessed from a local or remote UFS, typically mounted using Network File System (NFS). If this feature has not already been installed, use IPS to install and enable it:

```
# pkg install shadow-migration
# svcadm enable svc:/system/filesystem/shadowd:default
```

Then, on the destination Solaris 11 server:

```
# zfs create -o shadow=nfs://remoteS10system/export/home/{ufsdata} rpool/{destdata}
```

and the data will be gradually migrated from the UFS file system to the new ZFS file system. You can monitor the progress of this migration using the shadowstat command. Note that the source UFS file system should be *idle* or *read-only*, and the destination ZFS file system should be new and empty. This migration process may take many minutes or even hours depending on the amount of data to be transferred and the speed of your network.

Once you are using Solaris 11, however, updates from Solaris 11.1 to 11.2 and future updates can be accomplished with a few simple IPS commands. For example, if you are planning to use Oracle's *public* package repositories, first verify your IPS repository publisher using the pkg program:

```
# pkg publisher
PUBLISHER                    TYPE    STATUS P LOCATION
solaris                      origin  online F http://pkg.oracle.com/solaris/release/
```

If you have registered your system and have an active HW/SW support contract, you would update your system from Oracle's online repository at https://pkg.oracle.com/solaris/support/ or from an internal repository as described in Chapter 3. Whichever repository is being used, use the IPS pkg command to update your OS then execute the update as follows:

```
# pkg update --accept
```

and IPS will download and install any updates to the OS and system software. Additionally, IPS will create a new boot environment (BE) for the update; reboot your system to activate it. One nice feature of this approach is that if you don't like the results of the update, you can revert to an earlier BE as described in the next chapter.

Installing and Updating Application Software Using IPS

The IPS we described earlier provides tools and methods for installing and updating system software and updating OS releases.

Testing Solaris 10 Applications for Solaris 11 Readiness

Oracle guarantees that applications developed on earlier versions of Solaris will run on current and future OS releases given that standard Solaris APIs (application program interface) and development practices have been used. In order to verify this, Solaris 11.2 now includes the *Preflight Applications Checker*—a set of software tools that analyze Solaris 10 applications for compliance with Solaris development standards. In combination with the Oracle Solaris Studio development environment, you can validate your applications, device drivers, and kernel modules to ascertain that they will work properly on Solaris 11.2. Additionally, the included *Application Analyzer Tool* can check applications for inefficiencies and make recommendations for improvements based on new Solaris features. The Solaris Preflight Checker is available for both SPARC and x86 systems from http://www.oracle .com/technetwork/server-storage/solaris11/downloads/preflight-checker-tool-524493.html

To further assist Solaris application developers, Oracle provides a community Web site at http://www.oracle.com/technetwork/systems/solaris-developer/index.html that includes tutorials, best practice recommendations, ISV support programs, and help with migrating applications from other OS environments such as Linux, AIX, and HP-UX. This site also includes a list of the many ISV applications certified to run on Solaris 11.

Summary

In this chapter, we have described the various interactive methods for installing Solaris 11, including both graphical and text-based procedures; these are similar or identical on both x86 and SPARC systems. We have also highlighted some key tasks and features that assist in migrating your data and application environment from Solaris 10 to Solaris 11, with an emphasis on ZFS. In the following chapters, we focus on configuring and managing Solaris 11 systems after you have installed the OS.

References

Installing Oracle Solaris 11.2 Systems,
https://docs.oracle.com/cd/E36784_01/html/E36800/index.html

Updating to Oracle Solaris 11.2,
https://docs.oracle.com/cd/E36784_01/html/E39499/index.html

Adding and Updating Software in Oracle Solaris 11.2,
https://docs.oracle.com/cd/E36784_01/html/E36802/index.html

Oracle Solaris Studio,
http://www.oracle.com/technetwork/server-storage/solarisstudio/overview/
index.html

Installing Oracle Solaris 11.2 on VMware,
http://partnerweb.vmware.com/GOSIG/Solaris_11.html

Migrate to Solaris 11,
http://www.oracle.com/technetwork/server-storage/solaris11/overview/
evaluate-1530234.html

CHAPTER
3

Lifecycle Management

Oracle Solaris 11 includes a complete and integrated set of technologies for managing the end-to-end software lifecycle of systems in the data center. One of the biggest causes of system downtime in today's IT operations is due to human error. Solaris 11 technologies help to automate complex lifecycle management tasks at scale, helping administrators be more responsive and agile.

In this chapter, we will cover how the combination of boot environments (BEs) and the Image Packaging System (IPS) provide for fail-safe system update, allowing administrators to quickly ensure that systems are updated with the latest security fixes while minimizing system downtime. We will take a look at Unified Archives which allows administrators the ability to take a clone of an existing environment and rapidly deploy it at scale to other systems in the data center or restore a system in a disaster recovery scenario. Finally, we will cover the Automated Installer (AI) which provides secure end-to-end provisioning of systems in a hands-off manner.

Boot Environments

Boot environments are instances of a Solaris environment that can be booted. An instance includes the base operating system and any other application software that has been installed. This feature takes advantage of the fact that the ZFS File System is the default underlying file system in Solaris 11, and thus can be quickly cloned in a matter of minutes. BEs also have a low overhead in disk space usage by virtue of ZFS's copy-on-write architecture. BEs are a central part of the lifecycle management in Solaris 11 and allow a fail-safe procedure for applying updates to a system.

NOTE
Only one BE is active at any stage—the currently running operating system instance. It is recommended that administrators create a new BE for any administrative change so that they can quickly revert to their original state in the case where they are applying a change that adversely affects the current running environment.

Creating and Activating Boot Environments

We use the `beadm` command to directly manipulate BEs on a system. On a newly installed Solaris 11 system, one BE called `solaris` will have been created:

```
# beadm list
BE        Active Mountpoint Space Policy Created
--        ------ ---------- ----- ------ -------
solaris NR    /             1.17G static 2015-03-03 23:53
```

We can see that it is currently active (as indicated by `N`, for "Now") and that it will be active on next reboot (as indicated by `R`, for "next Reboot"). We can create a new BE using the `beadm create` command:

```
# beadm create new-be
# beadm list
BE        Active Mountpoint Space Policy Created
--        ------ ---------- ----- ------ -------
new-be  -      -            78.0K static 2015-03-04 03:51
solaris NR    /             1.17G static 2015-03-03 23:53
```

We can see that this new BE only consumes 84 K of disk space. If we wanted to make this BE active, we can use the `beadm activate` command:

```
# beadm activate new-be
# beadm list
BE        Active Mountpoint Space  Policy Created
--        ------ ---------- -----  ------ -------
new-be  R      -            1.17G  static 2015-03-04 03:51
solaris N     /             127.0K static 2015-03-03 23:53
```

We can now see that the `Active` column reads differently and that `new-be` will be the default BE on next reboot (an administrator can override the default BE to boot in the boot manager prompt).

TIP

Sometimes it can be a little confusing to know which BE is which, especially when you have many BEs to choose from. This is often the result of multiple system updates where the packaging system automatically creates a new BE for each

new update. To help with this, we can use the
-d option to beadm create and provide a
description of the BE. This description will be
used in the boot manager. We can manually set
the BE during a system update as we will see later
in this chapter.

Mounting and Destroying Boot Environments

We can also mount BEs easily using the beadm mount command. This is useful when you need to troubleshoot a problem with a BE failing to boot properly, or simply to retrieve files from an older BE.

```
# beadm mount new-be /mnt
# beadm list
BE        Active Mountpoint Space  Policy Created
--        ------ ---------- -----  ------ -------
new-be    R      /mnt       1.17G  static 2015-03-04 03:51
solaris   N      /          127.0K static 2015-03-03 23:53
# ls /mnt
bin       dev       export    lib    net    platform  rpool   tmp
boot      devices   home      media  nfs4   proc      sbin    usr
cdrom     etc       kernel    mnt    opt    root      system  var
```

Let's see how this maps to the ZFS datasets on this system:

```
# zfs list
NAME                          USED   AVAIL  REFER  MOUNTPOINT
rpool                         4.91G  10.7G  73.5K  /rpool
rpool/ROOT                    2.85G  10.7G  31K    legacy
rpool/ROOT/new-be             83K    10.7G  2.54G  /
rpool/ROOT/new-be/var         1K     10.7G  306M   /var
rpool/ROOT/solaris            2.85G  10.7G  2.54G  /
rpool/ROOT/solaris/var        308M   10.7G  306M   /var
rpool/VARSHARE                2.52M  10.7G  2.43M  /var/share
rpool/VARSHARE/pkg            63K    10.7G  32K    /var/share/pkg
rpool/VARSHARE/pkg/repositories 31K  10.7G  31K    /var/share/pkg/repositories
rpool/VARSHARE/zones          31K    10.7G  31K    /system/zones
rpool/dump                    1.03G  10.7G  1.00G  -
rpool/export                  63K    10.7G  32K    /export
rpool/export/home             31K    10.7G  31K    /export/home
rpool/swap                    1.03G  10.7G  1.00G  -
```

We can see that under our default ZFS pool rpool, there are a number of ZFS datasets that live under the rpool/ROOT dataset that coincide with our BEs. You will also notice that there are a number of datasets (/var/share and /export/home as good examples) that exist outside BEs—this means that they are shared across all BEs.

NOTE

Administrators can include additional ZFS datasets within a BE by creating it under the appropriate hierarchy. For example, to create a new non-shared dataset mounted at /apps for the new-be BE:

```
# zfs create -o canmount=noauto rpool/ROOT/new-be/apps
```

Let's now unmount this BE, reactivate the solaris BE, and destroy new-be:

```
# beadm unmount new-be
# beadm activate solaris
# beadm destroy new-be
Are you sure you want to destroy new-be?  This action cannot be undone(y/[n]): y
# beadm list
BE      Active Mountpoint Space Policy Created
--      ------ ---------- ----- ------ -------
solaris NR     /          1.17G static 2015-03-03 23:53
```

Boot Environment Snapshots and Clones

Administrators may choose to take a snapshot of a BE instead of a full clone; snapshots are not bootable until they have been promoted to a full clone. To create a BE snapshot, use the name@description syntax:

```
# beadm create solaris@mysnap
# beadm list -s
BE/Snapshot          Space Policy Created
-----------          ----- ------ -------
solaris
   solaris@install 1.52M static 2015-03-03 23:55
   solaris@mysnap  0     static 2015-03-04 03:57
```

To promote a BE snapshot, use the beadm create command with the -e option as follows:

```
# beadm create -e solaris@mysnap new-be
# beadm list -s
BE/Snapshot          Space Policy Created
-----------          ----- ------ -------
new-be
solaris
   solaris@install 1.52M static 2015-03-03 23:55
   solaris@mysnap  0     static 2015-03-04 03:57
```

Booting from a Boot Environment

Boot environments can also be selected from the boot managers on SPARC and x86 systems, though the procedure is slightly different.

For SPARC systems, first list the BEs that are available in the OpenBoot PROM and then choose the number of the BE to boot:

```
ok boot -L
Boot device: /pci@0/pci@0/pci@2/LSILogic,sas@0/disk@2,0:a  File and args: -L
1 Oracle Solaris 11.2 SPARC
2 Oracle Solaris 11.2 - SRU 7.4 SPARC
Select environment to boot: [ 1 - 2 ]: 2
```

For x86 systems, the GRUB menu reflects the BEs that are available, as shown in Figure 3-1.

Boot environments are also integrated into Oracle Solaris Zones, allowing administrators of non-global zones to manage their own BEs. For a standard non-global zone, BEs are linked with the parent global zone. This ensures that the software versions between the global zone and non-global zone are consistent between each other. As a result, some BEs that have been created in a non-global zone may be unbootable (as indicated by a ! in the Active column of a `beadm list` output) or orphaned (as indicated by an O in the Active column), until the appropriate BE has been selected in the global zone.

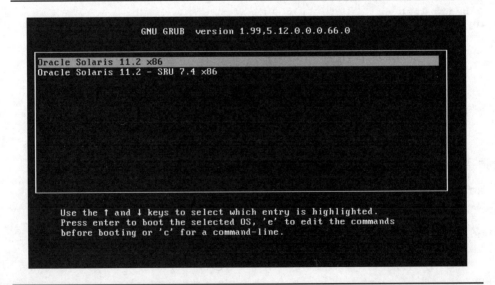

FIGURE 3-1. *GRUB boot menu showing available boot environments*

BEs in Oracle Solaris Kernel Zones do not have this restriction because they are running a separate kernel instance.

Image Packaging System

The Image Packaging System (IPS) is a modern, network-based package management solution included in Oracle Solaris 11. IPS has greatly simplified how administrators install software on their systems and ensure those systems are up to date with the latest bugs and security fixes. IPS helps to reduce the risk of system maintenance with full integration with BEs, helping to reduce both planned and unplanned downtime; if an administrator applies a critical patch that has an adverse effect on the system, they can simply reboot into the original BE to get back up and running quickly.

IPS uses a set of locally or remotely connected package repositories from which to install software, similar to most modern Linux-based offerings. Administrators can install systems with a basic set of software, and then later customize by installing extra software from the repository; this helps to avoid potential vulnerabilities in unnecessary software on the system and to encourage good data center minimization practices. Administrators can also create their own package repositories to deliver in-house software quickly to different systems in the data center with optimized lifecycle management.

Configuring IPS Publishers

IPS is a network-centric package manager. Software developers, or publishers, make their software available in software package repositories from which administrators can install to their systems. Administrators can install new software packages from this repository, search for package content, or mirror the contents of this repository locally if they are in a network-restricted environment within their data center. Administrators can quickly see what configuration a system has by using the `pkg publisher` command:

```
# pkg publisher
PUBLISHER     TYPE     STATUS P LOCATION
solaris       origin   online F http://pkg.oracle.com/solaris/release/
```

In a standard installation, a system will be configured with one publisher called `solaris`. In practice, a system may have multiple publishers depending on what other software has been installed. We can see that there is a URI (Uniform Resource Identifier) associated with this publisher that indicates the repository configured as shown in the `LOCATION` field. In this case, it is using the Solaris release repository hosted by Oracle, a set of packages that are made available with each new release of Oracle Solaris. This repository does not typically include bug or security fixes that are reserved for customers who have an Oracle support contract. The LOCATION field could equally point to an IPS repository on a local file system.

We can get more information about a particular repository using the pkgrepo command:

```
# pkgrepo info -s http://pkg.oracle.com/solaris/release
PUBLISHER  PACKAGES STATUS           UPDATED
solaris    4870     online           2015-01-14T22:32:02.217978Z
```

We can see that this repository has 4870 packages installed, its general network status, and when it was last updated.

NOTE
Administrators managing many systems in a data center should configure a local package repository that has its content synchronized with Oracle hosted package repositories. This is beneficial for speed of access and being able to provide a degree of version control over what software is installed onto the systems. Some data centers with network restrictions may require it.

To add a new publisher to the list, we use the pkg set-publisher command:

```
# pkg set-publisher -g http://mydomain.com/solaris/apps/ mydomain
# pkg publisher
PUBLISHER          TYPE    STATUS  URI
solaris            origin  online  http://pkg.oracle.com/solaris/release/
mydomain           origin  online  http://mydomain.com/solaris/apps/
```

To remove this publisher, simply use the pkg unset-publisher command:

```
# pkg unset-publisher mydomain
```

Administrators may wish to add or remove publisher configurations from systems as part of a typical lifecycle management of an application, say, as it goes from development, through test and finally to production.

Getting Information About a Package

Let's now look at what packages have been installed on this system:

```
# pkg list
NAME (PUBLISHER)                                  VERSION                   IFO
archiver/gnu-tar                                  1.27.1-0.175.2.0.0.42.1   i--
compress/bzip2                                    1.0.6-0.175.2.0.0.42.1    i--
compress/gzip                                     1.5-0.175.2.0.0.42.1      i--
compress/p7zip                                    9.20.1-0.175.2.0.0.42.1   i--
compress/pbzip2                                   1.1.6-0.175.2.0.0.42.1    i--
compress/pixz                                     1.0-0.175.2.0.0.42.1      i--
compress/unzip                                    6.0-0.175.2.0.0.42.1      i--
compress/xz                                       5.0.1-0.175.2.0.0.42.1    i--
... (output truncated) ...
```

Here, we can see a complete list of packages and versions that have been installed. The third column in the preceding output indicates whether a package has been installed (as indicated by i), frozen (as indicated by f), or obsoleted/renamed (as indicated by o or r). Administrators can freeze the version of individual packages to prevent them updating during a regularly scheduled system update. This is useful when there is in-house software that relies on a particular version of a package and may be sensitive to system updates.

We can get some more information about a particular package as follows:

```
# pkg info archiver/gnu-tar
          Name: archiver/gnu-tar
       Summary: GNU version of the tar archiving utility
   Description: Tar is a program for packaging a set of files as a single
                archive in tar format.
      Category: Development/GNU
         State: Installed
     Publisher: solaris
       Version: 1.27.1
 Build Release: 5.11
        Branch: 0.175.2.0.0.42.1
Packaging Date: June 23, 2014 01:01:57 AM
          Size: 1.80 MB
          FMRI: pkg://solaris/archiver/gnu-tar@1.27.1,5.11-
0.175.2.0.0.42.1:20140623T010157Z
```

We can see basic information about this package, including its name and description, where the package came from, its size, and the complete version or package FMRI (Fault Management Resource Indicator). We can also view what the package contents are, this time using a shorter version of the package name since `gnu-tar` is unique across all packages installed on the system:

```
# pkg contents gnu-tar
PATH
usr/bin/gtar
usr/gnu/bin/tar
usr/gnu/share/man/man1/tar.1
usr/sfw/bin/gtar
usr/share/info/tar.info
usr/share/info/tar.info-1
usr/share/info/tar.info-2
usr/share/info/tar.info-3
usr/share/locale/de/LC_MESSAGES/tar.mo
usr/share/locale/es/LC_MESSAGES/tar.mo
usr/share/locale/fr/LC_MESSAGES/tar.mo
usr/share/locale/it/LC_MESSAGES/tar.mo
usr/share/locale/ja/LC_MESSAGES/tar.mo
usr/share/locale/ko/LC_MESSAGES/tar.mo
usr/share/locale/pt/LC_MESSAGES/tar.mo
usr/share/locale/pt_BR/LC_MESSAGES/tar.mo
usr/share/locale/zh_CN/LC_MESSAGES/tar.mo
usr/share/locale/zh_TW/LC_MESSAGES/tar.mo
usr/share/man/man1/gtar.1
```

Installing Packages

Administrators will need to install additional software to supplement their requirements while running data center operations. We can use the `pkg install` command to install a package in the repository:

```
# pkg install wireshark
          Packages to install:  1
          Services to change:   1
      Create boot environment: No
Create backup boot environment: No
DOWNLOAD                    PKGS        FILES      XFER (MB)   SPEED
Completed                   1/1         8/8        1.3/1.3     20.8M/s

PHASE                                   ITEMS
Installing new actions                  27/27
Updating package state database         Done
Updating package cache                  0/0
Updating image state                    Done
Creating fast lookup database           Done
Updating package cache                  1/1
```

From the preceding listing, we can see that we have installed the `wireshark` package. It has installed a single package. This is also where we start to see BEs being used in the package manager. In this case we are not installing this package to a separate BE or creating a backup BE.

> **NOTE**
> *For package operations that affect the state of the system, administrators can choose to override the default behavior of whether a BE gets created or not. For example, using* `pkg install` `--require-new-be` *will always ensure that a new BE is created regardless of whether the software being installed affects the running kernel or not.*

IPS also has the ability to perform a dry run without modifying the system. This is useful for administrators to be able to see what packages would be installed or updated. Let's install the Ruby runtime using the `-nv` option to `pkg install`:

```
# pkg install -nv ruby
             Packages to install:           2
            Mediators to change:           1
       Estimated space available:   10.60 GB
Estimated space to be consumed: 531.54 MB
            Create boot environment:          No
Create backup boot environment:          No
             Rebuild boot archive:          No

Changed mediators:
  mediator ruby:
           version: None -> 1.9 (system default)

Changed packages:
solaris
  runtime/ruby
    None -> 1.9,5.11-0.175.2.4.0.2.0:20141010T203638Z
  runtime/ruby-19
    None -> 1.9.3.484,5.11-0.175.2.0.0.42.1:20140623T020752Z
```

Here we can see that there are two packages that are going to be installed – `runtime/ruby` and `runtime/ruby-19`. IPS includes package dependencies when it installs new packages; this ensures that necessary libraries or other components are installed in order for the package to function correctly. Assuming we want to continue with the installation, we can rerun this command without the -nv option.

TIP
Administrators needing to install the software packages into the global zone and all non-global zones can use the -r option to pkg install. Also available is the -z option to install into a specific set of non-global zones and -Z to exclude specific set of non-global zones.

Understanding the Package FMRI

Each software package is uniquely described by an FMRI string, which is used to define the name, version, and publisher of a package. For example, in the previous section we saw that the FMRI of the runtime/ruby package was

```
pkg://solaris/runtime/ruby@1.9,5.11-0.175.2.4.0.2.0:20141010T203638Z
```

We can break this version information down as follows in Table 3-1.

FMRI Segment	Description
pkg://	FMRI Scheme
solaris	Publisher
runtime/ruby	Package Name
1.9	Component Version
5.11	Build Version
0.175.2.4.0.2.0	Branch Version
20141010T203638Z	Timestamp (ISO 8601 format)

TABLE 3-1. *Understanding the Package FMRI*

The component, build, and branch versions are all sequences of dot-separated integers. This versioning scheme is used across all IPS packages and is fundamental to how IPS manages packages on a system and how it determines how to upgrade a system and ensure the result is a consistent and well-tested set of packages.

If there were alternative packages that also match the `ruby` package, you might need to further qualify what should be installed using any of the following commands, which are shown in increasing order of qualification:

```
# pkg install ruby
# pkg install runtime/ruby
# pkg install pkg:/runtime/ruby
# pkg install pkg://solaris/runtime/ruby
# pkg install pkg://solaris/runtime/ruby@1.9
# pkg install pkg://solaris/runtime/ruby@1.9,5.11-
0.175.2.4.0.2.0:20141010T203638Z
```

Searching for Packages

IPS has advanced search capabilities, allowing administrators to search for a variety of different things within the configured repositories—from simple package contents searches to more advanced searches such as looking for specific package dependencies. Let's search for what package includes the file `sshd_config` (a well-known configuration file for configuring the SSH server):

```
# pkg search sshd_config
INDEX      ACTION VALUE                PACKAGE
basename   file   etc/ssh/sshd_config  pkg:/service/network/ssh@0.5.11-0.175.2.0.0.42.2
```

We can see that we have found one match in the `service/network/ssh` package, located on the file system at /etc/ssh/ (as we would expect). Let's now find what package includes /usr/bin/java:

```
# pkg search /usr/bin/java
INDEX      ACTION VALUE         PACKAGE
path       link   usr/bin/java  pkg:/runtime/java/jre-6@1.6.0.75
path       link   usr/bin/java  pkg:/runtime/java/jre-8@1.8.0.5.13
path       link   usr/bin/java  pkg:/runtime/java/jre-7@1.7.0.60.19
```

This search finds three matches, representing the different versions of Java that are available in the repository. Rather than being a file as before, the `ACTION` column indicates it is a link. If we wanted to look at the contents of one of these packages, say the `runtime/java/jre-6` package, we could try the following:

```
# pkg contents jre-6
pkg: contents: no packages matching the following patterns you specified are
installed on the system.  Try specifying -r to query remotely:

    jre-6
```

We can see that this package isn't currently installed (which is the default behavior for a `pkg contents` command). If we use the `-r` option as indicated by the output, we get a different result:

```
# pkg contents -r jre-6
usr/jdk/instances/jdk1.6.0/bin/tnameserv
usr/jdk/instances/jdk1.6.0/bin/unpack200
usr/jdk/instances/jdk1.6.0/jre
usr/jdk/instances/jdk1.6.0/jre/COPYRIGHT
usr/jdk/instances/jdk1.6.0/jre/README
usr/jdk/instances/jdk1.6.0/jre/Welcome.html
... (output truncated) ...
```

The search command uses a field or structured query that takes the form of `pkg_name:action_type:key:token`. To understand this more fully, you will need to take a look at an IPS package manifest. A manifest describes how a package is assembled—some basic meta-data about a package, the package contents, and any package dependencies. We can see this manifest by using the `-m` option to the `pkg contents` command:

```
# pkg contents -m gnu-tar
set name=pkg.fmri value=pkg://solaris/archiver/gnu-tar@1.27.1,5.11-0.175.2.0.0.4
2.1:20140623T010157Z
set name=pkg.summary value="GNU version of the tar archiving utility"
set name=com.oracle.info.version value=1.27.1
set name=variant.arch value=i386 value=sparc
set name=com.oracle.info.description value="GNU tar"
set name=com.oracle.info.tpno value=16886
set name=com.oracle.info.name value=tar
set name=pkg.description value="Tar is a program for packaging a set of files as
 a single archive in tar format."
set name=info.classification value=org.opensolaris.category.2008:Development/GNU
set name=info.source-url value=http://ftp.gnu.org/gnu/tar/tar-1.27.1.tar.bz2
set name=org.opensolaris.consolidation value=userland
set name=info.upstream-url value=http://www.gnu.org/software/tar/
```

```
set name=org.opensolaris.arc-caseid value=PSARC/2000/488
depend fmri=pkg:/compress/bzip2@1.0.6-0.175.2.0.0.41.1 type=require
depend fmri=pkg:/compress/gzip@1.5-0.175.2.0.0.41.1 type=require
depend fmri=pkg:/network/ssh@0.5.11-0.175.2.0.0.41.0 type=require
depend fmri=pkg:/system/core-os@0.5.11-0.175.2.0.0.41.0 type=require
depend fmri=pkg:/system/library@0.5.11-0.175.2.0.0.41.0 type=require
file 6c1b664308058c996d6dd1282370944f538dc3bc chash=3218e15655c2853517c3790dbcad
edaae8ce3cd5 facet.locale.ca=true group=other mode=0444 owner=root path=usr/shar
e/locale/ca/LC_MESSAGES/tar.mo pkg.csize=20558 pkg.size=54344
... (output truncated) ...
```

From the preceding listing, we can see that each line specifies an *action*. The first section contains `set` actions that provide package meta-data. Following are `depend` actions which provide information about what other packages are required to run this package successfully. After this are other actions such as `file`, `dir`, `link`, `hardlink`, `user`, `group`, `license`, and `legacy`. This allows you to be very specific about what you are searching for. For example, let's find out what installed packages depend on the `library/libxml2` package. We will use the `-l` option to only list packages that are installed, and the `-o` option to only output the package name:

```
# pkg search -l -o pkg.name 'depend:require:library/libxml2'
PKG.NAME
system/management/ilomconfig
security/compliance/openscap
print/cups/filter/foomatic-db-engine
system/library/libdbus-glib
system/fault-management
system/core-os
system/library
... (output truncated) ...
```

We can see from the preceding listing, we are searching on `action _ type` being `depend`, the `key` being `require` (in this case a standard required dependency), and the search `token` being `library/libxml2`.

Updating a System

IPS integrates package and patch management allowing administrators to update their system for bug fixes and security alerts using the same set of commands—essentially just applying new package versions or updates to a system. IPS ensures that all the packages are brought forward in a consistent and well-tested state. The mechanism that controls this behavior is called package incorporations, whereby known groups of packages are constrained by their version using the incorporate dependency type. This forces parts of the system to update simultaneously. A good example of this is the kernel and C userspace library. IPS will look at what package versions have been installed on the system, check what new packages are available in the package repository and calculate how far it is able to update the system. In some cases it may not update to the absolute latest set of packages if it is constrained in some way.

To perform an update of the system, we use the `pkg update`:

```
# pkg update
            Packages to remove:   2
           Packages to install:   1
            Packages to update: 175
         Create boot environment: Yes
  Create backup boot environment:  No
DOWNLOAD                           PKGS          FILES     XFER (MB)    SPEED
Completed                       178/178      6782/6782  292.6/292.6  15.8M/s

PHASE                                          ITEMS
Removing old actions                       2656/2656
Installing new actions                     2816/2816
Updating modified actions                  6125/6125
Updating package state database                 Done
Updating package cache                       177/177
Updating image state                            Done
Creating fast lookup database                   Done
Reading search index                            Done
Building new search index                    544/544
Updating package cache                           1/1

A clone of solaris exists and has been updated and activated.
On the next boot the Boot Environment solaris-1 will be
mounted on '/'.  Reboot when ready to switch to this updated BE.

Updating package cache                           1/1

------------------------------------------------------------------------
NOTE: Please review release notes posted at:

http://www.oracle.com/pls/topic/lookup?ctx=solaris11&id=SERNS
------------------------------------------------------------------------
```

For most system updates, we are applying changes to the operating system kernel, device drivers and underlying system libraries. In this case, we can see that a new BE called `solaris-1` has been created. This means that a system update can be applied on a live production machine in parallel with the normal workload. When a maintenance window can be scheduled, the system can simply be rebooted into this new BE. We have applied updates to 175 packages, removed two packages, and added one new package.

NOTE

IPS is extremely bandwidth efficient. Rather than downloading the full contents of each new package, it is smart enough to determine the differences between package versions and only install those differences.

Once the system has performed the update, we can check the list of BEs that are installed on the system.

```
# beadm list
BE        Active Mountpoint Space Policy Created
--        ------ ---------- ----- ------ -------
new-be    -      -          84.0K static 2015-03-01 23:46
solaris   N      /          5.94M static 2015-03-01 23:03
solaris-1 R      -          5.68G static 2015-03-02 07:22
```

We can see that our new BE has been activated and that it will be the default on system reboot. If we do not want this BE to be default on the next reboot, we can use the `beadm activate` command as detailed earlier in this chapter.

Any non-global zones that are configured and installed on the system will be automatically updated during a package update. However, any kernel zones will required to be manually updated since it is a separate kernel version rather than shared in the case of a non-global zone.

TIP

Sometimes it may not be so obvious why an update fails to apply. If this happens, try using `pkg update entire@latest` *or* `pkg update entire@VERSION` *where VERSION is the specific version that you wish to apply. The entire package is the master incorporation for Oracle Solaris and constrains the overall version of the platform.*

Fixing a System

During day-to-day operations, it can be easy to make mistakes—perhaps by modifying or deleting a system file accidentally. IPS provides another way of recovering from this mistake with its built-in capability to fix packages. As an example, let's delete the `/usr/bin/ls` file:

```
# rm /usr/bin/ls
# ls
-bash: /usr/bin/ls: No such file or directory
```

We can use the `pkg verify` command to see if there are any changes to packages that have been made on the system that don't match the information stored in the configured repository.

```
# pkg verify
PACKAGE                                                         STATUS
pkg://solaris/system/core-os                                    ERROR
file: usr/bin/ls
            Missing: regular file does not exist
```

We can see that IPS has detected a problem. We can now use `pkg fix` to fix this package once again:

```
# pkg fix core-os
Verifying: pkg://solaris/system/core-os                         ERROR
file: usr/bin/ls
            Missing: regular file does not exist
Created ZFS snapshot: 2015-03-02-07:54:39
Repairing: pkg://solaris/system/core-os
Creating Plan (Evaluating mediators): |

DOWNLOAD                              PKGS        FILES     XFER (MB)    SPEED
Completed                             1/1          1/1      0.1/0.1    272k/s

PHASE                                       ITEMS
Updating modified actions                    1/1
Updating package state database             Done
Updating package cache                       0/0
Updating image state                        Done
Creating fast lookup database               Done
# ls /
bin       dev        export    lib      net      platform   rpool    tmp
boot      devices    home      media    nfs4     proc       sbin     usr
cdrom     etc        kernel    mnt      opt      root       system   var
```

And we can see we are back with a functional `/usr/bin/ls` once again.

Exact Installations

Sometimes it is useful to be able to restore a system to a particular baseline set of packages rather than completely reinstall it. One of the very useful features of IPS is the ability to do exact installations of package content.

This essentially allows the administrator to be able to install or update the specified packages as if installed onto a bare metal system—it will add any additional packages that are required and remove packages that are unnecessary. This is particularly useful tool in compliance auditing—we will take a look this in Chapter 7 *Secure Oracle Solaris 11 Deployment*.

To reset to a particular baseline, we use the `pkg exact-install` command:

```
# pkg exact-install solaris-minimal-server
```

In this case we are using the `solaris-minimal-server` package group, which defines an excellent boundary for a minimized Oracle Solaris server.

Managing IPS Repositories

IPS includes a number of commands to easily create and manage package repositories. Administrators will often create local package repositories to either publish packages for their own in-house applications, or to mirror the contents of Oracle hosted package repositories for local access. In this book we will only focus on setting up a local package repository that includes the bug fixes and security alerts issued by Oracle; for readers interested in creating their own package repositories and publishing packages to them, there are some great resources online at the Oracle Technology Network.

Oracle releases fixes for Oracle Solaris 11 every month in what are known as Support Repository Updates (SRUs). These take the form of package updates that can be applied either directly from the Oracle Solaris support repository or downloaded in a series of incremental repository zip files from My Oracle Support (MOS) at https://support.oracle.com/epmos/faces/MosIndex.jspx.

NOTE
The Oracle Solaris support repository can be reached at `https://pkg.oracle.com/solaris/support`. *To connect to this repository, an entitlement for Oracle Premier Support is required, and an SSL-based key and certificate to be associated in the IPS configuration. These credentials can be downloaded from* `https://pkg-register.oracle.com`.

Let's assume we have downloaded the Oracle Solaris 11.2 release repository images from MOS:

```
# ls -1 /mnt
install-repo.ksh
README-zipped-repo.txt
sol-11_2-repo-1of4.zip
sol-11_2-repo-2of4.zip
sol-11_2-repo-3of4.zip
sol-11_2-repo-4of4.zip
sol-11_2-repo-md5sums.txt
```

Let's use these to construct a local package repository. We'll first create a ZFS dataset at `mypool/repository` (assuming there is an additional ZFS pool called `mypool`) in which to host the repository. This means that the repository will exist independently outside the scope of BEs. We will then run our script (as indicated by the instructions in the README file):

```
# zfs create -o mountpoint=/repository mypool/repository
# cd /mnt
# ./install-repo.ksh -d /repository
Uncompressing sol-11_2-repo-1of4.zip...done.
Uncompressing sol-11_2-repo-2of4.zip...done.
Uncompressing sol-11_2-repo-3of4.zip...done.
Uncompressing sol-11_2-repo-4of4.zip...done.
Repository can be found in /repository.
```

Let's now take a look at the result:

```
# ls -1 /repository
COPYRIGHT
NOTICES
pkg5.repository
publisher
README-repo-iso.txt
```

Now that we have copied over the data, let's change our default publisher to point to this new repository:

```
# pkg set-publisher -G http://pkg.oracle.com/solaris/release -g /repository/ solaris
# pkg publisher
PUBLISHER                   TYPE     STATUS P LOCATION
solaris                     origin   online F file:///repository/
```

NOTE

IPS supports multiple different ways of making a repository available—over the network with HTTP or HTTPS using an IPS repository depot service or Apache proxy, or direct file access. For more information, see pkg.depotd(1M) *and* pkg.depot-config(1M).

In order to update systems with the latest fixes, we will want to synchronize this local repository with new updates that have been published by Oracle. There are a number of choices depending on your environment—directly syncing changes from the repository itself, or downloading incremental repository images that contain the latest updates from My Oracle Support.

To directly sync changes from the Oracle hosted package repository that represents the support repository, we use the pkgrecv command:

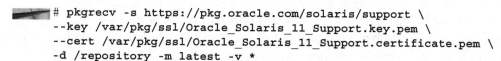

```
# pkgrecv -s https://pkg.oracle.com/solaris/support \
--key /var/pkg/ssl/Oracle_Solaris_11_Support.key.pem \
--cert /var/pkg/ssl/Oracle_Solaris_11_Support.certificate.pem \
-d /repository -m latest -v *
```

In this example we are providing the SSL key and certificate to gain access to the Oracle Solaris support repository to synchronize new package updates into our local package repository. If you choose the incremental repository images, make sure to check the relevant documentation provided with the download through MOS.

TIP

Administrators who have external network access can automatically sync their local repositories with the Oracle hosted repositories using the IPS repository mirroring service, svc:/application/pkg/mirror:default.

Unified Archives

Oracle Solaris 11 includes a new archive format called *Unified Archives* which provides the ability to create a snapshot of bare-metal environments and virtualized environments within a single archive for redeployment, either as clones within a cloud environment or for system backup and disaster recovery.

Under the hood, Unified Archives take advantage of ZFS snapshot and cloning capabilities, and use ZFS streams to capture the system image. This means that live production systems can be quickly captured using Unified Archives without fear of taking down the system. Unified Archives is also integrated into Oracle Solaris BEs, packaging and service management, having a full understanding of what software has been installed in a particular environment and what services have been run. This means that archives are completely portable across both bare-metal and virtualization boundaries, allowing physical-to-virtual or virtual-to-physical transforms. Thus, developers can work on smaller systems and then migrate these environments to larger scaling production ready systems.

Unified Archives are a multisystem archive, meaning that they can contain the bare-metal environment and any number of nested virtualized archives inside. Administrators can choose to selectively deploy parts of the archive as appropriate.

Unified Archives also have the ability to embed bootable media within the archive itself. This means that administrators can generate stand-alone bootable media in which to boot and install a system from the archive content at a later time—this greatly enhances archive portability.

Unified Archive Types

There are two types of archive that administrators can choose to create—a clone archive or a system recovery archive. The difference depends on how you want to use this archive after you create it.

Clone archives are used to rapidly deploy a golden image environment across the cloud. As such they only contain the system's active BEs and related ZFS datasets, including the BE and related datasets, including any zones that may be configured. During their creation, the archive is un-configured since each clone will want to assume a different identity when deployed across different VM environments. During clone archive creation, an administrator may choose to include or exclude specific systems.

Recovery archives are used to provide back up and disaster recovery of specific systems. They contain all the system's BEs and related ZFS datasets, including any zones that may be configured. The key difference is that this acts like a monolithic archive. The system configuration of the archive is preserved and the administrator can only deploy the entire archive at any time.

The `archiveadm` archive utility provides administrators with the ability to create clone and recovery archives of a running system, query the contents of an archive, and create bootable media from an archive.

On our system, let's assume we have a standard Oracle Solaris 11 system running on SPARC with two non-global zones as follows:

```
# zoneadm list -cv
  ID NAME            STATUS       PATH                     BRAND      IP
   0 global          running      /                        solaris    shared
   1 zone_one        running      /system/zones/zone_one   solaris    excl
   2 zone_two        running      /system/zones/zone_two   solaris    excl
```

Creating a Clone Archive

To create a clone archive, we will use the `archiveadm create` command with the -e option to exclude including bootable media in the archive:

```
# archiveadm create -e clonearchive.uar
Initializing Unified Archive creation resources...
Unified Archive initialized: /root/clonearchive.uar
Logging to: /system/volatile/archive_log.20102
Executing dataset discovery...
Dataset discovery complete
Preparing archive system image...
Beginning archive stream creation...
Archive stream creation complete
Beginning final archive assembly...
Archive creation complete
# ls -lh clonearchive.uar
-rw-r--r--   1 root       root         1.6G Mar  3 03:23 clonearchive.uar
```

We can see from the output that we have successfully created a clone archive (the default) with a size of 1.6 GB. We can now use the `archiveadm info` command to find out more details about this archive:

```
# archiveadm info clonearchive.uar
Archive Information
         Creation Time:  2015-03-03T03:09:35Z
           Source Host:  solaris
          Architecture:  sparc
      Operating System:  Oracle Solaris 11.2 SPARC
     Deployable Systems:  global,zone_two,zone_one
```

We can see details such as when and where the archive was created, its architecture and OS version, and what deployable systems are available within it. If we do the same command again with the -v option, we can see a more comprehensive output:

```
# archiveadm info -v clonearchive.uar
Archive Information
          Creation Time:  2015-03-03T03:09:35Z
            Source Host:  solaris
           Architecture:  sparc
       Operating System:  Oracle Solaris 11.2 SPARC
       Recovery Archive:  No
              Unique ID:  f6efe5a8-240b-c4b6-e3f1-b8782e773fd4
        Archive Version:  1.0

Deployable Systems
        'global'
             OS Version:  0.5.11
              OS Branch:  0.175.2.0.0.42.2
              Active BE:  solaris
                  Brand:  solaris
            Size Needed:  2.8GB
              Unique ID:  afd44b56-147c-4910-fb20-b3c8e56b5144
              Root-only:  Yes
        'zone_two'
             OS Version:  0.5.11
              OS Branch:  0.175.2.0.0.42.2
              Active BE:  solaris
                  Brand:  solaris
            Size Needed:  764MB
              Unique ID:  b26bd4ba-9342-4831-e967-cdfa0ab508ee
              Root-only:  Yes
        'zone_one'
             OS Version:  0.5.11
              OS Branch:  0.175.2.0.0.42.2
              Active BE:  solaris
                  Brand:  solaris
            Size Needed:  769MB
              Unique ID:  e0791fc0-0e5c-e72d-a5bb-97cba2d5b5eb
              Root-only:  Yes
```

In the preceding list, we can see a lot more information, including more detailed version information, the active BEs that were selected for each deployable system, the respective sizes of each deployable system, and whether any bootable media has been included.

Creating a Recovery Archive

Let's contrast the previous example by now capturing a recovery archive of the system. We will again use the `archiveadm create` command but with an added `-r` option which create a recovery archive instead:

```
# archiveadm create -r -e recoveryarchive.uar
Initializing Unified Archive creation resources...
Unified Archive initialized: /root/recoveryarchive.uar
Logging to: /system/volatile/archive_log.3828
Executing dataset discovery...
Dataset discovery complete
Preparing archive system image...
Beginning archive stream creation...
Archive stream creation complete
Beginning final archive assembly...
Archive creation complete
# ls -lh recoveryarchive.uar
-rw-r--r--   1 root       root           2.0G Mar  3 03:42 recoveryarchive.uar
```

The output is a little different, and the size of the archive is a little larger. Let's take a look at more information about this archive:

```
# archiveadm info recoveryarchive.uar
Archive Information
          Creation Time:  2015-03-03T03:27:19Z
            Source Host:  solaris
           Architecture:  sparc
       Operating System:  Oracle Solaris 11.2 SPARC
      Deployable Systems:  global
# archiveadm info -v recoveryarchive.uar
Archive Information
          Creation Time:  2015-03-03T03:27:19Z
            Source Host:  solaris
           Architecture:  sparc
       Operating System:  Oracle Solaris 11.2 SPARC
       Recovery Archive:  Yes
              Unique ID:  f0fe4b8a-e21a-6b2f-ca44-a0ddddalae9f
        Archive Version:  1.0

Deployable Systems
          'global'
             OS Version:  0.5.11
              OS Branch:  0.175.2.0.0.42.2
              Active BE:  solaris
                  Brand:  solaris
                  Zones:  zone_one,zone_two
            Size Needed:  8.9GB
              Unique ID:  1ca38aed-5f30-e501-febf-9f37891645a1
              Root-only:  Yes
```

We can immediately see a different. Rather than having three separate deployable systems (called `global`, `zone_one`, `zone_two`) in the clone archive, we only have a single deployable system called `global` which is our full-system recovery image.

Creating Bootable Media to Deploy an Archive

Assuming your archive includes bootable media, it is easy to create a USB image using the `archiveadm create-media` command:

```
# archiveadm create-media recoveryarchive.uar
Initiating media creation...
Preparing build environment...
Adding archive content...
Image preparation complete.
Creating USB image...
Finalizing media image: /root/AI_Archive.usb
```

Having created the bootable media, an administrator can copy this to a USB stick using the `usbcopy` or `dd` commands. Alternatively, you can specify that an ISO image should be created (so long as the resulting size is less than 4 GB) by using the `-f iso` option. Once an ISO image has been created, it can be burned to a DVD or booted directly from the system ILOM (Integrated Lights-Out Manager).

Archives can also be deployed directly through the Oracle Solaris Zone administration tools `zonecfg` and `zoneadm`, or through the Automated Installer for provisioning framework. We will cover zone deployment in Chapter 5 and deployment using the Automated Installer in the next section. Furthermore, when combined with immutable global and non-global zones, administrators can lock down a golden image in a read-only environment. This is an excellent way to ensure that application environments are compliant right through the process of development and test, through to production.

Automated Installer

The Oracle Solaris 11 Automated Installer (AI) provides administrators with a secure, automated, network-based, hands-off method for installing multiple systems in the data center. Having a fast deployment framework is critical for reliably and repeatedly getting systems online with secure end-to-end provisioning.

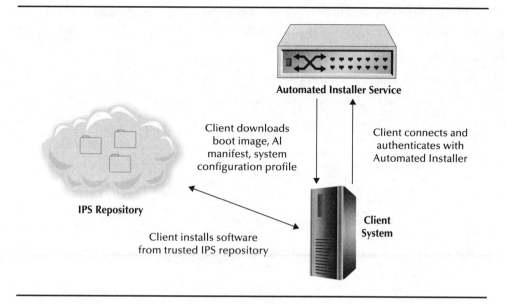

FIGURE 3-2. *How a client system is installed by the Automated Installer*

With the AI, client systems boot over the network, find the location of the Automated Installer server using DHCP, and get matched to a specific set of installation instructions called a service. An install service details how client system should get installed. Once a system is assigned an appropriate manifest based on a criteria match, it will then contact a package repository and finish the installation, as shown in Figure 3-2.

An install service consists of an AI manifest and usually a system configuration (SC) profile. The AI manifest includes information such as target disks and their layout, what software packages should be installed, and whether any Oracle Solaris Zones should be created. A system configuration profile (sometimes known as an SC profile) details initial user accounts that should be created, which services should be enabled or disabled, time zone and default locale, naming services, and basic networking configuration.

Creating an Automated Installer Service

All administration of an AI service is done using the `installadm` command. This provides administrators with the opportunity to create and modify install services, assign AI manifest and SC profiles to these services, and associate client criteria for a match. It can also provide assistance for editing AI manifests and setting properties on the AI server.

We will start by creating a simple AI service using the `installadm` `create-service` command as follows:

```
# installadm create-service
OK to use subdir of /export/auto_install to store image? [y|N]: y
   0% : Service svc:/network/dns/multicast:default is not online.  Installation services
will not be advertised via multicast DNS.
   0% : Creating service from: pkg:/install-image/solaris-auto-install
   0% : Using publisher(s):
   0% :       solaris: http://pkg.oracle.com/solaris/support/
   5% : Refreshing Publisher(s)
   7% : Startup Phase
  15% : Planning Phase
  61% : Download Phase
  90% : Actions Phase
  91% : Finalize Phase
  91% : Creating sparc service: solaris11_2_7_4_0-sparc
  91% : Image path: /export/auto_install/solaris11_2_7_4_0-sparc
  91% : Setting "solaris" publisher URL in default manifest to:
  91% :   http://pkg.oracle.com/solaris/support/
  91% : DHCP is not being managed by install server.
  91% : SMF Service 'svc:/system/install/server:default' will be enabled
  91% : SMF Service 'svc:/network/tftp/udp6:default' will be enabled
  91% : Creating default-sparc alias
  91% : Setting "solaris" publisher URL in default manifest to:
  91% :   http://pkg.oracle.com/solaris/support/
  91% : DHCP is not being managed by install server.
  91% : No local DHCP configuration found. This service is the default
  91% : alias for all SPARC clients. If not already in place, the following should
  91% : be added to the DHCP configuration:
  91% : Boot file: http://10.134.79.136:5555/cgi-bin/wanboot-cgi
  91% : SMF Service 'svc:/system/install/server:default' will be enabled
  91% : SMF Service 'svc:/network/tftp/udp6:default' will be enabled
 100% : Created Service: 'solaris11_2_7_4_0-sparc'
 100% : Refreshing SMF service svc:/network/tftp/udp6:default
 100% : Refreshing SMF service svc:/system/install/server:default
 100% : Enabling SMF service svc:/system/install/server:default
 100% : Enabling SMF service svc:/network/tftp/udp6:default
 100% : Warning: mDNS registry of service 'solaris11_2_7_4_0-sparc' could not be verified.
 100% : Warning: mDNS registry of service 'default-sparc' could not be verified.
```

From the output generated, we can see that a new directory at `/export/auto_install` has been created which will store our boot images and other configuration that will be used in our AI service. We have also enabled some SMF services including `svc:/system/install/server:default`, the core AI server. Finally, we have also downloaded a small boot image from the IPS repository that we will use to bootstrap any connecting clients initially. You will also notice that we have not configured a DHCP server in this setup. If you have an existing DHCP server on the network, you will need to manually configure it to ensure that it includes the location of the AI server and the appropriate boot files as indicated in the output.

NOTE

Oracle Solaris 11 includes ISC DHCP server. AI will automatically configure the DHCP server if it detects that one is running locally. It is also possible to install systems using Automated Installer without a DHCP server. This can be achieved by setting the appropriate `network-boot-arguments` variable in the OpenBoot PROM on SPARC. Support for x86-based systems is planned.

We can use the `installadm list` command to view our new AI service:

```
# installadm list
Service Name            Status Arch  Type Secure Alias Aliases Clients Profiles Manifests
------------            ------ ----  ---- ------ ----- ------- ------- -------- ---------
default-sparc           on     sparc pkg  no     yes   0       0       0        1
solaris11_2_7_4_0-sparc on     sparc pkg  no     no    1       0       0        1
```

From the preceding listing, we can see that there are two services that have been created, `solaris11_2_7_4_0-sparc` and `default-sparc`. One of the service names is simply an alias to another (as indicated by the `Alias` column). An alias service shares the same boot image as the service it aliases. This means we can apply our customizations to the alias service and swap out the underlying boot image to a later OS version by re-aliasing it to another service. We can also see from this summary what client criteria, SC profiles, and AI manifest have been associated with particular services.

Configuring an AI Manifest

An AI manifest, an XML-based file, provides details of how a system should be installed—disk target and layout, software package selection, and virtual environments. By default, an AI service will have a *derived manifest* associated with it. A derived manifest is actually a script that is able to generate an AI manifest on the fly—allowing for small customizations across a variety of systems depending on the system that is being installed. We can see what manifests have been associated with a given service by using the -m option, and giving the name of the service we are interested in with the -n option:

```
# installadm list -m -n default-sparc
Service Name  Manifest Name  Type     Status   Criteria
------------  -------------  ----     ------   --------
default-sparc orig_default   derived  default  none
```

We can see what this derived manifest looks like by using the `installadm export` command:

```
# installadm export -m orig_default -n default-sparc
```

As a very simple example of a derived manifest, it loads an XML manifest fragment and ensures we install the same version of Oracle Solaris that the client system is currently running within the boot image. By default, AI will install clients with the `group/system/solaris-large-server` package group using Oracle hosted Oracle Solaris release package repository. This is selection of software that is useful for most server situations.

TIP
Derived manifests are an important part of the AI. When installing at scale, some systems may require a different disk layout for example. Rather than using many different customized manifests, we can use derived manifests to dynamically generate an AI manifest based on environmental variables or other client configuration to accommodate these changes.

Let's create a custom manifest that installs clients with the minimal server configuration instead.

First we'll copy an example manifest from the AI image root into our local directory:

```
# cp /export/auto_install/solaris11_2_7_4_0-sparc/auto_install/default.xml /tmp
```

Next we'll edit the manifest—we can use standard command line editors or graphical XML editors if available for this. We need to find the section that looks similar to the following:

```
<software type="IPS">
  <source>
    <publisher name="solaris">
      <origin name="http://pkg.oracle.com/solaris/release"/>
    </publisher>
  </source>
  <software_data action="install">
    <name>pkg:/entire@0.5.11-0.175.2</name>
    <name>pkg:/group/system/solaris-large-server</name>
  </software_data>
</software>
```

Here we can see that our software source is an IPS repository and that we're installing the `entire` IPS incorporation (which indicates Oracle Solaris 11.2) and the `group/system/solaris-large-server` package group. We will need to replace the latter part of this with the following:

```
<software_data action="install">
        <name>pkg:/entire@0.5.11-0.175.2</name>
        <name>pkg:/group/system/solaris-minimal-server</name>
</software_data>
```

The AI manifest supports another way of installing a client system—directly from a Unified Archive. If we wanted to install from an archive instead, we would need to use the following AI manifest fragment:

```
<software type="ARCHIVE">
   <source>
     <file uri="/net/aiserver/archives/myarchive.uar"/>
   </source>
   <software_data action="install">
     <name>*</name>
   </software_data>
</software>
```

We can see that we're using an `ARCHIVE` type for our software source and providing a location to the Unified Archive. We also need to specify which deployable systems we wish to deploy. In the preceding case, we're deploying a recovery archive, so we indicate we choose all systems by using `*`.

Let's continue on with our previous example. Once we have successfully edited this manifest, save it, and use the `installadm create-manifest` command to associate it with our AI service. We will use the `-d` option to ensure it is the default manifest for this service.

```
# installadm create-manifest -n default-sparc -m newmanifest -d -f /tmp/default.xml
Created Manifest: 'newmanifest'
# installadm list -m -n default-sparc
Service Name  Manifest Name Type    Status   Criteria
------------  ------------- ----    ------   --------
default-sparc newmanifest   xml     default  none
              orig_default  derived inactive none
```

From the preceding listing, we can now see there are two manifests in place—our original derived manifest and also a new manifest called `newmanifest` which is of type XML manifest.

TIP
The installadm client supports an interactive mode that allows for easy administration of an AI server, including the ability to interactively edit AI manifests without having knowledge and experience of editing XML files. A web-based interface is also available to use.

Installing a Client System

Now that we have created a new AI service, it's time to boot our system over the network. In our case, we will use the Oracle ILOM to connect to a console. In the following listing, we can see the full steps of a typical AI install:

```
SPARC T5-2, No Keyboard
Copyright (c) 1998, 2014, Oracle and/or its affiliates. All rights reserved.
OpenBoot 4.36.1, 255.0000 GB memory available, Serial #107488122.
Ethernet address 0:10:e0:68:23:7a, Host ID: 8668237a.

{0} ok boot net - install
Boot device: /pci@300/pci@1/pci@0/pci@1/network@0  File and args: - install
100 Mbps full duplex Link up
<time unavailable> wanboot info: WAN boot messages->console
<time unavailable> wanboot info: configuring /pci@300/pci@1/pci@0/pci@1/network@0

100 Mbps full duplex Link up
<time unavailable> wanboot progress: wanbootfs: Read 368 of 368 kB (100%)
<time unavailable> wanboot info: wanbootfs: Download complete
Tue Mar  3 21:38:10 wanboot progress: miniroot: Read 249795 of 249795 kB (100%)
Tue Mar  3 21:38:10 wanboot info: miniroot: Download complete
SunOS Release 5.11 Version 11.2 64-bit
Copyright (c) 1983, 2014, Oracle and/or its affiliates. All rights reserved.
Remounting root read/write
Probing for device nodes ...
WARNING: /scsi_vhci/disk@g5000cca05692542c (sd4):
        primary label corrupt; using backup

Preparing network image for use
Downloading solaris.zlib
curl arguments --insecure for http://aiserver:5555//export/auto_install/
solaris11_2_7_4_0-sparc/solaris.zlib
  % Total    % Received % Xferd  Average Speed   Time    Time     Time  Current
                                 Dload  Upload   Total   Spent    Left  Speed
100  221M  100  221M    0     0  11.1M      0  0:00:19  0:00:19 --:--:-- 11.1M
Downloading solarismisc.zlib
curl arguments --insecure for http://aiserver:5555//export/auto_install/
solaris11_2_7_4_0-sparc/solarismisc.zlib
  % Total    % Received % Xferd  Average Speed   Time    Time     Time  Current
                                 Dload  Upload   Total   Spent    Left  Speed
100 18.0M  100 18.0M    0     0  11.0M      0  0:00:01  0:00:01 --:--:-- 11.0M
Downloading .image_info
curl arguments --insecure for http://aiserver:5555//export/auto_install/
solaris11_2_7_4_0-sparc/.image_info
```

```
       % Total    % Received % Xferd  Average Speed   Time    Time    Time  Current
                                      Dload  Upload   Total   Spent   Left  Speed
100    88 100    88     0      0     6931      0 --:--:-- --:--:-- --:--:--  8800
Done mounting image
Configuring devices.
Hostname: aiclient
Service discovery phase initiated
Service name to look up: default-sparc
Service discovery over multicast DNS failed
Service default-sparc located at aiserver:5555 will be used
Service discovery finished successfully
Process of obtaining install manifest initiated
Using the install manifest obtained via service discovery


client console login:
Automated Installation started
The progress of the Automated Installation will be output to the console
Detailed logging is in the logfile at /system/volatile/install_log
Press RETURN to get a login prompt at any time.

21:39:31    Install Log: /system/volatile/install_log
21:39:31    Using XML Manifest: /system/volatile/ai.xml
21:39:31    Using profile specification: /system/volatile/profile
21:39:31    Using service list file: /var/run/service_list
21:39:31    Starting installation.
21:39:31    0% Preparing for Installation
21:39:31    100% manifest-parser completed.
21:39:31    100% None
21:39:31    0% Preparing for Installation
21:39:32    1% Preparing for Installation
21:39:32    2% Preparing for Installation
21:39:32    3% Preparing for Installation
21:39:32    4% Preparing for Installation
21:39:40    22% target-discovery completed.
21:39:40    Selected Disk(s) : c0t5000CCA05692B8CCd0
21:39:41    27% target-selection completed.
21:39:41    30% ai-configuration completed.
21:39:41    33% var-share-dataset completed.
21:39:54    35% target-instantiation completed.
21:39:54    34% Beginning IPS transfer
21:39:54    Creating IPS image
21:40:02     Startup: Retrieving catalog 'solaris' ... Done
21:40:05     Startup: Caching catalogs ... Done
21:40:05     Startup: Refreshing catalog 'solaris' ... Done
21:40:05    Installing packages from:
21:40:05        solaris
21:40:06            origin:  http://pkg.oracle.com/solaris/support/
21:40:06     Startup: Refreshing catalog 'solaris' ... Done
21:40:15    Planning: Solver setup ... Done
21:40:15    Planning: Running solver ... Done
21:40:15    Planning: Finding local manifests ... Done
21:40:15    Planning: Fetching manifests:   0/276   0% complete
21:40:26    Planning: Fetching manifests: 276/276  100% complete
21:40:31    Planning: Package planning ... Done
21:40:31    Planning: Merging actions ... Done
21:40:33    Planning: Checking for conflicting actions ... Done
21:40:34    Planning: Consolidating action changes ... Done
21:40:35    Planning: Evaluating mediators ... Done
21:40:36    Planning: Planning completed in 30.08 seconds
```

```
21:40:36   The following licenses have been accepted and not displayed.
21:40:36   Please review the licenses for the following packages post-install:
21:40:36     consolidation/osnet/osnet-incorporation
21:40:36   Package licenses may be viewed using the command:
21:40:36     pkg info --license <pkg_fmri>

21:40:37   Download:      0/37086 items     0.0/279.9MB  0% complete
21:40:42   Download:   3474/37086 items    26.1/279.9MB  9% complete (5.3M/s)
21:40:47   Download:   5997/37086 items    66.3/279.9MB  23% complete (6.7M/s)
21:40:52   Download:  10910/37086 items    94.3/279.9MB  33% complete (6.8M/s)
21:40:57   Download:  14295/37086 items   124.1/279.9MB  44% complete (6.0M/s)
21:41:02   Download:  18868/37086 items   156.8/279.9MB  56% complete (6.2M/s)
21:41:07   Download:  23508/37086 items   176.2/279.9MB  62% complete (5.2M/s)
21:41:12   Download:  27254/37086 items   203.9/279.9MB  72% complete (4.7M/s)
21:41:17   Download:  33183/37086 items   238.7/279.9MB  85% complete (6.2M/s)
21:41:22   Download:  35856/37086 items   269.1/279.9MB  96% complete (6.5M/s)
21:41:24   Download: Completed 279.89 MB in 46.83 seconds (6.0M/s)
21:41:31    Actions:      1/53038 actions (Installing new actions)
21:41:36    Actions:  15570/53038 actions (Installing new actions)
21:41:41    Actions:  21529/53038 actions (Installing new actions)
21:41:46    Actions:  27410/53038 actions (Installing new actions)
21:41:51    Actions:  33067/53038 actions (Installing new actions)
21:41:56    Actions:  38680/53038 actions (Installing new actions)
21:42:01    Actions:  44137/53038 actions (Installing new actions)
21:42:06    Actions:  51946/53038 actions (Installing new actions)
21:42:11    Actions:  52163/53038 actions (Installing new actions)
21:42:12    Actions: Completed 53038 actions in 40.86 seconds.
21:42:13    Done
01:10:01    36% generated transfer 769 1 completed.
21:42:25    38% initialize-smf completed.
21:42:26    Setting boot devices in firmware
21:42:26    Setting openprom boot-device
21:42:27    47% boot-configuration completed.
21:42:27    48% update-dump-adm completed.
21:42:27    50% setup-swap completed.
21:42:28    52% device-config completed.
21:42:29    54% apply-sysconfig completed.
21:42:29    55% transfer-zpool-cache completed.
21:42:31    90% boot-archive completed.
21:42:31    92% transfer-ai-files completed.
21:42:32    100% create-snapshot completed.
21:42:32    100% None
21:42:32    Automated Installation succeeded.
21:42:32    You may wish to reboot the system at this time.
Automated Installation finished successfully
The system can be rebooted now
Please refer to the /system/volatile/install_log file for details
After reboot it will be located at /var/log/install/install_log

aiclient console login: root
Password: ########
Mar  3 21:43:35 dcsw-t52-1 login: ROOT LOGIN /dev/console
Oracle Corporation      SunOS 5.11      11.2    December 2014
# reboot
```

When the AI install finishes, you can drop down to the console login of the boot image by hitting the carriage return key. Here we can use the root/

`solaris` credentials to log in, optionally check the installation log file, and reboot the system.

Once the system has been rebooted, it will immediately enter into the System Configuration Tool and walk the administrator through some simple system configuration as shown in Figure 3-3. This is because we haven't yet associated an SC profile with our AI service.

TIP

You can enable an automatic reboot after the AI installation has finished by setting `auto_reboot="true"` as an attribute in the AI manifest as follows:

```
<ai_instance name="default" auto_reboot="true">
...
</ai_instance>
```

```
                    System Configuration Tool

    System Configuration Tool enables you to specify the following
    configuration parameters for your newly-installed Oracle Solaris 11
    system:
    - system hostname, network, time zone and locale, date and time, user
      and root accounts, name services, keyboard layout, support

    System Configuration Tool produces an SMF profile file in
    /etc/svc/profile/sysconfig/sysconfig-20150303-214636.

    How to navigate through this tool:
    - Use the function keys listed at the bottom of each screen to move
      from screen to screen and to perform other operations.
    - Use the up/down arrow keys to change the selection or to move
      between input fields.
    - If your keyboard does not have function keys, or they do not
      respond, press ESC; the legend at the bottom of the screen will
      change to show the ESC keys for navigation and other functions.

    F2 Continue  F6 Help  F9 Quit
```

FIGURE 3-3. *Initial post-installation configuration with System Configuration Tool*

Applying a System Configuration Profile

A system configuration profile (or SC profile) is an XML-based configuration file that details initial user accounts that should be created, which services should be enabled or disabled, time zone and default locale, naming services, and basic networking configuration. Based on an SMF service profile, they can either be manually created and edited, or generated using the `sysconfig` command as follows:

```
# sysconfig create-profile -o ./sc_profile.xml
```

Once we have walked through the configuration in the System Configuration Tool, we can check what has been output:

```
# cat sc_profile.xml
<?xml version='1.0' encoding='UTF-8'?>
<!DOCTYPE service_bundle SYSTEM "/usr/share/lib/xml/dtd/service_bundle.dtd.1">
<!-- Auto-generated by sysconfig -->
<service_bundle type="profile" name="sysconfig">
  <service version="1" type="service" name="system/identity">
    <instance enabled="true" name="node">
      <property_group type="application" name="config">
        <propval type="astring" name="nodename" value="aiclient"/>
      </property_group>
    </instance>
  </service>
  <service version="1" type="service" name="network/install">
    <instance enabled="true" name="default">
      <property_group type="application" name="install_ipv6_interface">
        <propval type="astring" name="stateful" value="yes"/>
        <propval type="astring" name="address_type" value="addrconf"/>
        <propval type="astring" name="name" value="net0/v6"/>
        <propval type="astring" name="stateless" value="yes"/>
      </property_group>
      <property_group type="application" name="install_ipv4_interface">
        <propval type="net_address_v4" name="static_address" value="10.134.79.160/24"/>
        <propval type="astring" name="name" value="net0/v4"/>
        <propval type="astring" name="address_type" value="static"/>
        <propval type="net_address_v4" name="default_route" value="10.134.79.1"/>
      </property_group>
    </instance>
  </service>
... (output truncated) ...
```

Now that we have created the SC profile, we need to associate it with our AI service. We use the `installadm create-profile` command:

```
# installadm create-profile -n default-sparc -p newprofile -f ./sc_profile.xml
Created Profile: 'myprofile'
# installadm list -p
Service Name  Profile Name Environment Criteria
------------  ------------ ----------- --------
default-sparc newprofile   system      none
```

We can now see that the profile has been associated with the `default-sparc` AI service. If we reboot our client and start the installation process again, the client will come up configured rather than having to walk through the System Configuration Tool again.

TIP

Since SC profiles are Service Management Facility (SMF) service profiles, we can use them to configure any part of the operating system that stores its configuration in the SMF repository. The `sysconfig` command only supports a small amount of common system configuration. If you want to provide more advanced configuration, you will need to manually edit the SC profile. A good approach is to use `sysconfig` to generate an SC profile first in which to be a base for further edits.

Applying Client Criteria

For managing multiple systems, administrators will need to map clients to the correct AI services. Only one manifest can be associated with a given client but multiple SC profiles can be associated. We do this through a set of client criteria on the AI service based on values that are determined by the client being installed. We can apply criteria based on architecture, CPU class or platform name, memory size, hostname, IP configuration, MAC address, and zone name.

Let's apply some client criteria to our existing service. We will use the `installadm set-criteria` command:

```
# installadm set-criteria -n default-sparc -m newmanifest \
-p newprofile -c mac=0:10:e0:68:23:7a
 53% : Changed Manifest: 'newmanifest'
100% : Changed Profile: 'newprofile'
# installadm list -m
Service Name            Manifest Name Type     Status            Criteria
------------            ------------- ----     ------            --------
default-sparc           newmanifest   xml      default / active  mac = 00:10:E0:68:23:7A
                        orig_default  derived  inactive          none
solaris11_2_7_4_0-sparc orig_default  derived  default           none
```

Final Configuration with First-Boot Scripts

The Oracle Solaris Automated Installer only supports a limited amount of system configuration (mostly through SMF) and doesn't generally support scripting during the install process. Any configuration that needs to be applied after an installation can be done through a series of first boot scripts that are triggered by SMF services—these are run once and then disabled. Administrators can integrate these scripts by creating their own SMF services using `svcbundle`, including them in a new IPS package and installing this as part of the AI manifest. Refer to the References at the end of this chapter for steps on how to perform this.

Alternatively, an administrator may choose to use the Puppet configuration manager for this purpose and enforce configuration from a central master. Puppet is covered in Chapter 9, *Oracle Solaris 11 Configuration Management*.

Secure End-to-End Provisioning

Installations can be secured using the Transport Layer Security (TLS) protocol. Private certificate and key pairs and Certificate Authority (CA) certificates can be generated and assigned to the install server and to clients. Using these methods, administrators can ensure that access to the install server is controlled, both the server and the client are trusted endpoints, data can be encrypted over the network and protected from other clients, and secure IPS repositories can be accessed over HTTPS connections.

Creating Custom Media

The Distribution Constructor is a tool that allows administrators to create their own customized media that can be used to install systems. Creating custom media is be important when systems have network or security restrictions and need additional software drivers to be present during system boot, for example. To use the Distribution Constructor, you will need to install the `distribution-constructor` package. The `distro_const` utility can be used to create ISO and USB install images based on a set of instructions included in a manifest (not to be confused with Automated Installer manifests). Sample manifests can be found in `/usr/share/distro_const` that are used to create the standard set of Solaris 11 installation media—LiveDVD images for x86, Text Install images for x86 and SPARC, and the AI boot images for x86 and SPARC. It is recommended that you start from these and modify as necessary. Building an image can take some time, so the tool also supports checkpoint and resume using ZFS snapshots.

Summary

In this chapter we have covered a variety of Oracle Solaris tools to help manage the software lifecycle of systems in the data center. Secure end-to-end provisioning with Automated Installer ensures total integrity of the system image. Comprehensive package management tools with IPS provide easy and fail-safe system updates, and powerful distribution of software across the data center. Finally, the flexible cloning and disaster recovery with Unified Archives allow the easy creation of an application environment with complete physical-to-virtual and virtual-to-virtual migration.

References

Oracle Solaris 11 Lifecycle Management Technologies — How to Articles, Cheat Sheets, Screencasts, Whitepapers and Presentations
http://www.oracle.com/technetwork/server-storage/solaris11/technologies/lifecycle-management-2237945.html

Boot Environments

Creating and Administering Oracle Solaris 11 Boot Environments
http://docs.oracle.com/cd/E36784_01/html/E36803/index.html

Image Packaging System (IPS)

Adding and Updating Software in Oracle Solaris 11
http://docs.oracle.com/cd/E36784_01/html/E36802/index.html

Copying and Creating Package Repositories in Oracle Solaris 11
http://docs.oracle.com/cd/E36784_01/html/E36805/index.html

Packaging and Delivering Software with IPS in Oracle Solaris 11
http://docs.oracle.com/cd/E36784_01/html/E36856/index.html

Unified Archives

Using Unified Archives for System Recovery and Cloning in Oracle Solaris 11
http://docs.oracle.com/cd/E36784_01/html/E38524/index.html

Automated Installer

Installing Using Automated Installer
http://docs.oracle.com/cd/E36784_01/html/E36800/useaipart.html#scrolltoc

Running a Custom Script During First Boot
http://docs.oracle.com/cd/E36784_01/html/E36800/firstboot-1.html#scrolltoc

Creating a Custom Solaris 11 Installation Image
http://docs.oracle.com/cd/E36784_01/html/E36804/index.html

CHAPTER
4

Oracle Solaris Zones

Solaris 10 introduced a new form of virtualization not based on, nor requiring, a hypervisor—zones. This form directly shares the base, or "global" kernel facilities, while providing secure separation of each zone's process namespace and execution environment, along with programs for zone administration like those for managing a complete OS kernel. Solaris 11 improves and extends this virtualization technology and includes zone variants that support earlier Solaris OS versions, read-only (or "immutable") environments, and, with Solaris 11.2, full Solaris OS kernels. In this chapter we discuss these variants; we describe how to create and configure native and kernel zones, how to relocate zones from a source server to a destination server, and how to set resource limits on a zone for performance and for licensing purposes. We conclude with a brief discussion of how to choose from among Oracle's various types of virtualization solutions.

Oracle's Virtualization Technologies

Oracle offers a complete range of virtualization technologies for its x86 and SPARC servers. For x86 servers, there is *Oracle Virtual Machine (OVM) for x86*, a Xen-based hypervisor that supports guest x86 operating systems including Linux, Windows, and Solaris. In that environment, *zones are available within the Solaris VMs*. For SPARC servers, there is *Oracle Virtual Machine (OVM) for SPARC*, which uses a custom hypervisor that supports SPARC/Solaris VMs called Logical Domains (LDoms). *Zones are also supported within LDoms*. With so many choices, there is great flexibility in selecting a Solaris virtualization technology. Since we are focusing on zones in this chapter, we highlight their typical use cases. This book does *not* cover *OVM for SPARC*; readers interested in that Oracle product for SPARC servers should consult the following resources:

- http://www.oracle.com/us/technologies/virtualization/oracle-vm-server-for-sparc/overview/index.html

- http://www.oracle.com/technetwork/server-storage/vm/ovmsparc-best-practices-2334546.pdf

What Are Zones?

A Solaris zone is a virtualized OS environment that securely encapsulates its process namespace and execution environment. It is configured to "look like" a traditional virtual machine (VM), in that it has a hostname and IP address, and includes typical system administration programs for managing, "booting," and configuring the zone and for installing applications within it. We prefer to call it a "virtual environment" (VE) rather than a "virtual machine" (VM) since it does *not* rely on a hypervisor to abstract its resources, although many zones users and even some documentation persist in that confusion. But that is an important distinction; since a zone is in essence just a collection of constrained processes, there is *no hypervisor overhead* to use up system resources. That means that zones are far more efficient and scalable than VMs; a single Solaris kernel can support dozens or hundreds of zones. Zones are very easy to create, deploy, and manage. And just like hypervisor-based virtualization, resources can be *shared* from the base OS and server hardware or they can be *dedicated* to specific zones. Figure 4-1 shows how zones are configured within the OS environment; the Solaris kernel runs several daemons to monitor zone services, states, and any resource caps.

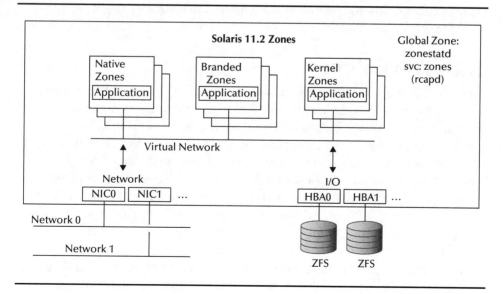

FIGURE 4-1. *Solaris 11.2 zones*

Another term often used for zones is "containers"; early Sun documentation described a Solaris container as a zone whose resource parameters were managed or explicitly constrained by the system administrator. That term—"container"—is also now commonly used for hypervisor-less VEs for Linux and for other operating systems and platforms like Docker. When describing Solaris VEs, we generally use the term "zones" to distinguish them from other workload partitioning technologies such as hardware partitions, logical domains (LDoms), and true, hypervisor-based VMs.

Solaris zones create VEs that securely isolate application environments from each other; their CPU, process, and memory resources can be restricted in order to fairly share server components or to restrict the number of OS-visible CPUs for licensing purposes. Users and applications in a zone can't observe or interact with other zones except through standard network services as if they were separate servers, although the administrator of the server's global zone can observe and monitor zones' internal activity. In fact, Solaris best practice recommendations suggest that *all* user applications should be installed and run within zones in order to take advantage of zone separation, mobility, and resource management. And, since zones are an integral part of the Solaris OS for both SPARC and x86 systems, there is *no additional cost* for using this form of virtualization.

If your system consolidation plans require lightweight VEs with high consolidation ratios and simple management, Solaris zones might be the ideal choice for virtualization.

The Global Zone

Typically an operating system is installed directly on the server hardware, or "bare metal." When Solaris is installed in this manner, its operating environment is called the "global zone" to distinguish it from other forms of zones. The global zone provides the primary kernel services and hardware access for non-global zones and for any applications running within them. Best practice for user applications, however, is to run them in non-global zones whenever possible to take advantage of zone mobility and management features. Additionally, running an application in the global zone can endanger all of the non-global zones if that application misbehaves or is compromised in some manner.

Updating and patching the global zone includes the necessary updates for the non-global zones within it. While this can provide an advantage, it precludes running different OS versions and kernel patches in those zones for Solaris 11.1 and earlier releases. But Solaris 11.2 now includes *kernel zones*, described later in this chapter, that *do allow* for different Solaris OS versions.

If you are familiar with zones on Solaris 10, you should recall that the
/etc/zones directory contains the default templates for several types of
zones. Solaris 11.2 has templates for "native zones," "branded zones," and
the new "kernel zones":

```
# cd /etc/zones
# ls
global.xml      SUNWdefault.xml                SYSsolaris-kz.xml
index           SYSblank.xml                   SYSsolaris.xml
keys            SYSdefault-shared-ip.xml       SYSsolaris10.xml
SYSdefault.xml
```

Additionally, the concept of "sparse" or read-only zones in Solaris 10 is no
longer applicable in Solaris 11, since the required file access features are now
provided by ZFS.

One final point: although virtualization technologies are useful for
consolidating multiple application environments on a single, powerful server,
you should recognize that a global zone (and a hypervisor as well!) represents
a *single point of failure*. Putting lots of eggs in one virtualized basket risks major
user and application disruption if the basket breaks. High availability (HA) and
redundancy practices are still relevant and necessary. Fortunately, Solaris zones
can be clustered and can be integrated with other availability solutions.

Basic Non-global (Native) Zones

Solaris zones are exceptionally easy to create, install, and manage. Since
they are essentially just a collection of constrained processes managed
by the global Solaris kernel, they have no additional performance impact
than those processes would have if they ran directly in the global zone.
So the scalability of multiple zones is determined by the underlying server
hardware, not by any limitations of a hypervisor. Additionally, any process
running in a zone is fully observable and even manageable from within the
global zone, unlike most true VMs.

The default installation of a zone is quite simple using the zonecfg and
zoneadm programs, for example, to create and initialize zone ngz01:

```
# zonecfg -z ngz01
Use 'create' to begin configuring a new zone.
zonecfg:ngz01> create
create: Using system default template 'SYSdefault'
zonecfg:ngz01> set zonepath=/system/zones/ngz01
zonecfg:ngz01> set autoboot=true
zonecfg:ngz01> verify
zonecfg:ngz01> commit
zonecfg:ngz01> exit
```

```
# zoneadm -z ngz01 install
        …(output deleted)…
# zoneadm -z ngz01 boot
# zoneadm list -cvi
   ID NAME          STATUS      PATH                     BRAND     IP
    0 global        running     /                        solaris   shared
    1 ngz01         running     /system/zones/ngz01      solaris   excl
```

In this simple example, we have specified the location of the root file system for the zone, and have configured the zone to boot when the global zone boots. After ngz01 boots, log into its console for further configuration and customization:

```
# zlogin -C ngz01
```

Administering the zone from *within* uses commands like those for a full OS; it can be "halted" or "rebooted," although those actions simply terminate or restart all the zone's processes. The administrator for the global zone can use the zoneadm command to "shutdown" or "reboot" the non-global zone as well.

By default, unless you specify otherwise, zonecfg creates a zone with a *virtual* NIC, using the "*exclusive-IP*" type. A *shared-IP* zone shares the network interface with the global zone and requires its own unique IP address; an *exclusive-IP* zone does *not* share the global zone's network interface. For a shared-IP zone, use zonecfg to add the IP address and NIC, for example:

```
# zonecfg -z ngz04 create -t SYSdefault-shared-ip
# zonecfg -z ngz04
zonecfg:ngz04> add net
zonecfg:ngz04:net> set physical=net1
zonecfg:ngz04:net> set address=192.168.1.230/24
zonecfg:ngz04:net> end
zonecfg:ngz04> verify
zonecfg:ngz04> commit
zonecfg:ngz04> exit
```

Creating New Zones Using Clones

Once you have created your first zone, you do not need to completely repeat all the same steps in order to create new ones; you can copy, or "clone" the original, modify the clone to suit other purposes, then boot and use it like any other zone.

To create a clone of an existing zone, first shut that zone down. Then use the `zoneadm` command to capture the zone's parameters, make any needed changes to the zonepath and IP addresses for the new zone, then create the clone. For example:

```
# zoneadm list -cvi
   ID NAME              STATUS        PATH                        BRAND        IP
    0 global            running       /                           solaris      shared
   ...
    - kzone01           installed     -                           solaris-kzexcl
    - ngz02             installed     /system/zones/ngz02         solaris      shared
# zoneadm -z ngz02 shutdown
# zonecfg -z ngz02 export -f /tmp/ngz02.cfg
...(edit the ngz02.cfg file to change the zonepath location and zone IP address)...
# zonecfg -z ngz03 -f /tmp/ngz02.cfg
# zoneadm -z ngz03 clone ngz02
...output not shown...
# zoneadm list -cvi
   ID NAME              STATUS        PATH                        BRAND        IP
    0 global            running       /                           solaris      shared
   ...
    - ngz02             installed     /system/zones/ngz02         solaris      shared
    - ngz03             installed     /system/zones/ngz03         solaris      shared
```

The newly cloned zone is now ready to use and to customize and is managed using `zoneadm` like any other zone.

Application Support in Zones

Installing and running an application in a zone is generally no different than doing so in the global zone, although this issue often comes up from ISVs who question whether their software will "run in a zone." Applications need to write to various files and directories during installation and execution; zones can be configured to allow such write permissions so that the application runs properly.

Solaris 10 Branded Zones

A "branded zone" is a Solaris VE that supports a previous release version of the OS. Solaris 10 supports Solaris 8 and Solaris 9 branded zones, and Solaris 11 supports Solaris 10 branded zones. This feature allows applications that still depend on the earlier OS version to run within the context of the new OS release.

Installing a Solaris 10 branded zone on a Solaris 11 server is a bit different from native zone installation, although it uses some of the same zone

management programs. First, verify that the IPS `pkg:/system/zones/`
`brand/brand-solaris10` package is installed on the server. Then to
create the zone, configure the target using `zonecfg` using the Solaris 10
template:

```
# zonecfg -z s10zone01 create -t SYSsolaris10
# zoneadm list -cv
  ID NAME            STATUS      PATH                        BRAND       IP
   0 global          running     /                           solaris     shared
   1 ngz01           running     /system/zones/ngz01         solaris     excl
   - s10zone01       configured  /system/zones/s10zone01     solaris10   excl
```

The usual next step for a new zone is to use `zoneadm` to install it. However,
a branded zone needs an appropriate installation source image that contains the
required Solaris 10 libraries.

NOTE
Ensure that the source image is at least at the
Solaris 10 9/10 release or later.

There are several methods for creating a Solaris 10 source image; typically
administrators will use the familiar `flarcreate` command on the source
system, for example:

```
# cd /
# flarcreate -n solaris10-image /tmp/s10-image.flar
```

This example creates an image named `solaris10-image` in a file
named `s10-image.flar` in the `/tmp` directory; specify a different directory
if necessary to ensure enough space is available. Copy the file to the target
server, for example into that system's `/tmp` directory. Then install the branded
zone using the `zoneadm` command:

```
# zoneadm -z s10zone01 install -a /tmp/s10-image.flar
    ...(installation output not shown)...
```

Once the Solaris 10 branded zone is created and installed, you administer
it in the same way as other non-global zones for booting, logging in, shutting
down, and managing installed applications. Additionally, the `zoneadm`
subcommands `detach` and `attach` described earlier and used for migrating a
non-global zone from one server to another will also work for branded zones.

Moving a Zone

Administrators familiar with VMware's *vMotion* often ask if there is a similar feature for Solaris zones that can *move* a live, running zone from one server to another without halting the zone. The short answer is no for non-global zones, since as we emphasized earlier a zone is not a VM it is an integral part of the global kernel. In a future release of Solaris, live migration will be supported for kernel zones. However, a zone can be easily "relocated"; that is, its configuration file can be copied (and edited for any required hardware differences) from the source server to the destination server and, the zone is restarted on the destination server. To capture a zone's configuration, use `zonecfg`, for example:

```
# zonecfg-z ngz01 export -f ngz01.cfg
```

Then copy the zone's configuration file to the destination server, editing it if necessary to reflect any hardware or device name differences between the source and destination servers. On the destination server, configure, install, and boot the zone:

```
# zonecfg -z ngz01 -f ngz01.cfg
# zoneadm -z ngz01 install
# zoneadm-z ngz01 boot
```

The preceding method is only one option for relocating a zone, and does *not* copy the zone's root file system. But if you are running zones in a logical domain (LDom) on a SPARC server and live migrate the LDom to a new server, the zones ride along with the migration. Also note that when relocating a zone, the destination must be at the same or later Solaris release as the source and must include the same required set of IPS packages.

A better way to relocate a zone is to use Solaris 11.2's new Unified Archive feature, which *will* copy the zone's contents to the destination. For example, create a *recovery archive* of the zone, deactivate the zone on the source by setting `autoboot=false` or by uninstalling the zone, copy the archive to the destination system, and configure the zone on the destination:

```
# zoneadm -z ngz02 halt
# archiveadm create -r -z ngz02 ngz02.uar
Initializing Unified Archive creation resources...
Unified Archive initialized: /root/ngz02.uar
Logging to: /system/volatile/archive_log.5932
Executing dataset discovery...
Dataset discovery complete
Creating install media for zone(s)...
```

```
Media creation complete
Preparing archive system image...
Beginning archive stream creation...
Archive stream creation complete
Beginning final archive assembly...
Archive creation complete

# ls -l *uar
-rw-r--r--   1 root      root        1293752320 Mar 27 20:51 ngz02.uar
```

Copy this file to the destination system, then use archiveadm to install it:

```
# zoneadm -z ngz02 install -a ngz02.uar
The following ZFS file system(s) have been created:
rpool/VARSHARE/zones/ngz02
Progress being logged to /var/log/zones/zoneadm.20150328T005705Z.ngz02.install
    Installing: This may take several minutes...
 Install Log: /system/volatile/install.5348/install_log
 AI Manifest: /tmp/manifest.ngz02.ZraOAk.xml
Zonename: ngz02
Installation: Starting ...

        Commencing transfer of stream: 2d65a5a3-30a1-4035-c717-c013e21b6756-0.zfs
torpool/VARSHARE/zones/ngz02/rpool
        Completed transfer of stream: '2d65a5a3-30a1-4035-c717-c013e21b6756-0.zfs'
from file:///root/ngz02.uar
        Archive transfer completed
Installation: Succeeded
… (output abbreviated) …
   Updating non-global zone: Zone updated.
                 Result: Attach Succeeded.

Done: Installation completed in 164.541 seconds.
  Next Steps: Boot the zone, then log into the zone console (zlogin -C)
to complete the configuration process.
Log saved in non-global zone as /system/zones/ngz02/root/var/log/zones/
zoneadm.20150328T005705Z.ngz02.install
```

Kernel Zones

Kernel zones are a new feature of the Solaris 11.2 release. While they are created and configured much like "native" non-global zones, they can implement a full Solaris 11 OS kernel version that differs from that of the global zone, and they can be updated and patched separately.

Kernel zones don't share the global 11.2 kernel, so they are in some sense like VMs running in a Type 2 hypervisor, but not exactly. Since the global zone OS and the kernel zone OS are both Solaris, significant performance and functionality optimizations are exploited, unlike general purpose hypervisor approaches.

In order to use kernel zones on Solaris 11.2, your server's processor must support the required hardware virtualization features. SPARC servers must have T4 or later processors and must have updated firmware; x86 servers must use modern Intel or Advanced Micro Devices (AMD) processors with VT-x enabled in the system's BIOS along with Nested Page Table or equivalent support. Additionally, using kernel zones requires more memory—at least 8 GB of random-access memory (RAM). Kernel zones retain the scalability benefits of native zones; you can configure hundreds of kernel zones on a single Solaris 11.2 server, assuming sufficient total server memory and processor resources.

You can check if your hardware is compatible and enabled for kernel zones using the Solaris 11.2 `virtinfo` command on either x86 or SPARC systems:
On SPARC servers:

```
# virtinfo
NAME CLASS
logical-domain current
non-global-zone supported
kernel-zone supported
logical-domain supported
```

and on x86 servers:

```
# virtinfo
NAME CLASS
non-global-zone supported
kernel-zone supported
```

You must also verify that the kernel zone software support is installed; if not, install it using IPS:

```
# pkg install brand/brand-solaris-kz
```

Configuring, installing, and booting a kernel zone is nearly identical to that of native zones; just use the familiar `zonecfg` and `zoneadm` programs. For example, to quickly create a kernel zone named `kzone01`:

```
# zonecfg -z kzone01 create -t SYSsolaris-kz
# zoneadm -z kzone01 install
       ...(IPS output not shown)...
# zoneadm -z kzone01 boot
# zlogin -C kzone01
       ...(configuration output not shown)...
```

From that point on, the installation process for the Solaris OS kernel is identical to that for the familiar bare-metal Solaris installation and configuration we described earlier.

The example above installs a Solaris 11.2 kernel zone and preconfigures several defaults. The kernel zone's `zonepath` is created in the /system/ zones ZFS, and cannot be changed. Additionally, the kernel zone's memory is initially capped at 2 GB as defined in the SYSsolaris-kz.xml template file and that memory is dedicated exclusively to that kernel zone at zone boot time. This value can be changed prior to installing the kernel zone using the `zonecfg` program. Note that for x86 systems, kernel zone capped-memory must be increased in 2 MB increments, and in 256 MB increments for SPARC systems. For example:

```
# zonecfg -z kzone01
zonecfg:kzone01> select capped-memory
zonecfg:kzone01:capped-memory> set physical=8g
zonecfg:kzone01:capped-memory> end
zonecfg:kzone01> exit
```

Kernel zones are fully independent of the server's global zone; this means the kernel zone's software image is independent from that of the global zone, and its kernel and system programs are separately patched and updated. So, while it is tempting to think of a kernel zone a traditional VM, that's not quite the case; kernel zones are a form of branded zone and use a similar framework.

The default configuration of a kernel zone has 2 GB of memory, one hardware thread (vCPU), one vNIC, and a 16 GB ZFS boot volume. Depending on the resource requirements for applications running in a kernel zone, you may need to increase these values. To allocate more storage at installation time, for example, use the `zoneadm` command:

```
# zoneadm -z kzone01 install -x install-size=64g
```

Additionally, depending on the total memory in your server and the number of active zones, you might need to limit the memory used by the *server's* ZFS cache. To do this, include a file in /etc/system.d with the content: "set zfs:zfs _ arc _ max=0x40000000" (1GB) or other desired number of bytes for the cache memory, and reboot the system. See the Recommended Oracle ZFS Practices document in the References section for further guidance on tuning ZFS.

The default kernel zone VE includes the `solaris-small-server` IPS group package; use the IPS `pkg` program to install other desired components, such as `group/system/solaris-desktop`.

One unique feature of kernel zones is the ability to suspend the execution of the zone and to persist its state into a compressed and encrypted file saved in the kernel zone's zonepath. The purpose of this feature is to enable migration of the kernel zone from one server to another. To use this feature, first use the `zonecfg` command to define a location for the file:

```
# zonecfg -z kzone01
zonecfg:kzone01> add suspend
zonecfg:kzone01:suspend> set path=/export/zones/suspend/kzone01.susp
zonecfg:kzone01:suspend> end
zonecfg:kzone01> exit
```

Additionally, you must save and transfer the kernel zone's configuration file from the source server to the destination server along with the suspension file:

```
# zonecfg -z kzone01 export -f /export/zones/suspend/kzone01.cfg
```

Copy that configuration file to the destination server, for example to its/ `tmp` directory, then on the destination server:

```
# zonecfg -z kzone01 -f /tmp/kzone01.cfg
```

Then you can suspend the kernel zone:

```
# zoneadm -z kzone01 suspend
```

The `zoneadm list` command then shows the suspended zone state as "installed." Use the '`-i`'(installed) and '`-s`'(state) flags together to observe the auxiliary "suspended" state of a kernel zone:

```
# zoneadm list -is
NAME                STATUS          AUXILIARY STATE
global              running
ngz01               running
kzone01             installed       suspended
```

To migrate the suspended kernel zone to a new server, detach it from the source server using `zoneadm detach`, transfer the suspend file to the destination server, reconnect it using `zoneadm attach`, then boot it. There is no explicit "resume" sub-command; the "boot" sub-command serves that purpose.

NOTE

Because kernel zones on x86 servers directly access the processor's virtualization hardware, you can't create and run them in hypervisor environments such as Oracle VM for x86 *or in* Oracle VM VirtualBox *which also want to use that virtualization hardware. Additionally, attempting to run Solaris 11.2 with kernel zones along with a VirtualBox instance at the same time might cause a kernel panic of the server's global zone.*

Immutable Zones

An *immutable* zone is one that has a *read-only* zone root file system. This prevents any changes to the zone's system binaries or configuration files from *within* the zone; the *global* zone administrator can access and alter the zone's files if needed.

Creating and updating immutable zones is a straightforward process. It uses the zone's `file-mac-profile` (file access control) property which is *not* set by default when the zone is created. That property can subsequently be set to values that control write access for IPS package updates, service configuration, and event audit logging. The "fixed" value allows write access to `/var` subdirectories but prevents IPS updates and service changes. The "flexible" value permits changes to both `/var` and `/etc` files and subdirectories and to the root home directory but still prevents IPS and service updates. The "strict" value implements complete immutability—read only—of the zone's files and configuration; only the global zone administrator can modify the zone. Set this property using the `zonecfg` program, for example:

```
# zonecfg -z ngz02
zonecfg:ngz02> set file-mac-profile=strict
zonecfg:ngz02> exit
```

Immutable *global* zones support has been added in Solaris 11.2 to extend the immutable zone capability to the global zone. If a system is configured to have an immutable global zone, files in the *root* file system are *read-only*. For example, to enable an immutable *global* zone:

```
# zonecfg -z global set file-mac-profile=fixed-configuration
```

A trusted path login allows access to perform maintenance tasks, such as system updates. That is, global zone maintenance can only be done through the server's console (directly attached, or through the server's ILOM interface). The global zone's ZFS `rpool` dataset is read-only, but writable sub-datasets can be created for unrestricted non-global zones. Immutable global zones are updated with IPS when they are first installed and booted, but then require a reboot to enable the immutability.

Hard Partitioning with Zones for Oracle Licensing

Many ISV software applications are licensed according to the number of CPUs presented by the processor hardware and operating system; the Oracle database and other Oracle software are licensed in this manner. But with the evolution of multicore/multithreaded processors, the number of CPUs seen by the OS and by the application is growing into the hundreds or even thousands. Oracle's SPARC T5-8 server, for example, presents more than 1000 hardware threads (CPUs) to the OS. In order for the per-CPU software licensing fees to avoid getting unmanageably expensive, especially on today's massively scalable servers, Oracle and other software vendors have implemented licensing policies that are based on the *capped* resources of VEs rather than on the full hardware thread (total "CPU") capacity of the server.

In particular, Oracle recognizes both LDoms and Solaris zones as "hard partitions" for the purpose of licensing database and other software. This is accomplished by explicitly limiting the number of server CPUs visible to the licensed application. For Oracle servers, there are three types of such limiting technologies: physical domains, logical domains, and zones.

Recall that modern servers may have multiple *processors* (chips, or "sockets"), each having multiple *cores*, with each core having multiple *hardware threads* ("CPUs," or "virtual CPUs"). For example, Oracle's T5-2 server has two T5 processors, each with sixteen 8-thread cores for a total of 256 "CPUs" ($2 \times 16 \times 8$). The T5-8 server has more than *1000* hardware threads, and future systems will have significantly more. Clearly, licensing according to total server CPU count is not ideal at present, so mechanisms to limit the number of visible CPUs have been provided.

To determine the number of hardware threads available, you can use the `psrinfo` command, for example on a SPARC T4-1 server:

```
# psrinfo -pv
The physical processor has 8 cores and 64 virtual processors (0-63)
The core has 8 virtual processors (0-7)
The core has 8 virtual processors (8-15)
The core has 8 virtual processors (16-23)
The core has 8 virtual processors (24-31)
The core has 8 virtual processors (32-39)
The core has 8 virtual processors (40-47)
The core has 8 virtual processors (48-55)
The core has 8 virtual processors (56-63)
SPARC-T4 (chipid 8, clock 2848 MHz)
```

There are several acceptable methods for limiting the number of hardware threads for licensing purposes. Use the `zonecfg` program to set and configure the zone's `dedicated-cpu` property or the `capped-cpu` property:

```
# zonecfg -z ngz01
zonecfg:ngz01> add dedicated-cpu
zonecfg:ngz01: dedicated-cpu> set ncpus=4-8
zonecfg:ngz01: dedicated-cpu> end
zonecfg:ngz01> verify
zonecfg:ngz01> commit
zonecfg:ngz01> exit
```

This sets the number of hardware threads for zone `ngz01` to a range of 4 to 8; the value used for the license in this case will be 8, the maximum of that range. Alternatively:

```
# zonecfg -z ngz01
zonecfg:ngz01> add capped-cpu
zonecfg:ngz01: capped-cpu> set ncpus=4
zonecfg:ngz01: capped-cpu> end
zonecfg:ngz01> verify
zonecfg:ngz01> commit
zonecfg:ngz01> exit
```

In this case, the number of hardware threads available for zone `ngz01` will be no more than 4, and that number is used for licensing purposes. Limiting assigned CPUs for Oracle software can save considerable licensing costs, so it is worthwhile accurately determining your zone sizing requirements. Be sure to review the document *Hard Partitioning with Oracle Solaris Zones* listed in the References section at the end of the chapter to better understand Oracle's licensing requirements.

Capping Zone Resources for Performance Management

Capping the number of hardware threads available to a zone can be done as we just described for licensing purposes, but that can also be used to limit hardware resources for performance management as well, that is, to avoid activity in one zone affecting the resources needed for other zones or for the global zone itself. In addition to limiting CPU usage for a zone, memory usage can be managed, along with the allowable number of process threads.

Use the zonecfg program to specify limits for the memory used by the zone and for the swap space used by the zone. For example:

```
# zonecfg -z ngz03
zonecfg:ngz03> add capped-memory
zonecfg:ngz03:capped-memory> set physical=2g
zonecfg:ngz03:capped-memory> set swap=4g
zonecfg:ngz03:capped-memory> end
zonecfg:ngz03> verify
zonecfg:ngz03> commit
zonecfg:ngz03> exit
```

One of the most commonly used resource controls for zones is the number of allowable execution threads—"lightweight processes" or LWPs. Although Solaris can run hundreds of thousands of threads, it may be desirable to limit the number of LWPs for each zone, lest one of the zones generates too many. Setting an appropriate value might require some experimentation depending on the type of application running in the zone. A zone itself might use almost 200 LWPs, and applications within it might want a few hundred more. So, for example, to cap the number of LWPs in zone ngz03at 500, use the following:

```
# zonecfg -z ngz03
zonecfg:ngz03> set max-lwps=500
zonecfg:ngz03> exit
# zoneadm -z ngz03 reboot
```

We will see in Chapter 6 how to monitor the activity of the global and non-global zones.

What Kind of Virtualization Should I Use?

Recall that there is a hypervisor-based VE solution from Oracle, in particular *OVM for SPARC*. Since that technology also provides for hosting different Solaris kernel versions on a server, albeit requiring multiple individually managed VMs, what are some general guidelines for selecting how to deploy applications in LDoms, native zones, branded zones, or kernel zones?

Hardware- and hypervisor-based LDoms can provide for the greatest level of direct resource separation and control, and can exploit the special server features of the SPARC systems for internal I/O path redundancy. Solaris zones, on the other hand, provide the highest consolidation potential and ease of management. Both can be optimized for maximum, "bare-metal" performance, and can be configured to enable various forms of live mobility or relocation. And recall that a Solaris 10 or 11 instance running on an LDom can have non-global zones of any type running within it.

The special case of branded zones allows applications dependent on the earlier Solaris 10 release to run in a VE within Solaris 11; so if your environment requires such support or if your applications are not yet ready to be moved to Solaris 11, branded zones are the logical option. But remember, the point of such branded zones is not to encourage you to run your applications on older OS versions forever, but to assist with eventually moving them to the current version. Also recall that with the Oracle Solaris Binary Compatibility guarantee, Solaris 10 applications should run unmodified in Solaris 11.

The choice between native and kernel zones is determined by the requirement to run different OS versions and the need for VE mobility. Native zones are the easiest to manage and can efficiently exploit resource sharing of memory, hardware threads, and virtualized I/O. Kernel zones provide for OS version variability if needed, are independently patched and updated, and are more easily relocated. The choice of a VE, therefore, is dependent on the requirements of the application(s) that will run within it, although in many cases the applications won't care. Even VE mobility is not a determining factor, since zones running within in an LDom or in a kernel zone can live migrate along with their host. The need for high consolidation ratios might determine which type of VE to implement; zones are considerably more scalable in that regard. And if you change your mind, Solaris 11.2's Unified Archive technology helps you redeploy one form of VE into another, as we described in Chapter 3.

Summary

In this chapter, we have described the various types of Oracle Solaris Zones, including how to create, configure, and manage them. We gave some general guidance on how to choose which type of zone to use for hosting applications and their operating system requirements. In later chapters, we cover system performance and security issues which includes further details related to zones.

References

Creating and Using Oracle Solaris 10 Zones,
https://docs.oracle.com/cd/E36784_01/pdf/E37630.pdf

Creating and Using Oracle Solaris Kernel Zones,
http://docs.oracle.com/cd/E36784_01/pdf/E37629.pdf

Hard Partitioning With Oracle Solaris Zones,
http://www.oracle.com/technetwork/server-storage/solaris11/technologies/
os-zones-hard-partitioning-2347187.pdf

Recommended Oracle Solaris ZFS Practices,
http://docs.oracle.com/cd/E36784_01/html/E36835/practice-1.html

CHAPTER
5

Configuring Solaris 11
Networking

As the Solaris operating system (OS) has evolved to provide richer and more scalable features such as virtualization, the traditional network stack and administration tools needed to be enhanced as well. Solaris 11 has, therefore, been significantly updated compared to earlier releases in order to simplify network administration of real and virtual components and to enhance network observability and resource management. In this chapter, we describe the new approaches to network configuration and administration, including basic hardware device setup and creating and using virtual network components. We show how to set up basic network hardware using new system commands, and then show how to use these command to set up and manage virtual network components. We also include details on monitoring hardware and virtual network traffic, and show how to allocate bandwidth resources among the network components.

Basic Network Setup

Basic network interface card (NIC) and Transmission Control Protocol/Internet Protocol (TCP/IP) setup for Solaris 11 has changed a bit, including some new and useful features and new commands for configuring and managing the network. The long-familiar `ifconfig` command has been superseded by two new commands, `dladm` for administering both physical network hardware and virtualized datalinks, and `ipadm` for configuring IP interfaces on those datalinks. An important new Solaris 11 feature is the *generic* naming of datalinks to support interoperability of network configurations for migration and easing of system upgrades. The older NIC device naming scheme, for example, `/dev/e1000g0`, now uses a more general `/dev/net/net0` "vanity" or descriptive linked name which can be set to any arbitrary name by the administrator, such as `/dev/net/production1` or `/dev/net/devtest0` – this allows greater portability of network configuration as the underlying devices change.

Network administration is also supplemented through the Service Management Facility (SMF) rather than through the older, less convenient manual editing of system configuration files in the `/etc` directory. This provides a mechanism using SMF profiles to deploy network configuration at scale across multiple systems.

Network monitoring and diagnostic tools have been enhanced as well, including integration with the Solaris Fault Manager (fmd), and two new programs: tcpstat for reporting on TCP and User Datagram Protocol (UDP) traffic statistics and ipstat for IP traffic.

Solaris 11 continues to support both IPv4 and IPv6 network configurations simultaneously, and includes tools for setup of both protocols.

The ifconfig command is still present and functional in Solaris 11, but all network configuration should now be done with the new dladm and ipadm commands. Generally, Solaris 11 preserves some of the "old ways" of OS administration, but strongly recommends or requires use of the new tools and methods. Table 5-1 shows comparisons of some typical network tasks using the old ifconfig and the new Solaris 11 programs.

Network Configuration Task	Using ifconfig	Using Solaris 11 Tools: ipadm and dladm
Display configuration info	# ifconfig -a	# ipadm
Set a static IP address	# ifconfig e1000g0 192.168.1.200/24 up	# ipadm create-ip net1 # ipadm create-addr -T static -a 192.168.1.200/24 net1
Set a NIC to use DHCP	# ifconfig e1000g0 plumb # ifconfig e1000g0 dhcp start	# ipadm create-addr -T dhcp net1
Display a NIC's MAC address	# ifconfig net0	# dladm show-linkprop -p mac-address net0

TABLE 5-1. *Network Configuration Tasks Using* ifconfig *and* ipadm/dladm

Identifying Physical Network Devices

The obvious first task for configuring a server's network is to identify the *physical* datalinks that are available. For this you use the dladm program, for example:

```
# dladm show-phys

LINK            MEDIA            STATE      SPEED   DUPLEX    DEVICE
net0            Ethernet         up         100     full      e1000g
net1            Ethernet         up         1000    full      rge0
```

This shows the generic names, device name and types of the datalinks, whether they are up, and their currently set speed (a good setting to check if there are network problems!). Additionally, automatic network configuration in Solaris 11 is done through *profiles*, using either the *Automatic* profile [for Dynamic Host Configuration Protocol (DHCP)] or the *Default Fixed* profile (for manual IP address assignment). You set and display the desired profile using the netadm program, for example:

```
# netadm enable -p ncp DefaultFixed
```

or

```
# netadm enable -p ncp Automatic
```

```
# netadm list

TYPE            PROFILE          STATE
ncp             Automatic        online
ncu:phys        net0             online
ncu:phys        net1             online
ncu:ip          net0             online
ncu:ip          net1             online
ncp             DefaultFixed     disabled
loc             Automatic        online
loc             NoNet            offline
```

NOTE

The two network configuration modes, DefaultFixed and Automatic, should be sufficient for most network setup. For static network address assignments, use DefaultFixed, and for DHCP, use Automatic.

Interfaces can be configured using profiles as given previously, or can be created directly for static or DHCP, for example:

```
# ipadm create-ip net1
# ipadm create-addr -a 192.168.1.220/24 net1
```

or

```
# ipadm create-ip net1
# ipadm create-addr -T dhcp net1
```

To set a default route, use the `route` command, for example:

```
# route -p add default 192.168.1.1
```

Name service configuration in Solaris 10 and earlier required editing of the /etc/resolv.conf and /etc/nsswitch.conf files. In Solaris 11, the name service information is now configured and maintained by SMF, for example:

```
# svccfg -s svc:/network/dns/client setpropconfig/nameserver=net_address: 192.168.1.1
```

which configures the /etc/resolv.conf file, and

```
# svc -s svc:/system/name-service/switch setpropconfig/default = "files nis"
# svc -s svc:/system/name-service/switch setpropconfig/host = "files dns nis"
```

which configures the /etc/nsswitch.conf file.

The name service files are created, but *should not be edited*; most files maintained by SMF contain this warning, *which should be heeded*:

```
# _AUTOGENERATED_FROM_SMF_V1_
#
# WARNING: THIS FILE GENERATED FROM SMF DATA.
#    DO NOT EDIT THIS FILE.   EDITS WILL BE LOST.
```

There are two Solaris technologies for improving network performance and availability: *Link Aggregation* and *IP Multi-Pathing* (IPMP). IPMP provides a failover connection for network traffic. It also increases aggregate network bandwidth, spreading outbound traffic among the NICs in the IPMP group, with each NIC having its own static IP address; the IPMP group is assigned a virtual NIC interface, such as `ipmp0`. If one of the IPMP group's NICs fails, traffic will be routed to another NIC in the group. Link aggregation provides similar bandwidth and failover features, and can load-balance both inbound and outbound network traffic; it functions at the datalink layer (L2), while IPMP does so at the protocol layer (L3). The `dlstat` program, discussed later, reports bandwidth statistics on link aggregations as well as on physical NICs.

Link aggregation is configured using the `dladm` and `ipadm` programs, for example:

```
# dladm create-aggr -l net0 -l net1 aggr0
# ipadm create-ip aggr0
# ipadm create-addr -T static -a 192.168.1.225/24 aggr0
```

and IPMP is configured using the `ipadm` program:

```
# ipadm create-ip net0
# ipadm create-ip net1
# ipadm create-ip net2
# ipadm create-ipmp ipmp
# ipadm add-ipmp -i net0 -i net1 -i net2 ipmp0
# ipadm create-addr -T static -a 192.168.1.200/24 ipmp0
# ipadm create-addr -T static -a 192.168.1.201/24 net0
# ipadm create-addr -T static -a 192.168.1.202/24 net1
# ipadm create-addr -T static -a 192.168.1.203/24 net2
```

Using the Network Preferences Graphical User Interface

If you have installed a system that includes the GNOME desktop environment (using the `group/solaris-desktop` package), network setup is easily done through the network preferences graphical user interface (GUI) as shown in Figure 5-1. Selecting the *Connection Status* (*Show:*) option displays the current network configuration of the available interfaces.

Selecting the *Network Profile* option allows you to create, activate, and manage profiles, as well as managing those created using the command, as in Figure 5-2.

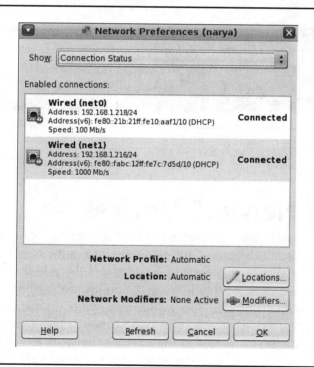

FIGURE 5-1. *The Solaris Network Preferences GUI*

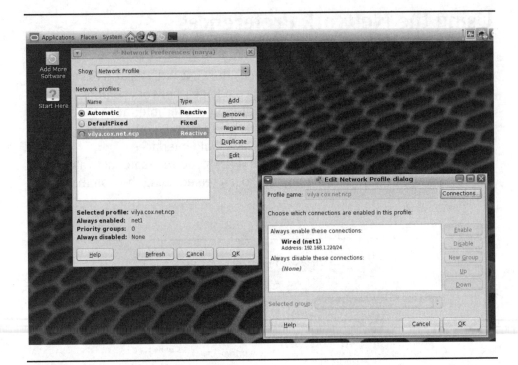

FIGURE 5-2. *Editing the Network Profile using the GUI*

Virtual Network Devices

Configuring *physical* network components in Solaris has not really changed that much from earlier versions other than the use of the new commands in Solaris 11. What has changed, significantly, is the addition of *virtual* network components that provide better flexibility and agility for networking in a virtualized environment. This evolution toward software defined network components provides a great opportunity to reexamine traditional network infrastructures and to eliminate certain network hardware, as well as to significantly improve inter-component bandwidth. For example, in a typical three-tier Web infrastructure with separate hardware for the Web server, application server, and database server, each component has its own physical server that communicates over the wired network at available Ethernet speeds, as in Figure 5-3. Contrast this with a single larger,

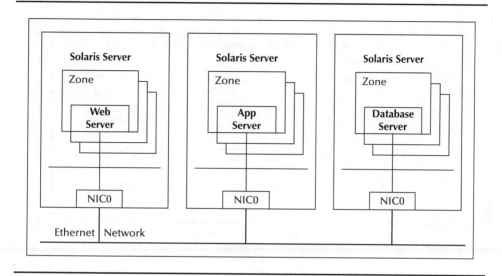

FIGURE 5-3. *A typical multi-server three-tier Web architecture*

virtualized system with each component running in a zone. Inter-zone communication among the components occurs at much faster system bus speeds and has no need to leave the server, does not require dedicated NICs for each tier, thus significantly reducing wired network traffic and improving Web application performance, as in Figure 5-4.

Additionally, virtual network components, along with virtual environments (VEs) [zones and virtual machines (VMs)], are a foundation of the elasticity and adjustable QoS technologies used in Oracle's cloud computing offerings and OpenStack implementations.

In this section, we describe the virtual network components available in Solaris 11 and show how to create and manage them using the new network commands.

Virtual Network Components

Virtual network components mimic their corresponding hardware counterparts in that they are designed to provide the same services and are configured with the same tools and parameters. Their benefit, however, is that they are *software*

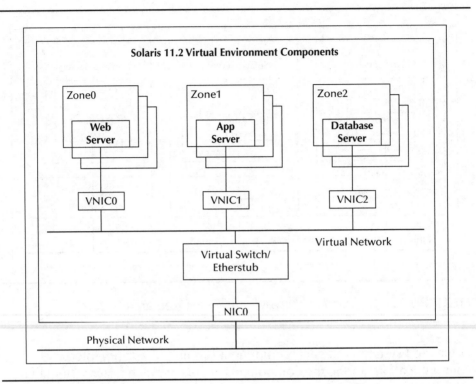

FIGURE 5-4. *A virtualized three-tier Web architecture*

constructs, easily created, modified, and activated *within* a physical server or VE. The basic virtual network components are as follows:

Virtual Network Interface Card (VNIC): This component acts like a physical NIC and is used in Solaris 11 to provide network connectivity among zones. Multiple VNICs can be associated with a physical NIC for addressing purposes; VNICs have unique media access control (MAC) addresses which can be automatically assigned or administrator assigned. Administrators can configure a VNIC's IP address statically or using DHCP.

Virtual Switch (VSWITCH): Like a physical network switch, a VSWITCH routes traffic among zones within the server. Such network traffic by default stays *within* the server unless forced to an external route. These are automatically created when VNICs are created and are not directly managed.

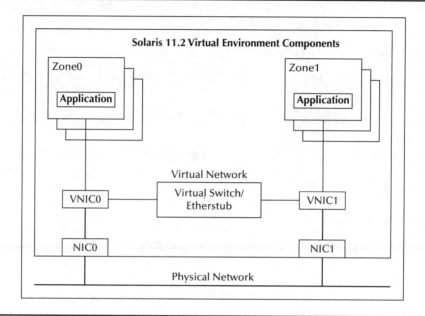

FIGURE 5-5. *Solaris 11 Virtual Network Components*

ETHERSTUB: An ETHERSTUB is a virtual Ethernet NIC which VNICs can use instead of linking to a physical NIC. This virtual device allows system administrators to build private networks within a server, isolated from any other network traffic.

The configuration and relationship of these virtual network devices are illustrated in Figure 5-5.

Creating Virtual Network Components

Recall that VNICs are associated with physical NICs, so first identify the physical NICs available on the server, for example:

```
# dladm show-phys
LINK               MEDIA              STATE      SPEED   DUPLEX    DEVICE
net0               Ethernet           up         100     full      e1000g0
net1               Ethernet           up         1000    full      rge0
```

Then, to create a VNIC for a particular physical NIC, use the `create-vnic` option for the `dladm` program, for example:

```
# dladm create-vnic -l net1 vnic0
# dladm show-vnic
LINK                OVER            SPEED   MACADDRESS          MACADDRTYPE VIDS
vnic0               net1            1000    2:8:20:ff:28:f4     random      0
```

Note that the VNIC has its own MAC address, and that it inherits the speed setting from the physical NIC.

Recall from Chapter 4 that when a zone is created it is given a VNIC associated with a physical NIC; we can see this using the `show-vnic` option, for example:

```
# dladm show-vnic
LINK                OVER            SPEED   MACADDRESS          MACADDRTYPE VIDS
kzone01/net0        net0            100     2:8:20:b1:c5:13     random      0
ngz01/net0          net0            100     2:8:20:98:da:f4     random      0
vnic0               net1            1000    2:8:20:ff:28:f4     random      0
```

Next, you need to assign an IP address to the VNIC using `ipadm`, for example:

```
# ipadm create-addr -a 192.168.1.222/24 vnic0
vnic0/v4
# dladm show-link
LINK                CLASS       MTU     STATE     OVER
net0                phys        1500    up        --
net1                phys        1500    up        --
kzone01/net0        vnic        1500    up        net0
ngz01/net0          vnic        1500    up        net0
vnic0               vnic        1500    up        net1
# ping 192.168.1.222
192.168.1.222 is alive
```

Alternatively, if you are creating an internal private network that won't interact with the external network, create an etherstub `estub0` in place of a physical NIC, for example:

```
# dladm create-etherstub estub0
# dladm show-link
LINK                CLASS         MTU     STATE     OVER
net0                phys          1500    up        --
net1                phys          1500    up        --
kzone01/net0        vnic          1500    up        net0
ngz01/net0          vnic          1500    up        net0
vnic0               vnic          1500    up        net1
estub0              etherstub     9000    unknown   --
```

When you create VNICs, Solaris automatically creates an internal VSWITCH to route the network traffic among the zones' VNICs. And VNICs created on an etherstub will use an internal VSWITCH for all network traffic.

The Elastic Virtual Switch

Solaris 11.2 now includes a new type of virtual network service, the *Elastic Virtual Switch* (EVS), which is used to manage multiple VSWITCH environments among multiple physical servers. Like the individual VSWITCH described earlier, the EVS routes network traffic among VNICS, but those VNICs can be on separate SPARC or x86 hardware servers or on VEs *anywhere on the network*, including on zones and on kernel zones. This feature enables centralized management of the virtual network resources, including MAC and IP address management and QoS resource settings on all of the virtual communication links.

The EVS consists of several components, including a Manager, Controller, Clients, and Nodes. The virtual network endpoints, clients and nodes, use VNICs as described in the previous section, but are configured and managed through the EVS that unifies the nodes under one virtual network, as shown in Figure 5-6.

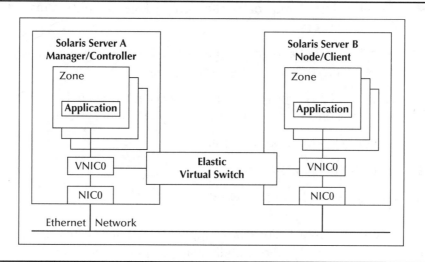

FIGURE 5-6. *A basic EVS configuration*

There are three major components in an EVS network:

EVS Manager: The EVS Manager defines the topology and IP addresses of the systems that comprise the network.

EVS Controller: The EVS Controller is the distributed switch that that routes the network traffic among the nodes and clients. It can (and usually does) reside on the same server as the EVS Manager, although it can be configured on a separate system for administrative or scalability purposes.

EVS Compute Nodes and Clients: EVS Nodes are systems on the network containing VNICs; EVS Clients are systems or zones associated with those VNICs.

Creating an EVS Network

There are several key steps to setting up an EVS network:

- Ensure that all systems can connect to each other over the net using their full domain names or host names.
- Using IPS, install and enable the `evs` package on all systems in the planned network.
- Using IPS, install and enable the `rad-evs-controller` package on the Manager/Controller system.
- Enable SSH password-less public key connections between the Manager/Controller system and the Node/Client systems.
- Configure the Manager/Controller.
- Configure the Nodes/Clients.
- Test and verify the EVS network.

In our example, we will illustrate a simple EVS network with one Manager/Controller node (`narya`) and one additional Compute/Client node (`vilya`). This example can be easily extended to multiple Compute/Client nodes.

The EVS components must first be installed using IPS on *each system* to be used as Manager, Controller, and Nodes, including zones and kernel zones:

```
# pkg install pkg:/service/network/evs
( ... output truncated ...)
# pkg list evs
NAME (PUBLISHER)                               VERSION              IFO
service/network/evs                            0.5.11-0.175.2.0.0.42.2   i--
# svcs evs
STATE        STIME     FMRI
online       11:48:21  svc:/network/evs:default
```

Upon installation on each system, IPS creates an EVS administrator user ID, evsuser, with a rights profile that allows EVS operations. On the Manager/Controller system:

```
# pkg install rad-evs-controller
( ... output truncated ...)
# svcadm restart rad:local
```

Next, set up an authenticated connection from the Node/Client system to the Manager/Controller system. This requires generating a password-less RSA SSH key pair on the Node/Client and copying it to the Manager/Controller, for example:

```
root@vilya:~# ssh-keygen -t rsa
Generating public/private rsa key pair.
Enter file in which to save the key (/root/.ssh/id_rsa):
Enter passphrase (empty for no passphrase):
Enter same passphrase again:
Your identification has been saved in /root/.ssh/id_rsa.
Your public key has been saved in /root/.ssh/id_rsa.pub.
The key fingerprint is:
35:62:55:c3:18:2b:3e:af:3b:ee:c6:0a:0a:79:20:93root@vilya
```

Copy the file, /root/.ssh/id_rsa, to the /var/user/evsuser/.ssh/authorized_keys file on the Manager/Controller system.

Test the evsuser SSH login connection from the Node/Client to the Manager/Controller:

```
# ssh evsuser@narya
The authenticity of host 'narya (192.168.1.216)' can't be established.
RSA key fingerprint is ea:57:9a:99:fa:28:b8:4f:62:f7:4e:d2:1a:10:5a:7f.
Are you sure you want to continue connecting (yes/no)? yes
Warning: Permanently added 'narya,192.168.1.216' (RSA) to the list of known hosts.
evsuser@narya:~$
```

In a similar way, set up authorized connection from the Manager/Controller to the Node/Client; generate the RSA key pair file and copy it to the Node/Client:

```
root@narya:~# su - evsuser
evsuser@narya:~$ ssh-keygen -t rsa
Generating public/private rsa key pair.
Enter file in which to save the key (/var/user/evsuser/.ssh/id_rsa):
Enter passphrase (empty for no passphrase):
Enter same passphrase again:
Your identification has been saved in /var/user/evsuser/.ssh/id_rsa.
Your public key has been saved in /var/user/evsuser/.ssh/id_rsa.pub.
The key fingerprint is:
36:2f:74:c7:b9:65:d0:d4:53:1b:40:61:87:1b:30:16
evsuser@narya:~$

root@narya:~# ssh evsuser@vilya
The authenticity of host 'vilya (192.168.1.207)' can't be established.
RSA key fingerprint is 48:52:91:77:7c:7d:15:55:fc:c1:be:a5:55:c7:81:1f.
Are you sure you want to continue connecting (yes/no)? yes
Warning: Permanently added 'vilya,192.168.1.207' (RSA) to the list of known hosts.
evsuser@vilya:~$
```

Configure and verify the EVS Controller using the evsadm program to point to the Manager/Controller system:

```
root@narya:~# evsadm set-prop -p controller=ssh://evsuser@narya
root@narya:~# evsadm show-prop
PROPERTY        PERM VALUE                      DEFAULT
controller      rw   ssh://evsuser@narya        --
```

Set the Controller property for the Node/Client:

```
root@vilya:~# evsadm set-prop -p controller=ssh://evsuser@narya
root@vilya:~# evsadm show-prop
PROPERTY        PERM VALUE                      DEFAULT
controller      rw   ssh://evsuser@narya
```

The EVS creates isolated multi-tenant virtual networks using virtual local area networks (VLANs) or virtual extensible local area networks (VXLANs). Set the EVS topology control property, VLAN range, and datalink ports for the VLAN using the evsadm program on the Manager system, for example:

```
root@narya:~# evsadm set-controlprop -p l2-type=vlan
root@narya:~# evsadm set-controlprop -p vlan-range=100-200
root@narya:~# evsadm set-controlprop -p uplink-port=net0
root@narya:~# evsadm set-controlprop -h vilya -p uplink-port=net0
```

At this point you can configure and verify the EVS Controller settings
directly or from any of the client nodes. For example:

```
root@narya:~# evsadm show-controlprop -p l2-type,vlan-range,uplink-port
NAME                    VALUE            DEFAULT            HOST
l2-type                 vlan             vlan               --
vlan-range              100-200          --                 --
uplink-port             net0             --                 --
uplink-port             net0             --                 vilya
```

You can now create an EVS and specify "tenants," which partition the
collection of VNICs into different name spaces; these name spaces confine
each tenant's network resources and traffic, and prevent other tenants from
viewing anything on each others' name spaces. For example, to create a
private EVS-managed set of systems and VNICs for a set of developers:

```
# evsadm create-evs -T tenant1 DEV
# evsadm create-evs -T tenant1 PROD
```

This will create a private VLAN network for DEV and PROD users within
the `tenant1` namespace. There can be multiple tenants on multiple EVSs,
each serving a different set of zones and VNICs, under each client's Node
Controller and a single, Central Master Controller. Figure 5-7 shows a general
schematic of a multiple EVS configuration.

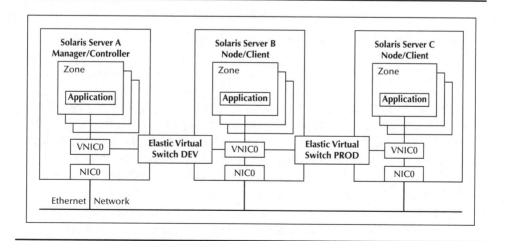

FIGURE 5-7. *A multi-tenant EVS configuration*

Managing and Monitoring Network Resources

Physical network devices have native bandwidth capabilities that can also auto-detect different settings depending on their connection to other network equipment. For example, a 10 GB Ethernet controller will auto-negotiate its bandwidth with a switch it's connected to and will reduce to 1 Gb/s if that is the maximum capability of the switch. Sometimes networks are explicitly designed to maximize throughput between some devices (like a server and a SAN), while throttling or minimizing network traffic for other purposes (like an archive file server for large downloads). Solaris 11 provides the ability to control bandwidth connections among VNICs to either limit the impact of network traffic or to guarantee a required level of bandwidth resource for critical applications.

Controlling Network Bandwidth

Network bandwidth on a physical or virtual network device is controlled using the `dladm` program to set the device's datalink properties. For example, to limit the bandwidth used for a VNIC, change its `maxbw` property:

```
# dladm show-vnic vnic0
LINK                    OVER            SPEED  MACADDRESS       MACADDRTYPE VIDS
vnic0                   net1            1000   2:8:20:ff:28:f4  random      0

# dladm set-linkprop -p maxbw=500 vnic0
# dladm show-vnic vnic0
LINK                    OVER            SPEED  MACADDRESS       MACADDRTYPE VIDS
vnic0                   net1            500    2:8:20:ff:28:f4  random      0
```

Note that this change is *immediate* and *dynamic*; no reboot or reset of the datalink is required for the new bandwidth setting to be recognized.

Another feature for managing network traffic in Solaris 11 is *flows*. A flow is a network device configuration setting that categorizes and filters network packets according to a specified protocol, for example, limiting the network bandwidth used by a particular IP address and service (such as an HTTP server). You must first create a named flow using the `flowadm` command, and then set the desired property for that flow. For example, to restrict the bandwidth from a remote system to a local Web server (by port and address):

```
# flowadm add-flow -l vnic0 -a transport=tcp,local_ip=192.168.1.205,
local_port=80,remote_ip=192.168.1.207 flow0
# flowadm set-flowprop -p maxbw=300 flow0
# flowadm
FLOW       LINK    PROTO LADDR              LPORT RADDR              RPORT DSFLD
flow0      vnic0   tcp   192.168.1.205      80    192.168.1.207      --    --
# flowadm show-flowprop
FLOW       PROPERTY     PERM VALUE       DEFAULT       POSSIBLE
flow0      maxbw        rw   300         --            --
flow0      priority     rw   medium      medium        low,medium,high
flow0      hwflow       r-   off         --            on,off
```

Monitoring Network Activity

Network bandwidth usage statistics are available using several utilities—
dlstat for datalinks, ipstat for IP traffic, and flowstat for flows. These
programs are useful for verifying network connectivity and performance
expectations, as well as for troubleshooting. All three of these programs
work similar to the familiar vmstat. That is, adding numeric parameters
n and r after the command will capture and display the statistics every
n seconds for r repetitions. For example, run the programs three times at
2-second intervals:

```
# dlstat 2 3
          LINK    IPKTS   RBYTES   OPKTS    OBYTES
          net1        0        0      17    2.23K
          net0    21.76K   2.53M   7.38K   627.78K
      vboxnet0        0        0       0        0
  kzone01/net0    16.40K   2.05M   2.35K   220.14K
    ngz01/net0    14.24K   1.82M       0        0
    ngz01/net1    14.24K   1.82M       0        0
(... output truncated ...)
```

```
# ipstat 2 3
SOURCE          DEST             PROTO         INT       BYTES
narya           192.168.1.202    TCP           vnic0     2431.0
192.168.1.202   192.168.1.255    UDP           net1      23.0
(... output truncated ...)
```

```
# flowstat 2 3
FLOW     IPKTS    RBYTES    IDROPS    OPKTS    OBYTES    ODROPS
flow0    1.2M     1.7G      996       536.34K  259.76M   0
flow1       0        0        0            0        0     0
(... output truncated ...)
```

These tools help you monitor network usage and detect any problems with your physical or virtual network device configurations. They should be run frequently and periodically to establish a baseline of normal activity and to help identify unusual spikes in network bandwidth usage.

Summary

Oracle Solaris 11 has a rich collection of network configuration and monitoring tools for both physical and virtual components. We have reviewed setting up physical NICs and virtual NICs and have shown examples of how to set parameters and how to observe and control network bandwidth.

Administrators should review the network architecture in their data centers and should reconsider the assumptions about how physical and virtual environments connect with each other. A better understanding of the virtual network services described in this chapter can lead to a faster and more efficient infrastructure as well as savings on external network hardware.

References

Managing Network Virtualization and Network Resources in Oracle Solaris 11.2,
http://docs.oracle.com/cd/E36784_01/html/E36813/

Managing Network Datalinks in Oracle® Solaris 11.2,
https://docs.oracle.com/cd/E36784_01/pdf/E37516.pdf

Transitioning From Oracle® Solaris 10 to Oracle Solaris 11.2,
http://docs.oracle.com/cd/E36784_01/pdf/E39134.pdf

Oracle Solaris SDN and Network Virtualization,
http://www.oracle.com/technetwork/server-storage/solaris11/technologies/
networkvirtualization-312278.html

CHAPTER
6

Performance and Observability

There was a time when system administrators and IT architects were concerned about the raw performance of servers having relatively few processors, little memory, and slow network and I/O connections, all supported by a single operating system (OS) running on "bare metal." With today's modern systems, however, featuring massive memories, hundreds of hardware threads (HWTs), and superfast I/O, one would think such concerns are fading. But because such systems are now typically partitioned into smaller subsystems using virtualization technologies, there is still a great need for understanding both total system *and* virtual environment (VE) performance and capacity issues. In fact, the ability to easily monitor and manage VE resources provides a great advantage over similar efforts for bare metal deployments, since VEs can be enlarged or reduced while physical servers are fixed in size.

The ability to observe and manage performance on Oracle's SPARC and x86 servers that are running Solaris 11 is of special interest due to unique features such as the ZFS File System, Oracle Solaris Zones, and massive scaling with high levels of virtualized consolidation. Therefore, in this chapter, we cover the most commonly used Solaris 11 performance and observability tools, along with a special focus on VEs.

Server Sizing

Selecting and configuring a server that supports an anticipated workload of multiple applications or VEs obviously depends on the hardware requirements of the applications, on the number and type of VEs used, if any, and on the desired level of performance. Additionally, any planned growth in system use needs to be factored in to the sizing decision. Certainly you would not want to waste money and resources on a system too large for your requirements, nor would you want to purchase and install a system inadequate from the start that would soon need to be replaced or upgraded. Server sizing decisions will generally be guided by past system experiences and growth patterns, as well as by the recommended requirements of the hosted applications. Public benchmarks, such as those published by *spec.org* or *tpc.org*, can be helpful in selecting server configurations and in comparing vendor offerings, although there is no simple formula for sizing complex collections of applications and VEs.

However, once a server has been acquired and installed, it is essential to understand its stated capabilities in order to efficiently maximize its use of existing hardware and OS resources. That is, what is the "normal" or expected behavior and capability of the system? Only then can you monitor, diagnose, and correct any deviations from that expected performance.

Modern Oracle hardware such as the T5 and M6 servers and the Oracle ZFS Storage Appliance (ZFSSA) and FS1 storage appliances take advantage of two important computing concepts—*parallelism* and *caching*. Combining these two, using highly threaded processors with large caches and memory along with solid state and flash storage devices, provides for extreme performance and scalability, and the ability to consolidate multiple workloads with a choice of virtualization options. Additional features and enhancements such as ZFS compression, on-chip encryption, and OS and database optimizations all work together to provide the highest potential performance. System administrators and architects must then ensure that potential is actually achieved.

Methodology

First, you must know your system's capabilities, and what the ideal performance profile looks like as it runs your applications. Are you running primarily CPU-bound processes, I/O-bound processes, or some mix of the two? Performance and functionality goals for individual applications and for the system as a whole need to be defined. Then, it's a continuous cycle of monitoring, diagnosing, and fixing deviations from expected performance. Be sure to concentrate on large-scale performance issues first: efficient I/O, and maximal use of parallelism and caching. That is, focus on the greatest return from your time investment; don't spend hours getting a few percent out of compiler options, for example, until the larger performance issues are addressed.

Solaris 11 includes a comprehensive set of programs for observing the states of the main components of the system—CPU, OS, memory, and I/O. Table 6-1 lists these programs, and Figure 6-1 illustrates their area of applicability in the overall OS environment; then we discuss how to use them and how to interpret their output.

Verifying Your System Configuration

A large proportion of server problems are due to misconfiguration or to misunderstanding the existing hardware and software environment. Therefore, although it may seem unnecessary, it's wise to check and verify the server's and OS's characteristics and configuration. If you need to request a service call, you will need this information anyway.

System Component	Observability Tools	What to Look for
CPUs (HWTs), applications, and operating system	Processes: `ps`, `prstat`, `top`, `pgrep`, `pkill`, `ptree`, `pfiles` Threads: `mpstat`, `cpustat`, `cputrack`, `latencytop` OS: `lockstat`, `dtrace`, `dispadmin`, `priocntl`, `uptime`	High CPU utilization, excessive context switching and interrupts, lack of parallelism, too many processes waiting
Memory	`vmstat`, `top`, `dtrace`	Low free memory, excessive paging, process memory leaks
I/O	Storage: `iostat`, `swap`, `dtrace`, ZFS Network: `netstat`, `nfsstat`	High disk utilization, lack of parallelism, high disk service times; long latencies, collisions
Zone virtualization	`zonestat`, `vmstat`, `prstat`	Excessive CPU or memory usage
Software/ hardware errors	`fmadm`, `fmstat`, `syslog`, `prtdiag`, `netstat`, `iostat`, `dmesg`, system log files	Hardware faults or disconnects, service failures

TABLE 6-1. *Oracle Solaris 11.2 System Observability Programs*

Check the Processor Type

Solaris 11 runs on both SPARC and x86 processors. Upon logging in to a Solaris server it may not be immediately apparent what type of system you are in, especially if you have a large number and variety of UNIX servers in your network. Use the uname program to display the current OS version and processor type, for example:

```
# uname -a (on an x86 server)
SunOS narya 5.11 11.2 i86pc i386 i86pc
# uname -a (on a SPARC server)
SunOS blade02 5.11 11.2 sun4v sparc SUNW,Sun-Blade-T6320
```

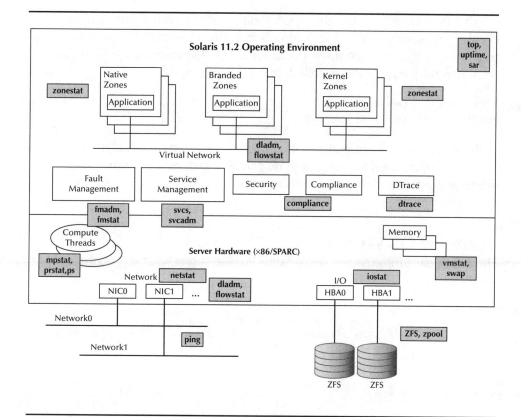

FIGURE 6-1.   *Observability and monitoring tools for Solaris 11*

More specific detail about a server's processor can be obtained using the psrinfo command. For example, on an x86 server:

```
# psrinfo -pv
The physical processor has 4 virtual processors (0-3)
x86 (GenuineIntel 306C3 family 6 model 60 step 3 clock 3193 MHz)
        Intel(r) Core(tm) i5-4460  CPU @ 3.20GHz
```

and on a SPARC server:

```
# psrinfo -pv(on a SPARC server)
The physical processor has 1 virtual processor (0)
  UltraSPARC-T2 (chipid 1, clock 1415 MHz)
```

The amount of installed and operational memory on a system can be checked in various ways. One common method is to run the /usr/sbin/ prtconf program which displays the server's full system configuration, and then search (grep) for the installed memory value:

```
# prtconf | grep Memory
Memory size: 16301 Megabytes
```

If this value does not match with what you know to be installed in the server, you may need to run system diagnostics to determine which memory modules are faulty. Other programs, such as /usr/bin/top, will also report total system memory.

Check the OS Version

The OS release information is contained in the server's /etc/release file. For example, on an x86 server:

```
# cat /etc/release
                         Oracle Solaris 11.2 X86
Copyright (c) 1983, 2014, Oracle and/or its affiliates.  All rights reserved.
                         Assembled 23 June 2014
```

and on a SPARC server:

```
# cat /etc/release
                         Oracle Solaris 11.2 SPARC
Copyright (c) 1983, 2014, Oracle and/or its affiliates.  All rights reserved.
                         Assembled 22 October 2014
```

Information about the IPS details for the installed Solaris OS is displayed using the pkg command; you might need this information when updating your OS kernel to refer to the appropriate matching repository, for example:

```
# pkg info entire
            Name: entire
         Summary: Incorporation to lock all system packages to the same build
     Description: This package constrains system package versions to the same
build. WARNING: Proper system update and correct package
selection depend on the presence of this incorporation.
                 Removing this package will result in an unsupported system.
        Category: Meta Packages/Incorporations
           State: Installed
       Publisher: solaris
         Version: 0.5.11
   Build Release: 5.11
          Branch: 0.175.2.1.0.2.1
  Packaging Date: September 23, 2014 10:49:40 PM
            Size: 5.46 kB
            FMRI: pkg://solaris/entire@0.5.11,5.11-0.175.2.1.0.2.1:20140923T224940Z
```

Optimizing Performance

When attempting to optimize Solaris 11 server performance or to diagnose a performance issue, it's crucial to characterize the perceived problem. Is it intermittent, periodic, or constant? Does it go away upon reboot and return later? Is the symptom an OS or application crash or merely a slowdown? Are there connectivity interruptions? Whenever possible, *monitor and diagnose on the production system showing the problem*, not on a "duplicate" or "test" system—"identical" usually isn't.

Two critical resources of a server are CPU (HWTs) and memory; generally what you'll be looking for is a "bottleneck" that's causing the problem. That is, there's very likely some system component that is at its maximum utilization and workload saturation. First, use diagnostic programs appropriate to those resources to get a gross characterization of the performance problem, then drill down with more specific tools and techniques like DTrace. We won't go into a full tutorial on using DTrace for such investigation in this book, but we will mention some useful examples of this powerful utility and we'll provide references for further instructions on how to use it.

Software and Hardware Errors

It's important to check first whether there is some hardware or software service component that is not functioning properly. That is, is something broken, or offline that should be online, or a service that should be running that's not? The main places to look for alerts and warnings about such issues are the log files in the `/var/log` and the `/var/adm` directories, and in the service-specific log files of the Service Management Facility (SMF). The `syslogd` daemon writes system error messages to the `/var/log/syslog` file, which can be inspected for OS service problems. Similarly, the `/var/adm/ messages` file can be checked for system service and hardware error alerts.

The Solaris Fault Manager interacts with the Oracle system hardware on both SPARC and x86 systems and reports on any system components diagnosed as faulty. To list such components, simply run the `/usr/sbin/ fmadm` program with the `faulty` parameter:

```
# fmadm faulty
```

SMF is also an important reporter of system health; run the `/usr/bin/ svcs` program to list online and offline services, and to display diagnostic information about OS service programs. For example, "`svcs -a`" will list all services and their states; "svcs -xv" will give specific details about any problematic services. Additionally, each SMF service has its own log file in the /var/svc/log directory where service startup, execution, and any error conditions are reported.

There can also be errors in the I/O subsystems and network; we'll show how to display and interpret them in the following sections.

CPU (Hardware Threads) and Operating System Issues

The primary task of any OS is to fairly and efficiently schedule processes onto the HWTs and to allocate sufficient memory for them. Diagnosing server performance problems therefore first focuses on the overall system load and how the OS is managing multiple demands for execution, memory, and I/O.

One useful and easy to run tool for continuously monitoring system activity is the /usr/bin/uptime program, which not only reports how long the system has been up since last boot, but also reports the average *system load*—the moving average number of processes in the OS's *run queue*—for the past 1, 5, and 15 minutes. For example:

```
# uptime
1:27pm  up 35 day(s),  3:15,  3 users,  load average: 0.36, 0.16, 0.07
```

A one-time, static observation of the load average is really not very informative; it must be viewed over a period of time and checked for very large and/or increasing 1-minute load averages. In such cases, the system might be experiencing a momentary heavy processing load. However, that number must be interpreted considering the number of HWTs available on the system. A 1-minute load average of 15.33 on a server with only 8 available HWTs would indicate a fairly busy OS; on a server with 16 HWTs the average number of waiting processes *per HWT* is lower and the system is therefore significantly less stressed. That is, if the load average is consistently and significantly greater than the number of HWTs, then the execution resources are *saturated*. Note that the top and prstat programs also report the system load averages, along with more detailed system activity metrics.

What do we mean when we say a system is "very busy" or "overloaded"? Generally that means the OS is either having trouble scheduling process requests and they are queuing up, or that some resource, such as storage hardware, is saturated and causing processes to wait for I/O service.

The reason processes must wait in the run queue might mean that there are too many requests for the processor to handle, or that there is not enough memory available to allocate to all the processes. In such cases, the OS will try valiantly to fairly allocate HWTs and memory among the requests, and may resort to paging or swapping processes out to slower storage resources. There are several useful observability tools to reveal such OS activity; we discuss several of them in the following sections.

NOTE

As we discuss performance, we will occasionally refer to "slower storage"; often this means traditional hard disk systems, but really includes any storage beyond dynamic random-access memory (DRAM), including flash memory and solid state "disks" (SSDs), both of which are significantly faster than hard disks but slower than DRAM. But be aware that OS observability tools reporting "disk" activity might refer to Flash or SSD devices as well as true disk devices.

Process Scheduling

The most commonly used Solaris system program for observing OS behavior is `vmstat`. It provides a wealth of information about process queuing, memory usage, disk activity, and average HWT utilization. Typically, it is run for some fixed time interval for a specified number of iterations. For example, to run it every 2 seconds for 4 iterations:

```
# vmstat 2 4
 kthr        memory                    page            disk          faults         cpu
 r b w   swap     free    re  mf pi po fr de sr  s0 s1  s2 s3   in      sy    cs us sy  id
 0 0 0 15356052 13514632   2   6  0  0  0  0  0   0  0   0  0  526     211   250 0  0 100
 7 2 1 13164108 12354320 520  74  0  0  0  0  0   8  0   0  0 5640   38495 18774 3 95   2
 3 0 0 13076292 12348848   0 283  0  0  0  0  0 138  0 146  0 5451   60765 23508 4 53  43
 0 0 0 13076292 12343232   0 706  0  0  0  0  0 279  0 335  0 5339  113471 20690 6 13  81
```

Note that the first line of the `vmstat` output is the average activity since the system was booted; this can be used as a baseline for comparison with current activity. In the example given previously, we see several key indicators of system distress: a period of very low CPU idle percent (`id`), very large number of context switches (`cs`), and several processes in the run queue (`r`), some of them blocked awaiting I/O (`b`) or fully swapped out (`w`). Together these metrics indicate a very busy system during the measurement period, although that level of activity was transient. A system consistently displaying such activity levels would be clearly overloaded.

Two additional tools are needed to understand system load: prstat, which reports statistics on individual processes and threads, and mpstat, which reports statistics for each HWT. The prstat program should be executed with flags that show per user stats (-a), individual threads (-L), and "microstate" details (-m), or some combination of these. For example:

```
# prstat -mL
  PID USERNAME USR SYS TRP TFL DFL LCK SLP LAT VCX ICX SCL SIG PROCESS/LWPID
17377 root       27  73 0.0 0.0 0.0 0.0 0.0 0.1   0  56 79K   0 prstat/1
16951 noaccess 0.5 0.1 0.0 0.0 0.0 0.0  99 0.1  27   2  1K   0 Xvnc/1
17230 root     0.1 0.0 0.0 0.0 0.0 0.0 100 0.0   2   0  22   0 firefox/1
17230 root     0.1 0.0 0.0 0.0 0.0 100 0.1 0.0   0   0   5   0 firefox/21
 2368 gdm      0.1 0.0 0.0 0.0 0.0 0.0 100 0.0   1   0  19   0 gdm-simple-g/1
 1357 root     0.0 0.0 0.0 0.0 0.0 0.0 100 0.0   1   0 126   0 Xorg/1
16515 pkg5srv  0.0 0.0 0.0 0.0 0.0 0.0 100 0.0   3   0  25   0 htcacheclean/1
17295 root     0.0 0.0 0.0 0.0 0.0 0.0 100 0.0   1   0   9   0 gnome-termin/1
17094 root     0.0 0.0 0.0 0.0 0.0 0.0 100 0.0   1   0   2   0 isapython2.6/1
17230 root     0.0 0.0 0.0 0.0 0.0 0.0 100 0.0   1   0   6   0 firefox/4
17084 root     0.0 0.0 0.0 0.0 0.0 0.0 100 0.0   1   0   4   0 updatemanage/1
17230 root     0.0 0.0 0.0 0.0 0.0 100 0.0 0.0   0   0   0   0 firefox/7
17092 root     0.0 0.0 0.0 0.0 0.0 0.0 100 0.0   0   0   5   0 xscreensaver/1
17100 root     0.0 0.0 0.0 0.0 0.0 0.0 100 0.0   0   0   0   0 clock-applet/1
23373 daemon   0.0 0.0 0.0 0.0 0.0 0.0 100 0.0   0   0   1   0 nfsmapid/4
```

On a system with multiple HWTs (that is, *all* current Oracle servers), it is critical to know whether *all* the HWTs are being used, as that is the whole idea of exploiting parallelism in processing. The mpstat program provides statistics on HWT usage. For example:

```
# mpstat 4
CPU minf mjf xcal intr ithr  csw icsw migr smtx srw syscl usr sys st idl
  0    2   0    0  615  104 1036  112  112 1531  29  7473   1   9  0  90
  1    6   0    0  354   19 1015  105  109 1535  26  7733   1   8  0  91
  2    5   0    1  757  582 1077  121  121 1503  30  6836   1  10  0  89
  3    3   0    0  352    9  976  110  111 1446  32  7290   1  10  0  90
...
```

This output shows that all four available HWTs are indeed in use and are not particularly busy (idl). Other key mpstat metrics to consider are cross-calls between HWTs (xcal) and migration of processes between HWTs (migr); processes that are moved among different HWTs can lose the efficiency of caching on the processor. Explicitly binding a process to a fixed set of HWTs can significantly improve that process's performance; Solaris 11.2 includes a new system call for application developers, processor _ affinity, that binds a process or thread to multiple HWTs.

```
● ● ●                            1. ssh
last pid: 18348;  load avg:  0.21,  0.22,  0.32;  up 36+04:39:20         14:50:58
157 processes: 153 sleeping, 3 zombie, 1 on cpu
CPU states: 96.4% idle,  2.4% user,  1.2% kernel,  0.0% iowait,  0.0% swap
Kernel: 1216 ctxsw, 1038 trap, 1201 intr, 3241 syscall, 1033 flt
Memory: 16G phys mem, 12G free mem, 2048M total swap, 2048M free swap
█
   PID USERNAME  NLWP PRI NICE   SIZE   RES STATE    TIME    CPU COMMAND
 18347 root        23  59    0   277M  121M sleep    0:06  1.40% appletviewer
 16951 noaccess     1  59    0    99M   89M sleep    2:05  1.12% Xvnc
 17230 root        26  59  -14   568M  305M sleep    2:30  0.56% firefox
  2368 gdm          1  59    0   150M   39M sleep   39:31  0.03% gdm-simple-gree
  1357 root         3  59    0    56M   32M sleep   25:57  0.02% Xorg
 17092 root         1  59    0    14M 4964K sleep    0:01  0.01% xscreensaver
 18330 root         1  59    0  4652K 2820K cpu/2    0:00  0.01% top
 17084 root         1   2   19    67M   38M sleep    0:03  0.00% updatemanagerno
 17094 root         1  59    0   133M   21M sleep    0:04  0.00% isapython2.6
  2369 gdm          1  59    0   129M   17M sleep    1:21  0.00% gnome-power-man
   231 daemon       1  59    0  2372K  872K sleep    0:02  0.00% utmpd
  1987 pkg5srv      1  59    0    13M 5532K sleep    1:18  0.00% httpd.worker
  1783 root         1  59    0    12M 3032K sleep    1:10  0.00% httpd
 16517 pkg5srv     24  59    0    21M 6392K sleep    0:01  0.00% httpd.worker
 16515 pkg5srv      1  59    0  6860K 5456K sleep    0:08  0.00% htcacheclean
 17085 root         1  59    0   128M   17M sleep    0:01  0.00% gnome-power-man
 17075 root         2  59    0   128M   15M sleep    0:00  0.00% nwam-manager
```

FIGURE 6-2.   *Solaris 11 `top` monitoring screen*

Solaris 11 includes the popular `top` utility that summarizes system activity in a constantly updated display. This program gathers OS data from multiple sources and is quite useful for general monitoring. Figure 6-2 shows a typical Solaris 11 top screen.

On this screen we can see the previously discussed load average, memory usage, kernel statistics, and key information about active processes. A quick inspection of the processes' CPU usage, memory usage, and total time of execution can point to performance issues, although the `prstat` program often provides finer detail about individual HWT usage.

Memory Issues

Insufficient system memory is one of the most common causes of poor performance. This is due to the OS needing to copy memory pages to slower storage in order to accommodate newly scheduled processes' memory needs. Various monitoring tools such as `vmstat`, `top`, and `prstat` report paging and swapping statistics that can indicate memory problems. A process memory space is partitioned into pages; when not all the pages can fit into available memory, or inactive pages are displaced by other processes, those memory pages are copied out to slower storage and copied back in when needed. Thus, too much paging can cause poor performance. Entire processes (along with their memory pages) can be copied out, or "swapped" to storage as well; this also occurs when there are too many processes than will fit in physical memory. Additionally, storage space for paging and swapping must be configured when the system is installed (although it can be changed later). For servers with small memory sizes (a few dozen gigabytes), swap space roughly equivalent to installed memory size is generally sufficient. But with larger, modern servers scaling to many terabytes, that "rule of thumb" is less useful; swap space for such systems should be no more than 50% of physical memory, and even half of that value might be sufficient depending on total application requirements. In any case, after monitoring the system in production, swap space can be increased if necessary. "vmstat -s" will provide detailed swap statistics, as will "swap -s" or "swap -lh":

```
# swap -s
total: 286688k bytes allocated + 119400k reserved = 406088k used, 17799876k available

# swap -lh
swapfile                    dev        swaplo   blocks   free
/dev/zvol/dsk/rpool/swap 285,1        4K       2.0G     2.0G
```

Running out of swap space can crash applications or even crash the kernel, so you should watch that metric carefully. Recall that Solaris 11 uses a ZFS volume for swap space, so it's quite easy to increase swap space if needed:

```
# zfs get volsizerpool/swap
NAME            PROPERTY    VALUE   SOURCE
rpool/swap   volsize     2G      local
# zfs set volsize=4G rpool/swap
# zfs get volsizerpool/swap
NAME            PROPERTY    VALUE   SOURCE
rpool/swap   volsize     4G      local
```

Storage I/O

Storage system components are often the primary performance bottlenecks, since they are very slow relative to DRAM and processor cache speeds. Therefore, the best strategy to maximize system performance is to minimize or even eliminate access to such devices. This is the philosophy behind *Oracle's Database In-Memory* product, which takes advantage of Oracle servers' massive memory capabilities. However, the majority of today's systems still depend heavily on hard disk subsystems, although there is a growing trend toward hybrid systems that use Flash and SSD components. For servers that use significant disk I/O, the primary observability tool is iostat. This program reports I/O statistics for terminals, tape subsystems, and "disks"; it includes CPU utilization, since HWTs are often idle as they wait for I/O requests to complete. The iostat program includes a large number of flags that give great detail on I/O activity. The most informative of these flags are as follows:

-x Displays extended disk statistics

-n Displays device names

-e Displays device error summary

-E Displays full device error stats

-D Displays device reads and writes per second, and utilization

To check for disk errors use the -E flag; this will report the device type, soft (recoverable) errors, availability errors, and any hard errors indicating a serious hardware problem:

```
# iostat -E
sd0        Soft Errors: 0 Hard Errors: 0 Transport Errors: 0
Vendor: ATA        Product: HITACHI H7210CA3 Revision: A39D Serial No: JP390VHQ19GPMA
Size: 1000.20GB <1000204886016 bytes>
Media Error: 0 Device Not Ready: 0 No Device: 0 Recoverable: 0
Illegal Request: 93 Predictive Failure Analysis: 0 Non-Aligned Writes: 0
```

To see how busy a server's disk devices are, including reads, writes, and any error stats, run the following, for example:

```
# iostat -xDen 2 8
                    extended device statistics      ---- errors ---
   r/s    w/s   kr/s    kw/s wait actv wsvc_t asvc_t  %w  %b s/w h/w trn tot device
   0.0  130.1    0.0 133196  9.0  1.0   69.1    7.6 100  99   0   0   0   0 c8t0d0
   0.0    0.0    0.0    0.0  0.0  0.0    0.0    0.0   0   0   0   0   0   0 c8t1d0
   0.0  127.6    0.0 130635  9.0  1.0   70.5    7.7 100  99   0   0   0   0 c8t2d0
   0.0    0.0    0.0    0.0  0.0  0.0    0.0    0.0   0   0   0   0   0   0 c7t0d0
...
```

In this example output, we see two very busy (mirrored) disks. Improving I/O in this case if such high write loads persist might involve modifying the writing applications, or installing SSDs or other faster storage devices.

Such disk activity statistics, in combination with other metrics from vmstat, for example, that show high idle HWT times and blocked processes, can be an indication of poor application design or insufficient server resources.

ZFS I/O Issues

Solaris 11's ZFS is designed to automatically spread disk writes across multiple disks in a pool. Additionally, ZFS uses available server DRAM for caching, using an *Adaptive Replacement Cache* (ARC). The idea behind this is to use available memory for data caching until some process needs the space, at which point ZFS ARC returns it to the OS. However, releasing that memory takes time, and can slow processing on the server. Therefore, it's a good practice to limit the size of the ARC, but remember, caching is good! So, if you know that an application like a database needs a certain amount of memory, don't let the ZFS ARC usage impact that need. To change the ARC size, add a kernel parameter file in the /etc/ system.d/ location; for example, to limit the ARC to 4 GB, create a file with the following content:

```
setzfs:zfs_arc_max = 4294967296
```

You can use decimal or hex values for the ARC size value; and when you change this value in the kernel parameter file, you'll need to reboot to have it take effect. You may have to experiment a bit to get an ideal value for your mix of applications. The ARC size can be changed dynamically; Solaris 11.2 provides a script (available from My Oracle Support) that dynamically sets the value using a replacement for zfs_arc_max:user_reserve_hintpct that reserves a specified percent of free physical memory for applications.

Another issue affecting ZFS I/O performance is the remaining capacity of the pool devices. Use the zpool program to display the pool's free space:

```
# zpool list
NAME    SIZE  ALLOC  FREE   CAP  DEDUP  HEALTH   ALTROOT
rpool   928G  51.7G  876G   5%   1.00x  ONLINE   -
```

ZFS performance degrades significantly when a pool is at 80% capacity or more; clean up your storage or add more disk devices to the pool to prevent this from happening.

Finally, consider using ZFS settings for deduplication and compression. Deduplication detects duplicate data blocks and avoids multiple writes of the same data. It's easy to set that feature for a specific pool, for example:

```
# zfs set dedup=on {poolname}
```

Additional ZFS performance improvement can be had by compressing the stored data, for example:

```
# zfs set compression=on {poolname}
```

Depending on the nature of your data, deduplication and compression can result in better performance and potential storage savings.

If your server has flash storage devices, setting the ZFS log and cache to use them can improve performance as well. For example, if your flash device name is c8t1d0, then

```
# zpool add {poolname} log c8t1d0
```

or

```
#zpool add {poolname} cache c8t1d0
```

Network Performance

Transmitting data over a network, even using a fast 10GE link, is relatively slow compared to disk I/O and is orders of magnitude slower than DRAM and processor caches. So, checking the network for proper configuration and usage is extremely important. Again, check the obvious! Verify that your network devices are operating at their intended speed; often there are components that default to lower speeds or whose rated speed is lower than expected. To check the speed of installed network interface cards (NICs), use the dladm program, for example:

```
# dladm show-phys
LINK            MEDIA           STATE   SPEED  DUPLEX   DEVICE
net0            Ethernet        up      100    full     e1000g0
net1            Ethernet        up      1000   full     rge0
```

Note that in this example, one of the NICs is at 100 MB/s, and the other at 1000 MB/s. Knowledge of which network component is faster in this case would help when transferring data. Of course, don't forget the simple but useful `ping` program that can be used to test network connectivity and also to check connection latencies to other systems. For example:

```
# ping -s brotherptr
PING brotherptr: 56 data bytes
64 bytes from brotherptr (192.168.1.108): icmp_seq=0. time=0.266 ms
64 bytes from brotherptr (192.168.1.108): icmp_seq=1. time=0.322 ms
64 bytes from brotherptr (192.168.1.108): icmp_seq=2. time=0.292 ms
64 bytes from brotherptr (192.168.1.108): icmp_seq=3. time=0.305 ms
...
----brotherptr PING Statistics----
6 packets transmitted, 6 packets received, 0% packet loss
round-trip (ms)  min/avg/max/stddev = 0.266/0.291/0.322/0.021
```

It's helpful to have earlier historical data on round-trip times between network components; changes in the average time can indicate problems with a component or with the entire network.

The `netstat` program will provide usage and diagnostic information about your server's network connections. One key metric is collisions; anything more than a few percent generally indicates an overloaded or misconfigured network.

```
# netstat -ai
```

Name	Mtu	Net/Dest	Address	Ipkts	Ierrs	Opkts	Oerrs	Collis
lo0	8232	loopback	localhost	1932768	0	1932768	0	0
lo0	8232	loopback	localhost	286	N/A	N/A	N/A	N/A
net0	1500	narya1	narya1	5443	0	2636	0	0
net0	1500	narya1	narya1	482	N/A	N/A	N/A	N/A
net1	1500	narya	narya	28044	0	24038	0	0
net1	1500	narya	narya	22547	N/A	N/A	N/A	N/A

Tunable Kernel Parameters

The usual advice about changing Solaris kernel parameters is...DON'T. That's because an enormous amount of engineering work has gone in to making the kernel as self-tuning as possible, and each iteration of Solaris improves upon the last. As we mentioned earlier, the best system performance tuning strategy is to go after the big benefits—I/O optimization, parallel processing, and sufficient memory. Tuning kernel parameters generally yields only small percentage points of improvement. That being said, there are a few changes that are often recommended, as well as ZFS ARC size adjustment we already discussed. For very busy systems with many users and user processes, there might be occasional "out of processes" error messages reported to the system console. Since the maximum number of processes is calculated by the OS using the maxusers kernel parameter, increasing that value is how to change the allowable number of processes. The default value for this parameter is calculated based on the size of server's memory and the number of HWTs. To display the current kernel's value of maxusers, *carefully* use adb:

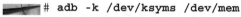

```
# adb -k /dev/ksyms /dev/mem
physmem 3f9cf3
maxusers/D
maxusers:       2048
```

Then, if a higher number is needed, add the desired kernel parameter setting to a file located in /etc/system.d/ and reboot, for example: set maxusers=4096.

NOTE
Do not directly modify or copy the contents of the /etc/system file from one system to another. This file is now automatically generated through a self-assembly process from files located in /etc/ system.d/. Change only what's necessary for each individual server, especially if they have different hardware configurations.

DTrace

One of the most remarkable observation tools for Solaris was introduced in 2005 with Solaris 10, DTrace. It is a non-intrusive dynamic tracing framework and language that can display high-granularity detail about any OS activity. DTrace has been ported to other OS such as FreeBSD, OS X, and even to Linux, including Oracle Linux. It forms the basis for some of the I/O analytics tools included with Oracle's storage systems and application software. DTrace includes a C-like scripting language for probing OS function calls.

DTrace is underutilized by many Solaris system administrators, likely due to the learning and practice required for its somewhat unfamiliar language and concepts. Fortunately, there has been a great deal of community development of pre-written scripts, tutorials, and books to assist with learning and using this powerful tool, much of that contributed by Brendan Gregg, one of the early Sun kernel engineers.

DTrace is only one tool, albeit an important one, for observing and analyzing system performance and behavior. It should be used *after* other basic tools have been used to get an idea of where a performance problem generally occurs; then you drill down to get more detail with DTrace.

DTrace is like a medical MRI for your OS; it's a non-invasive look at the OS inner workings. Then, it's like a scalpel, after you know where to cut. The DTrace infrastructure includes the D language used for writing scripts that monitor and display OS activity, everything from application function calls down to processor and system hardware activity. DTrace is *part of Solaris*—there is no need to install it—it's always there ready to be activated. As such, it is most useful for observing applications and system calls on production systems in real time; no need to alter the running environment in order to analyze performance issues.

The typical user of DTrace will be a system administrator or analyst familiar with performance concepts and tools on Solaris. After getting a general idea about a performance problem, they will write one or more DTrace scripts to investigate further.

A DTrace script, written in D, is automatically compiled by the `/usr/sbin/dtrace` command, checked for syntax and safety, then executed by the DTrace VM in the Solaris kernel. A DTrace script can take two forms: a single command "one-liner," or an executable similar to UNIX shell scripts.

The basic structure of a DTrace script includes a *probe*, an optional *predicate*, and one or more *action* statements, like this:

```
#!/usr/sbin/dtrace -s
probe description (provider:module:function:name)
/ predicate /
{
action statements
}
```

A key part of understanding DTrace is the probes. They are observation points attached to every Solaris kernel function, of which there are tens of thousands, and somewhat unique for each OS version and hardware platform.

A probe has four components: a *provider name, module name, function,* and *probe_name*, and the basic syntax is:

```
provider:module:function:probename
```

An example probe might look like this:

```
syscall::open*:entry
```

Wildcards in a probe can be blank (::), *, or ? In the preceding probe example, we reference the `syscall` provider, any module, any `open` function, and the `entry` event into the function.

Probes are available for system calls, virtual memory statistics, process scheduling events, I/O and network event tracing, and all kernel functions. You can list them all using the "`dtrace -l`" command, but there are so many that it's best to search that output using `grep` for the probes you are interested in. Probes are also available for instrumenting Python, Java, structured query language (SQL), HyperText Transfer Protocol (HTTP), Network File System (NFS), zones, ZFS, caches, CMT (Chip Multi Threading), CPUs, disks, and memory—*anything* the OS does in the kernel space or user space.

The DTrace language, "D," is a C-like language with additional features similar to the UNIX `awk` utility. It uses ANSI-C operators, and includes many built-in system variables and support for arrays and aggregations.

We present here just one example of how DTrace can assist with identifying performance issues. The example is derived from Gregg's *DTrace One-Liner* collection and helps identify what process is writing the most characters to storage. This example uses the `sysinfo` provider with the `writech` probe that traces character output; it gathers character output counts into an array indexed by the processes doing the writing and counts the characters output for each of the processes:

```
# dtrace -n 'sysinfo:::writech { @bytes[execname] = sum(arg0); }'
dtrace: description 'sysinfo:::writech ' matched 4 probes
^C
dtrace                                                       1
in.mpathd                                                    2
gnome-power-mana                                             4
sshd                                                        49
Xvnc                                                        96
clock-applet                                              400
Xorg                                                      576
sort                                                221430522
```

This simple script reports that the `sort` program was running and wrote more than 220 MB of data during the brief interval that DTrace was watching it. Clearly that would be useful information for an administrator seeking to identify what processes might be causing performance issues.

The `/usr/demo/dtrace` directory included with Solaris 11 contains nearly 100 sample DTrace scripts from Gregg's *DTrace Toolkit*. In addition, the toolkit itself is included in Solaris 11's `/usr/dtrace/DTT` directory, along with numerous annotated examples. In conjunction with the learning resources we mentioned earlier and those listed at the end of this chapter, system administrators can use these scripts to obtain further detail about server performance.

Virtualization (Zones)

There is a large "however" we need to add to all the previous discussion. That is, we have assumed in our examples that we are observing a single instance of Solaris 11 running directly on the server hardware. Well, that might not be the case.

Another major Solaris technology is zones, which we covered in Chapter 1. There are two performance viewpoints to consider when using Solaris zones: one, from the point of view of the *global zone administrator*, and the other from *within a non-global zone*.

The Global View of Zones

Recall that a zone is *not* a hypervisor-managed virtual machine (VM) (that's why we prefer to call it a VE!). In essence, a zone is a collection of processes, and the traditional Solaris tools for observing and managing processes are still largely relevant, although some have been enhanced to provide zone-specific information, typically by adding a flag for *all* zones (-Z) or a list of zones (-z). For example, the `prstat` program for displaying process statistics allows the global zone administrator to observe processes running within each zone using "`prstat -Z`" or "`prstat -z {zonename}`":

```
# prstat -Z
```

```
●  ○  ○                                    1. ssh
   PID USERNAME   SIZE    RSS STATE   PRI NICE      TIME  CPU PROCESS/NLWP
  6055 root       537M   128M sleep    59    0   0:11:13 0.1% java/26
  8224 root        11M  5632K cpu3     59    0   0:00:00 0.1% prstat/1
  2701 gdm        146M    38M sleep    59    0   0:06:07 0.0% gdm-simple-gree/1
  1474 root        54M    33M sleep    59    0   0:03:37 0.0% Xorg/3
    15 root        24M    18M sleep    59    0   0:00:18 0.0% svc.configd/22
    13 root        40M    33M sleep    59    0   0:00:05 0.0% svc.startd/13
   982 root      9060K  1028K sleep    59    0   0:00:00 0.0% cron/1
     9 root         0K     0K sleep    99  -20   0:00:00 0.0% postwaittq/1
     8 root         0K     0K sleep    60    -   0:00:00 0.0% vmtasks/5
ZONEID     NPROC  SWAP    RSS MEMORY      TIME  CPU ZONE
     0       126  986M   605M   3.7%   0:31:10 0.2% global
     1        16   70M    94M   0.6%   0:00:13 0.0% ngz01



Total: 142 processes, 733 lwps, load averages: 0.01, 0.01, 0.01
```

```
# prstat -z ngz01
```

```
●  ○  ○                                    1. ssh
   PID USERNAME   SIZE    RSS STATE   PRI NICE      TIME  CPU PROCESS/NLWP
  4117 daemon    2372K   632K sleep    59    0   0:00:00 0.0% utmpd/1
  4159 root      2948K   744K sleep    59    0   0:00:02 0.0% in.mpathd/1
  4225 root         0K     0K zombie    0    -   0:00:00 0.0% /0
  4124 netadm    4396K  1008K sleep    59    0   0:00:00 0.0% ipmgmtd/5
  4118 root      3156K   708K sleep    59    0   0:00:00 0.0% dbus-daemon/1
  4204 root         0K     0K zombie    0    -   0:00:00 0.0% /0
  4019 daemon    3352K   616K sleep    59    0   0:00:00 0.0% kcfd/2
  4191 root       106M    44M sleep    59    0   0:00:00 0.0% sysconfig/1
  3994 netcfg    3756K  1164K sleep    59    0   0:00:02 0.0% netcfgd/4
  3027 root         0K     0K sleep    60    -   0:00:00 0.0% zsched/1
  3969 root        18M    16M sleep    59    0   0:00:06 0.0% svc.configd/24
  4016 root      2016K   596K sleep    59    0   0:00:00 0.0% pfexecd/2
  4143 root      4660K  1660K sleep    59    0   0:00:00 0.0% milestone-confi/1
  3787 root      2344K   944K sleep    59    0   0:00:00 0.0% init/1
  3967 root        28M    24M sleep    59    0   0:00:03 0.0% svc.startd/13
Total: 16 processes, 61 lwps, load averages: 0.01, 0.01, 0.01
```

Because the global zone administrator can see inside each non-global zone's list of processes [whose Process IDs (PIDs) are listed along with those of the global zone], they have the power to terminate any wayward zone processes. A useful `vmstat`–like tool for zone observability is `zonestat`, which displays active zone statistics, for example:

```
# zonestat 4 2
Collecting data for first interval...
Interval: 1, Duration: 0:00:04
SUMMARY                   Cpus/Online: 4/4    PhysMem: 15.9G  VirtMem: 19.9G
                     ---CPU----  --PhysMem-- --VirtMem-- --PhysNet--
            ZONE  USED %PART   USED %USED   USED %USED PBYTE %PUSE
         [total]  0.05 1.32%  6636M 40.7%  7406M 36.3%   212 0.00%
        [system]  0.01 0.33%  1845M 11.3%  6207M 30.4%     -     -
         kzone01  0.02 0.51%  4121M 25.2%  7184K 0.03%     0 0.00%
          global  0.01 0.46%   605M 3.71%  1131M 5.54%   212 0.00%
           ngz01  0.00 0.00%  63.5M 0.38%  61.1M 0.29%     0 0.00%

Interval: 2, Duration: 0:00:08
SUMMARY                   Cpus/Online: 4/4    PhysMem: 15.9G  VirtMem: 19.9G
                     ---CPU----  --PhysMem-- --VirtMem-- --PhysNet--
            ZONE  USED %PART   USED %USED   USED %USED PBYTE %PUSE
         [total]  0.07 1.75%  6636M 40.7%  7406M 36.3%  1640 0.00%
        [system]  0.01 0.40%  1845M 11.3%  6207M 30.4%     -     -
          global  0.03 0.99%   605M 3.71%  1131M 5.54%  1640 0.00%
         kzone01  0.01 0.34%  4121M 25.2%  7184K 0.03%     0 0.00%
           ngz01  0.00 0.01%  63.5M 0.38%  61.1M 0.29%     0 0.00%
#
```

As we described in Chapter 4, if the resources used by a non-global zone need to be constrained for licensing or performance reasons, `zonestat` statistics will reveal those settings and metrics. Note also that the `/var/log` directory we discussed earlier in this chapter includes the `/var/log/zones` directory that contains startup and error message files for each of the server's configured zones.

The Insider's View of a Zone

Non-global zone administrators, or global zone administrators who have logged in to a non-global zone, need to be aware that they are sharing server OS and hardware resources with other users and processes. The process observability tools discussed earlier are specifically limited in what they can display from within the zone. Tools such as `vmstat` and `iostat` will only report statistics for the processors that a zone is bound to, and they are unaware of other system activity. The `dtrace` program, which can examine detailed kernel activity, is also specifically constrained in non-global zones, although limited functionality can be granted to non-global zone administrators, for example:

```
# zonecfg -z ngz01
zonecfg:ngz01> set limitpriv="default,dtrace_proc,dtrace_user"
zonecfg:ngz01> exit
```

then reboot the zone to enable that privilege setting.

Graphical View of Performance Monitoring

Solaris 11's GUI toolset includes graphical monitors for performance and file system capacity. The *System Monitor* shown in Figure 6-3 produces a running display of CPU activity, memory and swap usage, and network bandwidth. These displays can be quite useful for alerting administrators to

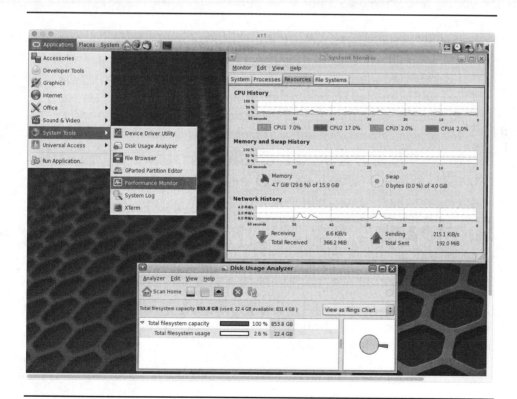

FIGURE 6-3. *Solaris 11 graphical monitoring tools*

potential performance issues. For a more comprehensive tool for monitoring and managing multiple Oracle Solaris and Oracle Linux servers, IT architects and infrastructure managers should consider *Oracle Enterprise Manager Ops Center*, which includes features for hardware fault detection, active performance monitoring, and resource management.

NOTE
Since partitioning an Oracle T* or M* server using logical domains (LDoms) or physical domains (PDoms) essentially results in dedicated (unshared) memory, processor, and I/O components, observing and managing performance in such configurations is nearly identical *to that for typical "bare metal" approaches. Since we do not cover those technologies in this book, see* Oracle VM Server for SPARC Best Practices, Oracle White Paper, December 2014, *http://www.oracle.com/ technetwork/server-storage/vm/ovmsparc-best-practices-2334546.pdf and* How to Get the Best Performance from Oracle VM Server for SPARC, *http://www.oracle.com/technetwork/articles/ servers-storage-admin/solaris-network-vm-sparc-2275380.html for advice on configuring LDoms for optimal performance and availability.*

Summary

Server performance monitoring and management is a complex task for system administrators and IT architects. This chapter has summarized many of the tools and procedures available in Solaris 11 for that purpose. Diagnosing and correcting server performance problems generally requires significant experience; we strongly recommend further self-study and practice using the References listed.

References

*Managing System Information, Processes, and Performance in Oracle®
Solaris 11.2,*
http://docs.oracle.com/cd/E36784_01/html/E36819/index.html

Solaris 11.2 Dynamic Tracing Guide,
http://docs.oracle.com/cd/E36784_01/pdf/E36846.pdf

Systems Performance, Enterprise and the Cloud, Brendan Gregg, 2014,
Prentice Hall

DTrace: Dynamic Tracing in Oracle Solaris, Mac OS X, and FreeBSD,
Brendan Gregg and Jim Mauro, 2011, Prentice Hall

Oracle Enterprise Manager Ops Center,
http://www.oracle.com/technetwork/oem/ops-center/index.html

CHAPTER
7

Oracle Solaris 11
Security Features

S olaris has a long history and excellent reputation for innovation in UNIX security and deployment in the most demanding security environments such as those used by the US Department of Defense and by the various US Intelligence communities. Solaris has included important technologies like auditing, role-based access control, labeled security, hardware-assisted encryption, access control lists, operating system (OS) memory protection, and many other features to ensure safe execution environments for critical applications in banking, health care, and government. These technologies provide comprehensive, defense-in-depth protection for Oracle applications and for other application environments running on Solaris 11.

As serious security incidents have been increasing dramatically in recent years, commercial and government organizations find themselves in need of trusted environments and tools which detect intrusions and prevent data theft and compromise. Without such capabilities, these organizations are subject to serious loss of user trust, as well as potential legal liabilities. Solaris 11 incorporates modern security features not found in other operating systems that enhance user trust and help protect organizations' data integrity and reputation.

In this chapter, we cover the most common and important OS security–related administrative tasks and system configuration settings, including initial secure Solaris 11 installation, Image Packaging System (IPS) Security, ZFS File System (ZFS) Security, privileged user control, file system access, secure virtualization, observing and auditing security events, and ensuring security policy compliance.

Secure Installation and Configuration

Solaris 11 upon initial installation is "secure by default," meaning it is pre-hardened by disabling non-essential network services with the exception of console access; auditing is enabled from the start, and initial package installations are minimized. No inbound network services other than Secure Shell (SSH) are active and listening; direct root logins are disabled, there are no default passwords, and log file and audit file access is restricted. This approach is important since systems are most vulnerable when they are being installed and configured if their network services are exposed; Solaris 11's secure installation processes address this risk. Additionally, IPS in Solaris 11.2, covered in Chapter 3, includes the "solaris-minimal-server" install group package for initial installations, providing a minimal command-line environment and the smallest required set of OS packages.

NOTE

The Solaris Security Toolkit for Solaris 10 and earlier releases (also known as the JumpStart Architecture and Security Scripts or "JASS") is no longer needed nor relevant to Solaris 11, since many of its features have been incorporated into the new OS release.

For legal or policy purposes, it is sometimes useful or even required to provide a warning about unauthorized usage to those who connect to your system. In that case, edit the /etc/issue file to provide a *pre-login* warning message, and edit the /etc/motd file for *post-login* alerts, for example:

```
$ ssh 192.168.1.218
WARNING:
This machine is for authorized users only.
Your actions are monitored and recorded.
Password:########
Last login: Fri Feb 20 08:39:22 2015 from 192.168.1.205
Oracle Corporation     SunOS 5.11     11.2    June 2014
This system serves authorized users only.
```

One of the key tasks in ensuring secure system use is monitoring and controlling privileged users, in particular the root user. Solaris 11 by default denies direct root logins by treating root as any other user role whose privileges can be fully specified. No longer is root the all-powerful (and dangerous) user. And while it is possible to configure Solaris 11 for direct root logins, such practice is unwise and strongly discouraged. Instead, control privileged user access with the usermod, rolemod, and auths programs. For example, to add root privileges to users johndoe and janedoe:

```
# usermod -R +root johndoe
# usermod -R +root janedoe
```

This will add root privileges to those two users, requiring them to first log in as themselves and then use "su –" with the appropriate password to become a root user whose actions will be audited.

Image Packaging System Security

Since IPS and ZFS are key foundation technologies in Solaris 11, they include features for validating system programs and files and their sources. IPS has additional security features for ensuring that package contents and updates have been digitally signed and have not been corrupted or modified. For example, "pkg verify" will validate the installation of all packages in the current OS image. It will report differences between the expected and actual signatures (hashes), file sizes, and group assignment for package contents. The "pkg fix" command can then be used to download and update any package contents reporting errors using the default or specified repository. For example:

```
# pkg verify
PACKAGE        STATUS
…( output truncated)…
pkg://solaris/system/display-manager/gdm ERROR
file: etc/gdm/custom.conf
            Group: 'root (0)' should be 'sys (3)'
…
# pkg fix pkg://solaris/system/display-manager/gdm
Verifying: pkg://solaris/system/display-manager/gdm            ERROR
file: etc/gdm/custom.conf
            Group: 'root (0)' should be 'sys (3)'
Created ZFS snapshot: 2015-03-12-15:27:25
Repairing: pkg://solaris/system/display-manager/gdm
# pkg verify -v pkg://solaris/system/display-manager/gdm
PACKAGE                        STATUS
pkg://solaris/system/display-manager/gdm OK
file: etc/gdm/custom.conf
editable file has been changed
```

ZFS Security

Solaris 11's ZFS data management framework now supports encryption at the file system level. Creating an encrypted ZFS data set is a simple procedure; ZFS pools can contain both encrypted and unencrypted data sets. Note that you must first create a data set and enable encryption on it; then subsequent writes to that data set will be encrypted. That is, you can't just turn on encryption for an existing data set. One useful option with this

feature is creating encrypted $HOME directories. First, add the following
lines to the: `/etc/security/pam_policy/unix` file:

```
## pam_zfs_key auto-creates an encrypted home directory
##
otherauth required               pam_zfs_key.so.1 create
```

then, use that file when you create a new user's login, for example:

```
# useradd -K pam_policy=/etc/security/pam_policy/unix mrsmith
# passwd mrsmith
New Password:########
Re-enter new Password:########
passwd: password successfully changed for mrsmith
# su - mrsmith
Creating home directory with encryption=on.
Your login password will be used as the wrapping key.
Enter passphrase for 'rpool/export/home/mrsmith':########
Enter again:########

Oracle Corporation      SunOS 5.11      11.2     June 2014

This system serves authorized users only.
-bash-4.1$
```

Verify that the user's home directory ZFS data set is indeed created and
encrypted:

```
# zfs get encryption,keysourcerpool/export/home/mrsmith
NAME                         PROPERTY     VALUE               SOURCE
rpool/export/home/mrsmith    encryption   on                  local
rpool/export/home/mrsmith    keysource    passphrase,prompt   local
```

Other encrypted ZFS data sets are easily created simply by specifying the
required option at creation time, for example:

```
# zfs create -o encryption=on rpool/export/crypt_data
Enter passphrase for 'rpool/export/crypt_data':########
Enter again:########
```

ZFS creates and automatically mounts the new encrypted data set; any
new data written to that data set will be encrypted, and any newly created
file systems under that data set will inherit the encryption setting. To securely
delete an encrypted data set, change its encryption key and destroy the ZFS
data set.

User Privilege Control

A convenient way to manage the numerous user profiles and privileges is the *Solaris 11 graphical user interface (GUI) User Manager*. Assuming you have used IPS to install the `solaris-desktop` group package (which we recommend), you can call it up from the Solaris desktop menu as seen in Figure 7-1, or from the command line (as root) using the Visual Panels utility:

```
# vp usermgr &
```

The User Manager will display the system's list of current users, and allows for assigning or editing each user's name, group memberships, home directory, and login shell, and password, as seen in Figure 7-2.

From that window, select *Advanced Settings* in order to manage a user's group memberships, roles, and profiles, as shown in Figure 7-3. For example, you click on an available setting, then add or remove it from the user's list of settings. The benefit of this approach is that you can see all the available settings and easily add or delete them.

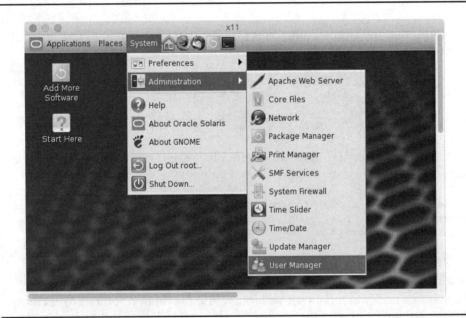

FIGURE 7-1. *Selecting the Solaris 11 User Manager GUI*

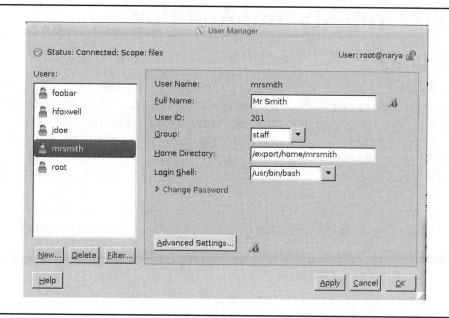

FIGURE 7-2.   *The User Manager GUI*

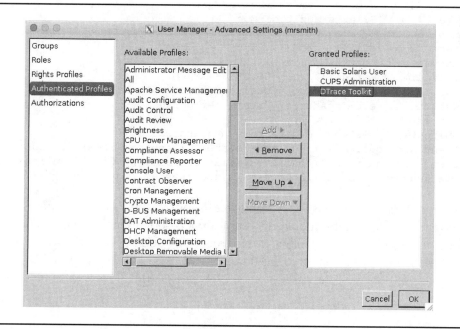

FIGURE 7-3.   *User Manager Advanced Settings*

Observability and Auditing

Auditing

The Solaris 11 audit service is enabled by default. Its purpose, of course, is to monitor and report data about the use of system resources as specified by your organization's data protection policies. Auditing's goal is to uniquely assign specific user responsibility to system events; that is why it is so important to control privileged (root) use as we discussed earlier in this chapter. Auditing is necessary to detect and report any unauthorized system activity or misuse, or any user attempts to bypass security mechanisms.

To verify that system auditing is active, one method is to use the `auditconfig` program to display the current audit condition, for example:

```
# auditconfig -getcond
audit condition = auditing
```

Additionally, the Service Management Facility (SMF) state of the audit daemon can also be displayed:

```
# svcs -l auditd
fmri          svc:/system/auditd:default
name          Solaris audit daemon
enabled       true
state         online
next_state    none
state_time    March 13, 2015 09:38:33 AM EDT
logfile       /var/svc/log/system-auditd:default.log
restarter     svc:/system/svc/restarter:default
contract_id   133
manifest      /lib/svc/manifest/system/auditd.xml
dependencyrequire_all/none svc:/system/filesystem/local (online)
dependencyrequire_all/none svc:/milestone/name-services (online)
dependencyoptional_all/none svc:/system/system-log (online)
```

This latter method has the advantage of showing the location of the `auditd` log file and the required system service dependencies that auditing requires. Note that the log file is *not* for recording audit events, but for recording any issues related to starting `auditd`.

Use the `auditconfig` program to set the type of events you need to audit. The most common audit settings are for login/logout events, process start/stop events, and file write events. To set these, for example:

```
# auditconfig -setflags lo, ps, fw
user default audit flags = ps,lo,fw(0x101002,0x101002)
```

and to display the default settings:

```
# auditconfig -getflags
active user default audit flags = ps,lo,fw(0x101002,0x101002)
configured user default audit flags = ps,lo,fw(0x101002,0x101002)
```

The hex numbers in the preceding output are *additive* and correspond to the codes listed in the /etc/security/audit_class file. Additional audit settings can be activated by adding the mnemonic codes listed in that file; flags can be set for individual users.

The audit events are recorded locally in the /var/audit directory and are tokenized (a kind of compression) to save disk space. Auditing can generate enormous amounts of data, which generally must be saved for later analysis. Solaris auditing can be configured to send events to a remote auditing server.

To read/display the events recorded in the audit log, special programs— auditreduce and praudit—are used to extract data from the tokenized file and display it in human-readable form. The auditreduce program is used to select records from the audit logs which are recorded in the /var/ audit directory. The naming convention for those log files includes the starting and ending dates and times for the log and the system's hostname, for example:

```
# ls -l /var/audit/*
-rw-r----- 1 root    root         304 Jan 13 10:11 /var/audit/20150113150432.20150113151124.narya
-rw-r----- 1 root    root       10201 Feb 18 14:59 /var/audit/20150113151245.20150218195949.narya
-rw-r----- 1 root    root        8400 Mar 12 14:19 /var/audit/20150218200130.20150312181948.narya
-rw-r----- 1 root    root        3275 Mar 13 09:37 /var/audit/20150312182122.20150313133705.narya
-rw-r----- 1 root    root       65320 Mar 13 19:39 /var/audit/20150313133833.20150313233930.narya
-rw-r----- 1 root    root     4990592 Mar 14 10:30 /var/audit/20150313233932.not_terminated.narya
```

Note that the currently active audit log has not been closed and is still appending data. The praudit program is used to translate the tokenized audit data into human readable form and can format that output in short form or in XML format for further processing by browsers or other display programs. For example, to extract file write (fw) events from the current log and generate short form output into a temporary file:

```
# auditreduce -c fw 20150313233932.not_terminated.narya | praudit -s >temp.aud
```

When we inspect the temp.aud file, we might see for example that the user mrsmith has apparently copied the /etc/passwd file and written a modified copy to his home directory, something that should require further investigation:

```
(… output truncated …)
header,157,2,AUE_OPEN_WT,,narya,2015-03-14 09:48:01.098 -04:00
path,/export/home/mrsmith/passwd
attribute,100644,mrsmith,staff,65565,9,18446744073709551615
subject,mrsmith,mrsmith,staff,mrsmith,staff,6237,1085247025,10546 136704 192.168.1.205
return,success,4
```

Auditing system activity is a complex and continuous task, more involved than we have illustrated here with our simple example. For additional detail and instruction on administering auditing, see *Managing Auditing in Oracle Solaris 11.2* listed in the references at the end of this chapter.

Observing Virtual Operating System Activity

It is difficult or impossible to manage and secure what you can't see. We have already discussed Solaris 11's rich set of monitoring tools in Chapter 6. One of the great advantages of using Solaris zones is that process activity in a zone can be directly observed by the administrator of the global zone. Such visibility is generally not available with hypervisor-based virtualization. Administrators of non-global zones can be delegated to audit activity within their zones, or the global zone administrator can audit the entire system including activity within all zones. Auditable events set by the auditconfig program can be configured to capture data separately for each active zone, for example:

```
# auditconfig -setpolicy +perzone
```

This will start a separate auditd daemon in each zone.

Zone Security

Solaris non-global zones, with the exception of kernel zones, share the resources of the global kernel, which enforces namespace and memory boundaries between zones and maintains separate user ID lists for each zone. The Solaris zones technology is derived from earlier work on Trusted Solaris (now Trusted Extensions), which has been used for years in critical military and intelligence environments. Users logged in to a non-global zone cannot observe nor affect processes running in other zones or the global zone, even if they acquire root privileges. Moreover, processes running in a non-global zone run with a reduced set of privileges, although the global zone administrator can enhance a zone user's privileges for certain purposes, such as allowing a limited use of the DTrace tools, for example:

```
# zonecfg -z ngz01 set limitpriv=default,dtrace_proc,dtrace_user
```

which sets the `ngz01` zone's root privileges to include only a few providers like `pid` and `syscall`, which are limited to the scope of that zone.

Solaris 10 included a feature called "sparse root zones," where a minimal subset of global zone components were installed and the remainder mounted read-only from the global zone. That feature provided a way for reducing zone disk usage as well as preventing certain system files and binaries (in /usr, for example) from being written by zone processes. Since Solaris 11 is based on ZFS, sharing read-only file systems in non-global zones is a bit different.

Immutable Non-Global Zones

Solaris 11 supports the creation of "immutable" zones. That is, the zone root is read-only, and system binaries and configuration files cannot be altered except through the global zone. Immutable zones are created in the same way native non-global zones are created (see Chapter 4). The difference is that the file access policy, `file-mac-policy`, is set to one of four values: `none`, `strict`, `fixed-configuration`, and `flexible-configuration`. These set the following properties for the zone:

- `none`: The zone's root file system is read-write

- `strict`: The zone's root file system is read-only, no IPS packages can be installed, SMF services cannot be modified, auditing data must be logged remotely

- `fixed-configuration`: Directories in /var can be updated, including audit logs

- `flexible-configuration`: Directories in /var and files in /etc can be updated

Before booting the zone, use the `zonecfg` program to set the zone's file access policy to one of the preceding (`none` is the default). For example, to create a fully immutable zone:

```
# zonecfg -z ngz01
zonecfg:ngz01> set file-mac-profile=strict
zonecfg:ngz01> end
```

Since zones appear as if they were a full OS environment (like a "server," having a hostname and IP address), immutable zones are ideal for certain applications such as Web servers where the content is not writable from within the zone, protecting it from any security exploits or defacements. The immutable zone's content must be managed from the global zone.

Immutable Global Zone

Solaris 11.2 extends the idea of immutable zones to the global zone. An immutable global zone is configured in much the same way as for non-global zones, setting the file access policy to one of the four listed previously:

```
# zonecfg -z global
zonecfg:global> set file-mac-profile=strict
zonecfg:global> end
```

The system (global zone) must be rebooted for this change to take effect. And in order to make any changes to the now read-only global zone, you must reboot it using `zoneadm` with the -w flag to temporarily enable any needed changes or updates and then reboot again to re-enable the immutable global zone state:

```
# zoneadm -z global boot -w
```

Future releases of Oracle Solaris will remove this restriction by allowing changes to the system (such as a system update) without reboot using the Trusted Path.

Compliance

Solaris 11.2 now includes a tool that reports on compliance to security policies; it's based on the National Institute of Standards and Technology (NIST) Security Content Automation Protocol (SCAP), and is used for verifying critical security updates, checking security-related configuration settings, and reporting on potential security problems.

To use the compliance tool, you might need to install the IPS package, `pkg:/security/compliance`. That package is normally installed along with the `solaris-small-server` or `solaris-large-server` package groups. Check that it is installed, for example:

```
# pkg list compliance
NAME (PUBLISHER)     VERSION                  IFO
security/compliance 0.5.11-0.175.2.0.0.42.2   i--
```

The compliance tool can generate a report for the *Oracle Solaris Security Policy* benchmark, or for the *Payment Card Industry Data Security Standard* (PCI DSS) benchmark. List these as follows, showing the available benchmarks and profiles:

```
# compliance list -v
Benchmarks:
pci-dss
        Payment Card Industry Data Security Standard
solaris
        Oracle Solaris Security Policy
Assessments:
No assessments available
# compliance list -p
Benchmarks:
pci-dss:       Solaris_PCI-DSS
solaris:       Baseline, Recommended
Assessments:
        No assessments available
```

To run an assessment, choose a benchmark and run the compliance tool, for example:

```
# compliance assess -p Baseline -b solaris
Assessment will be named 'solaris.Baseline.2015-03-16,11:06'
        Package integrity is verified
        Test_1.1
pass

        The OS version is current
        Test_1.2
pass
( ... output truncated ... )
```

The compliance check might take several minutes to complete and will output a variety of test results to the console. Tests include checking the current OS version, ZFS, SSH access, root role and login settings, and numerous other system configuration settings. A report is created in the `/var/share/compliance` directory:

```
# compliance list
Benchmarks:
pci-dss
solaris
Assessments:
solaris.Baseline.2015-03-16,11:06
# compliance report
/var/share/compliance/assessments/solaris.
Baseline.2015-03-16,11:06/report.html
```

Note that the report's directory name includes the profile and benchmark types, and the date/timestamp. The generated report file by default is an HTML document, which can be viewed with a Web browser, as shown by the Solaris Compliance Report in Figure 7-4.

The Compliance Report provides details on all the compliance tests for the requested benchmark and profile. By clicking on any of the test links, administrators can view the results of the tests and see recommendations for correcting any reported failures. For example, in this sample report, the "root is a role" test has failed. Clicking on that link will bring up details for that failed test, along with remediation instructions, as shown in Figure 7-5.

After following the recommended remediation for any of the failed tests, rerun the compliance tool to verify the security profile for the system.

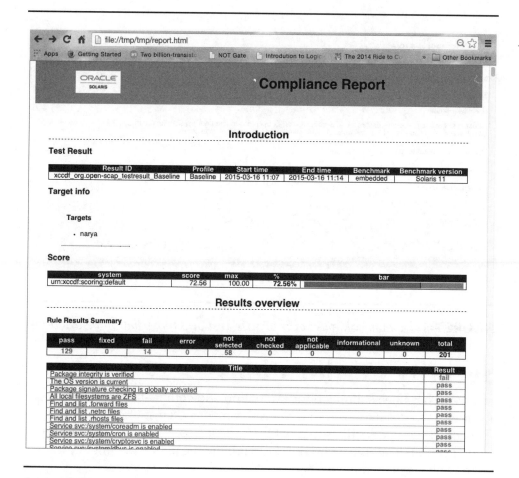

FIGURE 7-4.   *Solaris Compliance Report*

This compliance review process should be repeated regularly and preferably automatically using the `cron` service.

To display the contents of the compliance guides, simply run the command

```
# compliance guide -a
```

which will create HTML files in the `/var/share/compliance/guides` directory that you can read using any browser.

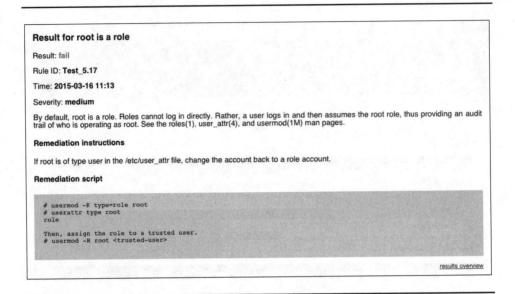

Result for root is a role

Result: fail

Rule ID: **Test_5.17**

Time: **2015-03-16 11:13**

Severity: **medium**

By default, root is a role. Roles cannot log in directly. Rather, a user logs in and then assumes the root role, thus providing an audit trail of who is operating as root. See the roles(1), user_attr(4), and usermod(1M) man pages.

Remediation instructions

If root is of type user in the /etc/user_attr file, change the account back to a role account.

Remediation script

```
# usermod -K type=role root
# userattr type root
role

Then, assign the role to a trusted user.
# usermod -R root <trusted-user>
```

results overview

FIGURE 7-5 Details of failed compliance test and remediation instructions

Security Certifications

Solaris 11 has been submitted for evaluation and certification of several key security standards for use in the US Government systems. Not all Solaris users need such evaluations to meet their security policies, but even those among commercial users who don't require them gain the benefit of the testing and strengthening of OS protections.

Oracle Solaris 11.1 has been certified under the Common Criteria standard at EAL4+, including the Labeled Security and Virtualization profiles. The US Government's Defense Information Systems Agency (DISA) publishes evaluations and compliance recommendations for operating systems and applications which include Oracle Solaris 11. They publish a *Security Technical Implementation Guide* (STIG) for Solaris 11.1 for both x86 and SPARC systems that reviews OS security services (see the References section at the end of this chapter).

Additionally, the *Center for Internet Security*, which provides objective, vendor-neutral evaluations of operating systems, database servers, and other IT infrastructure hardware (HW) and software (SW) components, has published the CIS Oracle Solaris 11.1 Benchmark that provides best-practice recommendations and *instructions* for hardening the OS and meeting the benchmark requirements, and is well worth reviewing and implementing its guidelines.

Complete Oracle Stack Security

Solaris 11 includes built-in kernel security features that don't need any administrative intervention. For example, by default, application stacks are non-executable, reducing the potential for buffer-overflow exploits. The Oracle Solaris Cryptographic Framework provides transparent, hardware-accelerated encryption for security-related applications and functions on SPARC and Intel processors with cryptographic components.

In addition to OS security features, many of Oracle's applications have security and data protection capabilities. We won't cover them in this book, but they are worth mentioning and investigating, such as data encryption and masking, database firewalling, and user access control and auditing, along with a security configuration menu in *Oracle Database 12c*. See the *Oracle Database 12c Security and Compliance* whitepaper listed in the References for further details.

Summary

We have summarized some of the key Oracle Solaris 11 features that system administrators need to use to ensure a secure and compliant environment for users' data and applications. We introduced new Solaris 11.2 features like immutable global zones and the Compliance Framework for enhancing security in distributed systems such as those in cloud computing infrastructures. We have covered only some of the many security features that Solaris 11 provides for protecting data, users, and applications; we strongly recommend additional review of the References listed.

References

Oracle Solaris 11.2 Security Compliance Guide,
https://docs.oracle.com/cd/E36784_01/pdf/E39067.pdf

Oracle Solaris 11 - Engineered for Public Sector,
http://www.oracle.com/us/products/server-storage/solaris/solaris11/solaris-for-public-sector-ds-2618450.pdf

User and Process Rights Provide an Alternative to the Superuser Model,
http://docs.oracle.com/cd/E36784_01/html/E37123/rbac-28.html

Managing User Accounts by Using the User Manager GUI,
http://docs.oracle.com/cd/E36784_01/html/E36818/usersetupgui-1.html

Managing Auditing in Oracle Solaris 11.2,
http://docs.oracle.com/cd/E36784_01/html/E37127/index.html

Solaris 11 SPARC Manual STIG,
http://iase.disa.mil/stigs/Documents/U_Solaris_11_SPARC_V1R2_STIG.zip

Solaris 11 x86 Manual STIG,
http://iase.disa.mil/stigs/Documents/U_Solaris_11_X86_V1R2_STIG.zip

CIS Security Benchmarks,
https://benchmarks.cisecurity.org/

Oracle Database 12c Security and Compliance,
http://www.oracle.com/technetwork/database/security/security-compliance-wp-12c-1896112.pdf

CHAPTER
8

Installing Applications
Using Templates and IPS

Solaris 11 for x86 systems can be installed as a virtual machine (VM) on several popular hypervisor environments, including *Parallels Desktop for Mac*, *VMware Workstation* and *VMware Fusion for Mac*, the open source *Xen* hypervisor, on Oracle's Xen-based *OVM for x86*, and on *VirtualBox*. The most common use of cases for such virtualized environments is for learning about operating system (OS) features and for creating test and development environments. Installing Solaris 11 in a VM enables learning how to set up and explore new OS features and frameworks like OpenStack and Puppet using multiple Solaris VMs and/or zones. In this chapter, we describe how to create a Solaris 11 VM using *VirtualBox*; the setup decisions and concepts will also generally apply to other hypervisors that support Solaris VMs although the user interfaces, of course, will differ.

Solaris applications can be deployed in VirtualBox VMs, or they can be deployed in zones. Installing an application in a Solaris VM is essentially identical to installing it in a bare metal OS environment, although there may be questions about support. We'll also show how to deploy an Oracle application in a zone, which is a best practice recommendation, and how to create an IPS package for the application.

Installing Oracle VirtualBox

You can download VirtualBox from Oracle's Web site at http://www.oracle .com/technetwork/server-storage/virtualbox/downloads/index.html, or from https://www.virtualbox.org/. The former includes links to a variety of pre-built VirtualBox VMs that include pre-configured software "appliances" such as Oracle's database and application server.

VirtualBox is an application, specifically a "Type 2" hypervisor, that installs and runs like any other application on a host OS. Supported *host* operating systems include Microsoft Windows, Apple OS X, Linux, and Solaris itself. Creating guest VMs on any of these platforms involves a common set of tasks that includes configuring the VM's memory allocation, virtual disk size, number of virtual CPUs, network connections, and local file system access. Installation of an OS in a VirtualBox VM requires a source file on removable media or a boot/install file downloaded from an appropriate source and might also require a license key to activate the OS. For Microsoft Windows hosts (laptop, desktop, or server), select, download, and install the current `VirtualBox*Win.exe` version; for Apple laptops or desktops, select, download, and install the current `VirtualBox*OSX.dmg` version.

You should also download and install the current *Extension Pack* which includes VM support for certain USB devices and for remote desktop support. Execute VirtualBox as you would for any other application on your host OS, from the "Programs" menu on Windows or from the "Applications" menu on OS X.

NOTE

A "Type 1 hypervisor" is installed directly on a system's hardware. Examples include VMware's ESX, Microsoft's Hyper-V, and Oracle's VM for SPARC and for x86. A "Type 2 hypervisor" is an application that runs within a host OS and provides many of the same virtualization services as Type 1.

Creating Solaris Virtual Machines Using *VirtualBox*

There are two options for creating a Solaris 11 VM in VirtualBox: download and create the VM using Solaris 11 Installation media, or download, import, and activate a pre-built VM. For the former method, go to http://www.oracle .com/technetwork/server-storage/solaris11/downloads/install-2245079.html and download one of the Solaris 11.2 installation images as we described in Chapter 2; make note of where this image resides on your host system. For the following example, we will create a Solaris 11.2 VM using the `sol-11_2-text-x86.iso` installation file, which is an image of an installation DVD that we have saved in our `Download` directory. Remember that the tasks for creating a VirtualBox VM are the same for all host operating systems, although the user interface and certain options will vary.

Start up VirtualBox on your system; you will see a display similar to the one in Figure 8-1. Click on the "New" icon to start the VM creation process. Fill in a name for your VM, and select the OS type and version (Solaris 11 in our example) as shown in Figure 8-2. You will need to specify the required memory and virtual disk sizes for your VM: at least 2 GB of memory and 9 GB of disk space for the Text Installer version of Solaris 11, more of each for any anticipated application and storage requirements. And note that you are

FIGURE 8-1. *The VirtualBox Manager*

allocating resources from your host OS and must leave sufficient memory and disk space for that (don't allocate more than half of your host OS memory to the VM, for example). Then click the *Create* icon; when asked about the drive file type, select VDI and select Dynamically allocated, and select the desired size of the virtual disk you want to use.

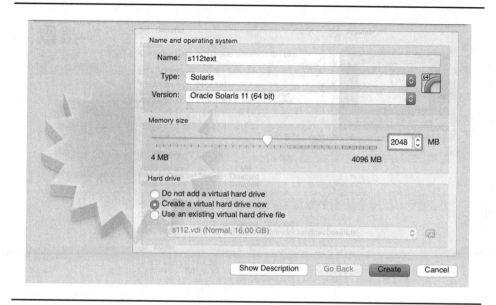

FIGURE 8-2.   *Create the Solaris 11 VM*

Note that the virtual disk is just a file on your host system, not a "real" disk. VirtualBox then displays the specification screen for the new VM, as shown in Figure 8-3. Clicking on any of the main headings in this display brings up additional options for configuring the VM. For example, the *System* section lets you configure the VM's number of virtual CPUs (hardware threads). Allocating more than one virtual central processing unit (vCPU) is useful for VM performance but you need to reserve some for the host OS, so don't allocate more than half of your processor's available vCPUs to the VM (Figure 8-4).

The key step in installing the VM is telling the VirtualBox where to find the OS install file. Click on the Storage section, then on the DVD icon, and locate you install file, as shown in Figure 8-5. To begin the install process, click on the VirtualBox *Start* icon, and the process will begin. It will continue just like a typical installation described in Chapter 2, but the Solaris

FIGURE 8-3. *Configuring the Solaris VM*

VM will be installed on the virtual disk and will run as a guest OS under the VirtualBox hypervisor.

An alternate and perhaps easier Solaris VM installation method is to download the pre-configured Solaris 11.2 VM template, `sol-11_2-vbox.ova`, from http://www.oracle.com/technetwork/server-storage/solaris11/downloads/vm-templates-2245495.html, and import it into VirtualBox (select *File, Import Appliance* from the VirtualBox menu, as shown in Figure 8-6).

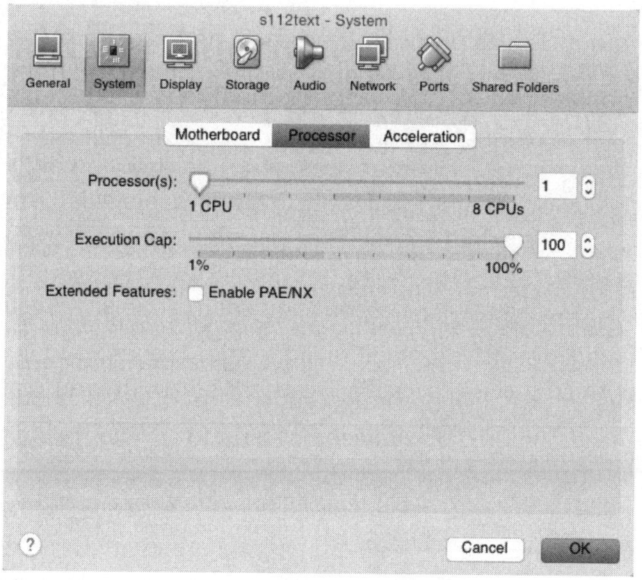

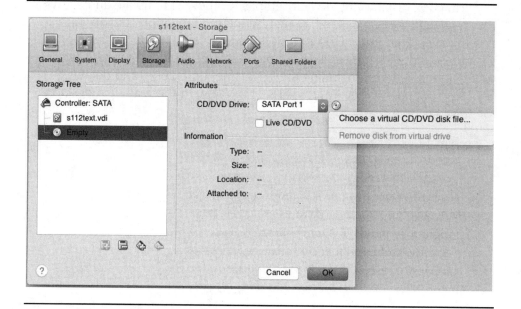

FIGURE 8-4. *Configuring the VM resources*

FIGURE 8-5. *Selecting the VM installation file*

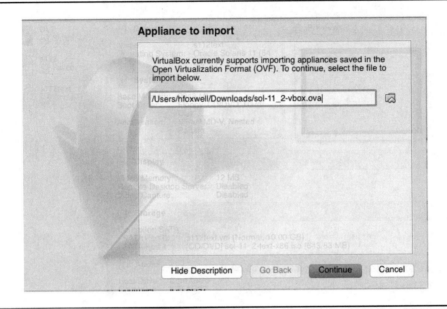

FIGURE 8-6. *Import the VM template file*

VirtualBox displays the default settings for the VM template and allows you to change them if desired (remembering the limitations of your host system); click the *Import* icon to install the VM. You can then *Start* the VM as you did with the earlier example; it will prompt you for additional configuration settings, including the hostname, time zone, and default user and root passwords. Your Solaris 11.2 VM with the graphical desktop (GNOME) is now ready.

NOTE
There are more pre-built template VMs for developers at http://www.oracle.com/ technetwork/community/developer-vm/ index.html. They include VMs for the Oracle Database 12c, MySQL, Oracle Linux, Solaris 10, and other Oracle application software. These templates are installed using the same VirtualBox Import Appliance method described in this section.

Installing Oracle Applications in Zones

The traditional method of deploying applications is to install them directly in the OS kernel environment that runs on the system's hardware; for Solaris, we call this the "global zone" to distinguish it from virtual environments called "non-global zones." Deploying applications in non-global zones has several benefits, including features we discussed in Chapter 4 such as secure separation from other application environments, the ability to easily manage and migrate the zone, dynamic expansion and/or capping of zone resources, and even hosting the application on a different OS release when using kernel zones. For these reasons, it is considered a "best practice" to deploy Solaris application in zones rather than on "bare metal" in the global zone unless there is some compelling technical reason. A misbehaving or compromised application running in the global zone can endanger all the other zone environments.

Installing Oracle WebLogic Server 12c in a Zone

To deploy an application such as *Oracle WebLogic Server 12c* in a zone, first create, install, and boot the zone as we described in Chapter 4; we will use the zone ngz01 created earlier for this example. Log in to the zone's console and become the root user, for example:

```
# zlogin -C ngz01
ngz01 console login: hfoxwell
Password: ########
Oracle Corporation        SunOS 5.11     11.2     June 2014
$ su -
Password: ########
Apr 15 20:56:39 ngz01 su: 'su root' succeeded for hfoxwell on /dev/console
Oracle Corporation        SunOS 5.11     11.2     June 2014
#
```

An Oracle application might require other software to be installed; this is the case with WebLogic, which requires Java. So, confirm that Java is not yet installed in the zone, then use IPS to install it. The Java developer package requires a license agreement to install and run, so include the –accept flag:

```
# pkg list jdkpkg list: No packages matching 'jdk' installed
# pkg install --accept developer/java/jdk
... (output truncated) ...
# java -version
java version "1.7.0_60"
Java(TM) SE Runtime Environment (build 1.7.0_60-b19)
Java HotSpot(TM) Server VM (build 24.60-b09, mixed mode)
#
```

Oracle WebLogic Server 12c requires a default user to run it, so we add that user and log in:

```
# useradd -d /export/home/wladmin -m wladmin
80 blocks
# passwd wladmin
New Password: ########
Re-enter new Password: ########
passwd: password successfully changed for wladmin
# su - wladmin
Oracle Corporation      SunOS 5.11      11.2      June 2014

$
```

Next you need to download and install the WebLogic software; obtain this from the Oracle Technology Network (OTN) site at http://www.oracle.com/technetwork/middleware/weblogic/downloads/index.html (clicking the checkbox to accept the OTN license agreement enables the software to be available for downloading), and then copy the install file into the wladmin user's home directory and install the .jar file:

```
$  ls -l
total 1804497
-rw-r-----   1 wladmin  staff    923179081 Apr 15 21:30
fmw_12.1.3.0.0_wls.jar
$ java -jar ./ fmw_12.1.3.0.0_wls.jar
... (output truncated) ...
```

After an application like WebLogic is installed, follow its specific startup and configuration instructions (we won't get into WebLogic setup in this chapter; for a more detailed example, see the Hands-On-Lab listed in the References section at the end of this chapter).

Installing Oracle Database 12c in a Zone

The *Oracle Database 12c* is supported on various hardware and OS environments, although it is best to run "Oracle on Oracle" to take advantage of the many optimizations that have been developed for the database on Solaris 11 for SPARC servers. Moreover, when installing the database on Solaris 11, it is generally recommended best practice to install the application in a zone. Such deployment has several advantages including the ability to cap the CPU resources used for licensing cost calculations. Additionally, deploying the Oracle Database in a zone, or any application for that matter, enables better encapsulation of the environment for security and performance isolation, management, development and testing, and resource management. This also allows for multiple database versions to be run in different zones and makes moving the database zones to other systems much easier.

The installation process for Oracle Database 12c is relatively straightforward, though prior to installing the software there are a number of considerations we will need to make—particularly if we want to implement hard partitioning to conform to the Oracle licensing policies for partitioned environments. Hard partitioning can be implemented using Oracle Solaris Zones resource management using a processor-based resource metric based on the number of cores that the application runs on. Oracle Solaris 11.3 introduced a new way to configure this resource management allowing administrators to allocate based on CPUs, cores, and sockets. See *Hard Partitioning with Oracle Solaris Zones* in the References section for more information.

Administrators may want to create a shared file system for multiple database instances that can be centrally managed by the database administrator—this is especially useful when applying database patches and updates. This in turn can be made available to a zone using the following zone configuration:

```
# zonecfg -z ngz01
Use 'create' to begin configuring a new zone
zonecfg:ngz01> create -t SYSdefault
zonecfg:ngz01> add fs
zonecfg:ngz01:fs> set dir=/u01
zonecfg:ngz01:fs> set special=/u01
zonecfg:ngz01:fs> set type=lofs
zonecfg:ngz01:fs> end
zonecfg:ngz01> verify
zonecfg:ngz01> exit
```

Once we have successfully created and installed the zone (see Chapter 4 for further details of this), we will need to prepare the environment for installing the Oracle Database. We need to perform some additional steps that are prerequisites such as creating an `oracle` user and assigning it to two new groups, the Oracle inventory group `oinstall` and the DBA administration group `dba`.

```
# useradd -m oracle
80 blocks
# groupadd oinstall
# groupadd dba
# usermod -g oinstall -G dba oracle
```

We will also need to configure kernel parameter defaults that the Oracle Database requires. We use the *projects* resource management mechanism to label workloads and separate them from other aspects of the operating system. These workloads can then be appropriately controlled. Most kernel parameter defaults in Oracle Solaris 11 are appropriate for the Oracle Database, but we will need to adjust a few parameters by creating a new project called `user.oracle`:

```
# projadd user.oracle
# projmod -U oracle -sK "process.max-file-
descriptor=(basic,65536,deny)" user.oracle
# projmod -U oracle -sK "project.max-shm-
memory=(priv,8589934592,deny)" user.oracle
```

NOTE
If we are using the Oracle Database graphical installer and these kernel parameters are not set, the installer will create a script that administrators can run to make these changes.

Oracle Database has a few software dependencies in order to run the installer. For convenience, a group package `oracle-rdbms-server-12-1-preinstall` has been made available that allows an administrator to quickly remedy possible missing software. Administrators can install it as follows:

```
# pkg install oracle-rdbms-server-12-1-preinstall
        Packages to install: 19
        Services to change:   2
   Create boot environment: No
```

```
Create backup boot environment: No
DOWNLOAD                             PKGS        FILES    XFER (MB)    SPEED
Completed                           19/19      349/349     7.5/7.5    1.0M/s

PHASE                                           ITEMS
Installing new actions                        897/897
Updating package state database                  Done
Updating package cache                            0/0
Updating image state                             Done
Creating fast lookup database                    Done
Updating package cache                            1/1
```

Once this has been installed, we are ready to install and configure the database. We will need to log in as the `oracle` user:

```
# su - oracle
Oracle Corporation      SunOS 5.11      11.2      June 2014
oracle@ngz01:~$
```

Assuming that the appropriate installation files have been downloaded from the OTN and unzipped into the home directory, we are ready to run the installer using the `runInstaller` script to launch the Oracle Universal Installer. Administrators can choose to either run the graphical interactive installer or run the installer in a non-graphical silent mode using a response file template, `db_install.rsp`, that is provided in the `response` directory that can be easily customized.

In the following example, we have downloaded and unpacked the zip files into /u01 to run the installer:

```
oracle@ngz01:~$ cd /u01/database
oracle@ngz01:/u01/database/$ ./runInstaller
```

Once the installer starts you will see a window popping up as the Oracle Universal Installer starts, as shown in Figure 8-7.

NOTE
The graphical installer requires an X11 environment to display the installation screens. Administrators can choose to install the GNOME desktop environment by installing the `solaris-desktop` *package, or display to a remote host using* `ssh -X` *for example.*

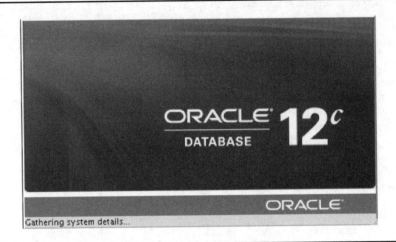

FIGURE 8-7. *Running the Oracle Database Universal Installer*

The installer will perform prerequisite checks on the system. If any of these fails, the administrator will need to fix and restart the installer. Once the installation is complete, the administrator will be asked to run two scripts as the root user, `orainstRoot.sh` and `root.sh`, to modify file permissions and copy over some scripts. After this has been completed, the installer may run the Oracle Database Assistant to create database instances as required.

Packaging and Deploying Applications Using IPS

Administrators will often need to reliably deploy in-house applications to a wide range of systems in their data center, and provide means to update those systems as and when new versions of the application are released. There are many approaches to this problem that can be taken, but one recommended approach on Solaris 11 systems is to take advantage of the Image Packaging System (IPS).

Image Packaging System provides a way to manage the complete software lifecycle of an application, particularly as that application moves between development, test, and production environments. We covered how to use IPS to update Solaris 11 systems in Chapter 3. By choosing to package application in IPS, administrators can take advantage of more seamless updates using built-in versioning and package dependencies, automated deployment during install time, and the ability to roll back to previous versions if required. Creating an IPS package can be a little more work, but the benefits outweigh the costs of doing so.

Creating an Image Packaging System Repository

Before we start to create a package for our application, we will need to create an IPS repository in which we will publish it to. IPS repositories can be hosted locally on the file system, or made available through HyperText Transfer Protocol (HTTP) and HyperText Transfer Protocol Secure (HTTPS). We will first create a new ZFS file system data set that can host our repository. This is recommended best practice because it allows us to quickly snapshot or clone the repository as required.

```
# zfs create rpool/export/repository
```

Once we have created the data set, we can now go ahead and create an IPS package repository. In Chapter 3, we saw how we can use `pkgrepo` to query a repository for packages. We can also use it to create repositories as follows:

```
# pkgrepo create /export/repository
# ls /export/repository
pkg5.repository
```

From the above output, we can see that it has created a `pkg5.repository` file in this data set. As we start publishing packages, we'll see that the contents of this data set will change. When we create a repository, we need to set the appropriate publisher prefix—for example, this corresponds to `solaris` for the Oracle hosted package repositories for both the release and support repositories. In our case, we will set it to `mycompany` as follows:

```
# pkgrepo set -s /export/repository publisher/prefix=mycompany
```

We can query this newly recreated repository and ensure that it has zero packages as follows:

```
# pkgrepo -s /export/repository info
PUBLISHER PACKAGES STATUS       UPDATED
mycompany 0        online       2015-05-26T23:22:48.330087Z
```

Creating a Package Manifest

In order to create an IPS package and publish it to a repository, we will need to create a package manifest. A package manifest describes how a package is put together. We briefly touched on this during Chapter 3 when we looked at the package manifest for the gnu-tar package:

```
# pkg contents -m gnu-tar
set name=pkg.fmri value=pkg://solaris/archiver/gnu-tar@1.27.1,5.11-0.175.2.0.0.4
2.1:20140623T010157Z
set name=pkg.summary value="GNU version of the tar archiving utility"
set name=com.oracle.info.version value=1.27.1
set name=variant.arch value=i386 value=sparc
set name=com.oracle.info.description value="GNU tar"
set name=com.oracle.info.tpno value=16886
set name=com.oracle.info.name value=tar
set name=pkg.description value="Tar is a program for packaging a set of files as
a single archive in tar format."
set name=info.classification value=org.opensolaris.category.2008:Development/GNU
set name=info.source-url value=http://ftp.gnu.org/gnu/tar/tar-1.27.1.tar.bz2
set name=org.opensolaris.consolidation value=userland
set name=info.upstream-url value=http://www.gnu.org/software/tar/
set name=org.opensolaris.arc-caseid value=PSARC/2000/488
depend fmri=pkg:/compress/bzip2@1.0.6-0.175.2.0.0.41.1 type=require
depend fmri=pkg:/compress/gzip@1.5-0.175.2.0.0.41.1 type=require
depend fmri=pkg:/network/ssh@0.5.11-0.175.2.0.0.41.0 type=require
depend fmri=pkg:/system/core-os@0.5.11-0.175.2.0.0.41.0 type=require
depend fmri=pkg:/system/library@0.5.11-0.175.2.0.0.41.0 type=require
file 6c1b664308058c996d6dd1282370944f538dc3bc chash=3218e15655c2853517c3790dbcad
edaae8ce3cd5 facet.locale.ca=true group=other mode=0444 owner=root path=usr/shar
e/locale/ca/LC_MESSAGES/tar.mo pkg.csize=20558 pkg.size=54344
... (output truncated) ...
```

Each line of the package manifest represents an *action*—the set action provides some basic meta-data about the package, the file action indicates what files are included in the package, the dir action indicates what directories are included in the package, the depend action lists the package dependencies a particular package might have, and so on. We will need to do the same for the application we wish to package.

As a simple application example to package, let's assume we have a very simple Bash script called `check_space.sh` that periodically checks the status of the root ZFS pool called `rpool` and notifies us if the pool reaches greater than 80% capacity. Such a script might do something as basic as the following:

```bash
#!/bin/bash

# Get the current date
timestamp() {
date +"%Y/%m/%d"
}

# Who are we sending to
MAILTO="admin@mycompany.com"


# What the subject of the mail is

SUBJECT="Disk Quota : $HOSTNAME ($(timestamp))"


# Get the status of ZFS pool called rpool

ZPOOL_STATUS=$(zpool list -H -o capacity rpool)

# Strip off the percentage

SPACE_CONSUMED="${ZPOOL_STATUS//%}"


# If we are over 80%, let's send an email

if [ "$SPACE_CONSUMED" -gt "80" ]

then


echo "Root pool capacity: $ZPOOL_STATUS" | mailx -s "$SUBJECT" $MAILTO
fi
```

We would like it to be installed into `/usr/local/bin`. We won't worry at this time how this script is called—we could achieve this either by using a `cron` entry (automated using Puppet for example) or by using a simple SMF service that periodically runs the script. Fortunately, there are IPS tools to help us generate an initial manifest based on a listing of directories and files. To prepare for running this tool, we need to create a *proto* area that provides a mockup of how the package should look from a directory structure. We can quickly create this using the following commands:

```
# mkdir -p proto/usr/local/bin
# cp check_space.sh proto/usr/local/bin/
# find proto -name '*'
proto
proto/usr
proto/usr/local
proto/usr/local/bin
proto/usr/local/bin/check_space.sh
```

As we can see from this code, the proto directory contains a directory structure that models what we'd like to see. The next step is to run the pkgsend generate command on the proto directory to generate an initial manifest. We will also pass it through the pkgfmt command to provide a prettier looking format that is easier to read and output it to a file called check-space.p5m.1.

```
# pkgsend generate proto | pkgfmt> check-space.p5m.1
# cat myapp.p5m.1
dir  path=usr owner=root group=bin mode=0755
dir  path=usr/local owner=root group=bin mode=0755
dir  path=usr/local/bin owner=root group=bin mode=0755
file usr/local/bin/check_space.sh path=usr/local/bin/check_space.sh owner=root \
group=bin mode=0755
```

One best practice of packaging is to avoid including directories that have already been provided by the base set of system packages. In this case, /usr, /usr/local, and /usr/bin are already included in other packages so we can remove them from our manifest. In doing so, our manifest changes to only having a single line as follows:

```
# cat myapp.p5m.1
file usr/local/bin/check_space.sh path=usr/local/bin/check_space.sh owner=root \
group=bin mode=0755
```

Now that we have captured what files we would like to include, we now need to create some meta-data for this package. Meta-data can be added manually to the preceding manifest using set actions. The recommended best practice is to store your meta-data separately to a generated manifest—this is particularly true when the application you want to package contains many files and directories and could change over the course of new versions. We will follow this best practice and capture the meta-data separately in a file called check-space.mog.

```
# cat check-space.mog
set name=pkg.fmri value=site/check-space@1.0
set name=pkg.description value="ZFS root pool capacity check"
set name=pkg.summary value="Checks if ZFS root pool is over 80%"
set name=variant.arch value=$(ARCH)
```

You will notice from this code that each set of action uses a different set of attributes and values. `pkg.fmri` tells us what the package name is and its version. `pkg.description` provides a short description for the package. `pkg.summary` provides a longer summary for the package. `variant.arch` tells us what architecture this package is for—in this case we're using a variable that we will substitute for the platform that we are on. The next step is to take this package meta-data and merge it with our manifest to create a new file. The `pkgmogrify` command is used to achieve this and provides programmatic editing of package manifests—not essential in this simple example, but very useful where you may want to filter content, move files and directories around, and more. We will output to a new file `check-space.p5m.2`.

```
# pkgmogrify -DARCH=`uname -p` check-space.p5m.1 check-space.mog \
| pkgfmt> check-space.p5m.2
# cat check-space.p5m.2
set name=pkg.fmri value=site/check-space@1.0
set name=pkg.summary value="Checks if ZFS root pool is over 80%"
set name=pkg.description value="ZFS root pool capacity check"
set name=variant.arch value=i386
file usr/local/bin/check_space.sh path=usr/local/bin/check_space.sh owner=root \
group=bin mode=0755
```

Now that we have regenerated our manifest, we can see that the meta-data is now included with the file action. When we ran the `pkgmogrify` command, we provided an additional option of DARCH='uname -p' which substituted in the value of `i386` for the `variant.arch` attribute.

The final step before we can publish this package is to generate dependencies for the package, so as to ensure that any dependent software is installed along with this package. We use the `pkgdepend generate` command and provide it a pointer to our *proto* area and manifest as follows:

```
# pkgdepend generate -md proto check-space.p5m.2 | pkgfmt> check-space.p5m.3
# cat check-space.p5m.3
set name=pkg.fmri value=site/check-space@1.0
set name=pkg.summary value="Checks if ZFS root pool is over 80%"
set name=pkg.description value="ZFS root pool capacity check"
set name=variant.arch value=i386
file usr/local/bin/check_space.sh path=usr/local/bin/check_space.sh owner=root \
group=bin mode=0755
```

```
depend type=require fmri=__TBD pkg.debug.depend.file=bash \
pkg.debug.depend.path=usr/bin \
    pkg.debug.depend.reason=usr/local/bin/check_space.sh \
pkg.debug.depend.type=script
```

We can see from this code that we now have a depend action added to our manifest. It's a little complicated to read, but it has essentially detected that there is a dependency on /usr/bin/bash. IPS recursively looks through the files planned to be included in the package. If our package had compiled C code, the pkgdepend generate step would look at the symbols and determine what was being linked in. Similarly, IPS can also detect any Python modules that are being used. From here we will need to trace this file dependency on /usr/bin/bash back to its origin package. We use the pkgdepend resolve step to do this work. This can take some time, particularly if there are a number of dependencies listed. When the command completes, it creates a new file check-space.p5m.3.res.

```
# pkgdepend resolve -m check-space.p5m.3
# cat check-space.p5m.3.res
set name=pkg.fmri value=site/check-space@1.0
set name=pkg.summary value="Checks if ZFS root pool is over 80%"
set name=pkg.description value="ZFS root pool capacity check"
set name=variant.arch value=i386
file usr/local/bin/check_space.sh path=usr/local/bin/check_space.sh owner=root \
group=bin mode=0755
depend fmri=pkg:/shell/bash@4.1.11-0.175.2.0.0.41.1 type=require
```

We can see that the depend action now has a package associated with it, shell/bash. We now are in the position that we can use this manifest to publish our first package.

Publishing the Package Manifest

The last stage is to publish this package to the repository. We use the pkgsend publish command to achieve this, and provide it the location of our *proto* area and final package manifest as follows:

```
# pkgsend publish -s /export/repository -d proto check-space.
p5m.3.res
pkg://mycompany/site/check-space@1.0,5.11:20150527T002832Z
PUBLISHED
# pkgrepo -s /export/repository info
PUBLISHER  PACKAGES  STATUS      UPDATED
mycompany  1         online      2015-05-27T00:28:32.603360Z
```

From this code, we can see that the package has been successfully published to the IPS repository. We can now test it out by adding this repository configuration using the `pkg set-publisher` command and trying to install the `check-space` package as follows:

```
# pkg set-publisher -p /export/repository
pkg set-publisher:
  Added publisher(s): mycompany
# pkg publisher
PUBLISHER               TYPE     STATUS P LOCATION
solaris                 origin   online F https://pkg.oracle.com/solaris/support/
mycompany               origin   online F file:///export/repository/
# pkg install check-space
          Packages to install:  1
     Create boot environment: No
Create backup boot environment: No
DOWNLOAD                        PKGS          FILES     XFER (MB)    SPEED
Completed                       1/1           1/1       0.0/0.0      0B/s

PHASE                                ITEMS
Installing new actions                6/6
Updating package state database       Done
Updating package cache                0/0
Updating image state                  Done
Creating fast lookup database         Done
Reading search index                  Done
Updating search index                 1/1
Updating package cache                2/2
# ls /usr/local/bin/
check_space.sh
```

Providing Wider Access to Your Repository

In the previous example we created a file-based IPS repository. This can be accessed from other systems over Network File System (NFS). Another way to access it is to host it over HTTP or HTTPS. To do this, we use the `svc:/application/pkg/server` SMF service to provide access to the repository. We can quickly use the `svccfg` command to tell the default service instance where to look for a repository, what port to use, and then enable it using `svcadm` as follows:

```
# svccfg -s application/pkg/server:default \
setprop pkg/inst_root=/export/repository
# svccfg -s application/pkg/server:default setprop pkg/port=9001
# svcadm enable application/pkg/server:default
# svcs application/pkg/server:default
STATE           STIME    FMRI
online          17:44:35 svc:/application/pkg/server:default
```

FIGURE 8-8. *The Web interface to an IPS package repository*

We can now see that the service is online. This means that we can reach this repository over HTTP using the `pkgrepo` command.

```
# pkgrepo -s http://10.0.0.5:9001 info
PUBLISHER PACKAGES STATUS     UPDATED
mycompany 1        online     2015-05-27T00:28:32.603360Z
```

We can also use our Web browser to display `http://10.0.0.5:9001`. This is a Web-based interface that allows viewing and searching of package content as shown in Figure 8-8.

Summary

Installing applications on Solaris 11 depends on the server architecture (SPARC or x86) and on the desired deployment, for example, in zones; the tools for such installation vary also—using pre-built templates, or by creating your own IPS software repositories. In this chapter, we have presented examples of several of these methods, showing how to install

Solaris 11 in VirtualBox both directly and using templates, as well as showing how to install Oracle WebLogic and the Oracle 12c Database. We also describe how to create and access a local IPS repository for installing packages locally. Collectively, these methods provide a great deal of flexibility for installing and updating software on Solaris 11.

References

Hands-On-Lab: Using Unified Archives to Deploy an Oracle WebLogic Server Cluster on Oracle Solaris 11.2,
http://www.oracle.com/technetwork/systems/hands-on-labs/using-ua-deploy-weblogic-solaris11-2492481.html

Hard Partitioning with Oracle Solaris Zones,
http://www.oracle.com/technetwork/server-storage/solaris11/technologies/os-zones-hard-partitioning-2347187.pdf

Five Steps for Installing Oracle Database 12c on Oracle Solaris 11,
https://community.oracle.com/docs/DOC-910652

Packaging and Delivering Software with IPS in Oracle Solaris 11,
http://docs.oracle.com/cd/E36784_01/html/E36856/index.html

Oracle Solaris 11 Unified Archives,
http://www.oracle.com/technetwork/server-storage/solaris11/downloads/unified-archives-2245488.html

Oracle VM Templates,
http://www.oracle.com/technetwork/server-storage/solaris11/downloads/vm-templates-2245495.html

CHAPTER
9

Configuration
Management

Oracle Solaris 11 includes a number of different technologies to allow administrators to configure systems at scale within their data centers. The Service Management Facility (SMF) provides service and configuration management for systems. It is the foundation for applying configuration in an automated way at deployment time, and managing configuration seamlessly across system updates. With more and more system configuration being managed through SMF, a good understanding of how it works is essential.

Administrators can also choose a variety of other mechanisms to complement the configuration management they can achieve using SMF—whether through customized scripting, or using popular open source configuration management tools. One such tool, Puppet, has been recently included in Oracle Solaris 11 to allow administrators to enforce configuration with support for a verity of different Solaris technologies. Puppet is a widely used tool to allow administrators to manage a complete heterogeneous data center of different technologies and platforms, especially useful to ensure compliance or other regulatory requirements.

In this chapter, we will also highlight the Remote Administration Daemon (RAD), a relatively recent addition to Oracle Solaris as a way to programmatically manage systems through a set of Application Programming Interfaces (APIs).

Service Management

Oracle Solaris 11 uses the SMF to manage system and application services. SMF dramatically improves the overall availability of the operating system by ensuring that essential services run continuously, even in the event of hardware and software failures. SMF is a part of Oracle Solaris' predictive self-healing capability, and closely integrates with the Fault Management Architecture (FMA) that also helps to isolate faulty hardware components and notifying administrators of their failure. SMF provides significant benefits over the legacy RC scripting mechanism such as the ability to support service dependencies and a central logging mechanism.

A typical Oracle Solaris system will include many different application and system services. Most services typically only have one service instance associated with them, though some services can have many instances (e.g., a web server with multiple document roots). Each service instance has a state—online, disabled, maintenance, or offline. A service instance will also have a relationship to other services, allowing the system to start instances in parallel during boot according to a defined dependency graph. If a service instance is interrupted for any reason, the system will know what other services instances need to be running to meet these dependencies. Each service instance is started by a master restarter daemon called `svc.startd`, though this task can also be delegated to an alternate restarter.

SMF stores service configuration data in a configuration repository, including the state of a given service instance and configuration related to that service instance. The configuration repository is managed by a central repository daemon called `svc.configd`. Each service is described using an XML-based file called a service manifest. This manifest details some basic information about the service, what dependencies it has, configuration it includes, and how that particular service should be started and stopped. A service, once started, can start several different processes that are tied together as part of a service contract. This means that an administrator needs to only manage the higher level service and service instance, rather than worry about a collection of processes.

Each service instance on a system can be described using a Fault Management Resource Indicator (FMRI) that shows the service name, the service instance, and associating category. Administrators use these FMRIs to manipulate service instances on a system. In some cases, we can use the abbreviated forms of the FMRI to refer to the same service or service instance assuming it is unique. Table 9-1 shows a breakdown of an FMRI for the SSH server service, `svc:/network/ssh:default`.

NOTE
Site-specific SMF services should begin with the FMRI, `svc:/site` to ensure they aren't confused with vendor-provided services.

svc:/	FMRI scheme for SMF
network	SMF category
ssh	Service
default	Service instance

TABLE 9-1. *Breakdown of the SMF FMRI for SSH Server*

Basic Service Management

To generate a list of services running on a system, we can use the `svcs` command as follows:

```
# svcs
STATE         STIME    FMRI
legacy_run    22:45:24 lrc:/etc/rc2_d/S47pppd
legacy_run    22:45:24 lrc:/etc/rc2_d/S81dodatadm_udaplt
legacy_run    22:45:24 lrc:/etc/rc2_d/S89PRESERVE
disabled      22:45:12 svc:/platform/i86pc/acpihpd:default
disabled      22:45:26 svc:/system/sp/management:default
online        22:44:58 svc:/system/early-manifest-import:default
online        22:44:58 svc:/system/svc/restarter:default
online        22:45:03 svc:/network/connectx/unified-driver-post-upgrade:default
online        22:45:03 svc:/network/ib/ib-management:default
online        22:45:03 svc:/network/netcfg:default
... (output truncated) ...
```

This command shows the list of service instances that are online. It also shows service instances that have been temporarily disabled until next reboot (as indicated by `disabled` in the STATE column) and legacy rc services (as indicated by `legacy _ run` in the STATE column). We can get a list of all services, including those that are permanently disabled by using the `-a` option to the `svcs` command:

```
# svcs -a
STATE         STIME    FMRI
legacy_run    22:45:24 lrc:/etc/rc2_d/S47pppd
legacy_run    22:45:24 lrc:/etc/rc2_d/S81dodatadm_udaplt
legacy_run    22:45:24 lrc:/etc/rc2_d/S89PRESERVE
disabled      22:44:59 svc:/system/device/mpxio-upgrade:default
disabled      22:44:59 svc:/system/labeld:default
disabled      22:45:00 svc:/network/ipfilter:default
disabled      22:45:00 svc:/network/ipsec/ike:default
disabled      22:45:00 svc:/network/ipsec/ike:ikev2
disabled      22:45:00 svc:/network/ipsec/manual-key:default
disabled      22:45:00 svc:/network/ldap/client:default
... (output truncated) ...
```

To get information about a particular service instance, we use the `-l` option to `svcs` command:

```
# svcs -l ssh
fmri         svc:/network/ssh:default
name         SSH server
enabled      true
state        online
next_state   none
state_time   April  7, 2015 10:46:39 PM UTC
```

```
logfile        /var/svc/log/network-ssh:default.log
restarter      svc:/system/svc/restarter:default
contract_id    141
manifest       /etc/svc/profile/generic.xml
manifest       /lib/svc/manifest/network/ssh.xml
dependencyrequire_all/none svc:/system/filesystem/local (online)
dependencyoptional_all/none svc:/system/filesystem/autofs (online)
dependencyrequire_all/none svc:/network/loopback (online)
dependencyrequire_all/none svc:/network/physical:default (online)
dependencyrequire_all/none svc:/system/cryptosvc (online)
dependencyrequire_all/none svc:/system/utmp (online)
dependencyoptional_all/error svc:/network/ipfilter:default (disabled)
dependencyrequire_all/restart file://localhost/etc/ssh/sshd_config (online)
```

From the previous output, we can see more detailed information about the service instance, including a description, the service instance state, what file the service instance logs to, who is responsible for executing the methods of this service instance, and some information about the instance dependencies it has. You will also note that we have used the abbreviated form ssh to refer to this service instance.

We can list the service instances upon which the SSH server depends on using the -d option:

```
# svcs -d ssh
STATE          STIME     FMRI
disabled       22:45:00  svc:/network/ipfilter:default
online         22:45:05  svc:/network/loopback:default
online         22:45:05  svc:/system/cryptosvc:default
online         22:45:12  svc:/system/utmp:default
online         22:45:16  svc:/network/physical:default
online         22:45:18  svc:/system/filesystem/local:default
online         22:45:21  svc:/system/filesystem/autofs:default
```

We can use the -D option to show what services instances depend on SSH server:

```
# svcs -D ssh
STATE          STIME     FMRI
online         22:45:23  svc:/milestone/self-assembly-complete:default
online         22:45:25  svc:/milestone/multi-user-server:default
```

We can see what processes have been started by this service instance by using the -p option to svcs:

```
# svcs -p ssh
STATE          STIME     FMRI
online         22:46:39  svc:/network/ssh:default
               22:46:39      1384 sshd
```

To enable service instances, we use the `svcadm enable` command. In the following example, we will enable the Apache web server:

```
# svcadm enable apache22
# svcs apache22
STATE          STIME    FMRI
online          1:25:04 svc:/network/http:apache22
```

To disable this service instance again, we use the `svcadm disable` command:

```
# svcs http:apache22
STATE          STIME    FMRI
disabled        1:26:14 svc:/network/http:apache22
```

If something goes awry with a given service instance, SMF puts the instance into a maintenance state (as indicated in the STATE column), meaning that some administrative intervention is required to get it successfully running again. For example, let's take a look at the DHCP server IPv4 service instance:

```
# svcs dhcp/server:ipv4
STATE          STIME    FMRI
maintenance     1:28:02 svc:/network/dhcp/server:ipv4
```

We will need to look at the logs for this service to determine why it is failing to run—likely due to a mistake in the configuration for this service.

We can also check the overall state of the system for service instances that are enabled but not running by using the -xv options to `svcs`:

```
# svcs -xv
svc:/network/dhcp/server:ipv4 (ISC DHCP Server)
 State: maintenance since April  8, 2015 01:28:02 AM UTC
Reason: Start method exited with $SMF_EXIT_ERR_FATAL.
   See: http://support.oracle.com/msg/SMF-8000-KS
   See: man -M /usr/share/man -s 1M dhcpd
   See: /var/svc/log/network-dhcp-server:ipv4.log
Impact: This service is not running.
```

In the previous example, we can see that the start method of the service instance failed. We could check the log to get more details about why this is the case.

TIP

We can use `svcs -xL` *to display part of the log file since the last successful method exit without errors. This can be a useful short cut to save time in troubleshooting problems.*

Finally, SMF milestones are service instances that aggregate multiple service and service instance dependencies and describe a specific state of readiness of a system on which other service instances can depend. Administrators can see a list of milestones using the `svcs` command:

```
# svcs milestone*
STATE          STIME    FMRI
online         22:45:12 svc:/milestone/config:default
online         22:45:12 svc:/milestone/unconfig:default
online         22:45:15 svc:/milestone/devices:default
online         22:45:16 svc:/milestone/network:default
online         22:45:17 svc:/milestone/name-services:default
online         22:45:17 svc:/milestone/single-user:default
online         22:45:23 svc:/milestone/self-assembly-complete:default
online         22:45:24 svc:/milestone/multi-user:default
online         22:45:25 svc:/milestone/multi-user-server:default
```

Some milestones correspond to traditional system run levels. For example: `svc:/milestone/single-user:default` corresponds to run level S, `svc:/milestone/multi-user:default` corresponds to run level 2, and `svc:/milestone/multi-user-server:default` corresponds to run level 3. Other milestones correspond to internal implementation for how an Oracle Solaris system is configured.

NOTE

We recommend that administrators use `init` *to switch milestones rather than switching them using* `svcadm`*.*

Setting Service Properties

Service configuration is stored in SMF. One of the significant changes in Oracle Solaris 11 was to move a lot of system configuration to SMF and replace traditional configuration files stored in `/etc`. The primary drivers for this change was to ensure seamless configuration management during a system upgrade—by preserving administrative customizations and merging in new vendor-provided default configuration. SMF stores its configuration in a number of different configuration layers with each layer having a priority order, each of higher priority overriding those with lower priority. Table 9-2 shows the discrete layers used in decreasing priority order.

Service configuration is achieved through property groups and properties. A service or service instance has an arbitrary number of these that are used to describe a service instance, its state, and how it should be configured. Property groups are a set of properties that have been logically grouped within a namespace. Properties can store different configuration types, including simple strings, integers, booleans, and network addresses. SMF uses a technique called inheritance (or composition), meaning that configuration can be shared across services instances from the parent service. During a configuration lookup, if a property is not found within the service instance, SMF will search for the same property in the parent service that contains the instance.

NOTE

SMF services and service instances include a number of framework property groups. These property groups will typically not be displayed to administrators.

Layer	Description
admin	Administrative changes made directly through the command line or running applications that are using `libscf(3LIB)` interfaces.
site-profile	Changes made through SMF profiles in `/etc/svc/profile/site`
system-profile	Vendor-provided changes made through SMF profiles in `/etc/svc/profile/generic.xml` or `/etc/svc/profile/platform.xml` Do not edit these files.
manifest	Default configuration through SMF manifests in `/lib/svc/manifests`

TABLE 9-2. *Configuration Layers in the SMF Repository*

We use the svcprop command to list properties and values of services and service instances. We can either list properties by property group or properties themselves. In the following example, we list all properties of the pkg property group in the svc:/application/pkg/server:default service instance. By default, it will use a composed view, that is, it will include any inherited properties of the parent service if they are not overridden by the same property in the instance:

```
# svcprop -p pkg application/pkg/server:default
pkg/inst_root astring /repositories/solaris
pkg/address net_address
pkg/cfg_file astring ""
pkg/content_root astringusr/share/lib/pkg
pkg/debug astring ""
pkg/file_root astring ""
pkg/log_access astring none
pkg/log_errors astring stderr
pkg/mirror boolean false
pkg/pkg_root astring /
pkg/port count 80
pkg/proxy_base astring ""
pkg/readonly boolean true
pkg/socket_timeout count 60
pkg/sort_file_max_size astring ""
pkg/ssl_cert_file astring ""
pkg/ssl_dialog astring smf
pkg/ssl_key_file astring ""
pkg/standalone boolean true
pkg/threads count 60
pkg/writable_root astring ""
```

We can use the -C option to only list the properties without composition and we will notice that there are many less properties listed:

```
# svcprop -C -p pkg application/pkg/server:default
pkg/inst_root astring/repositories/solaris
```

We can confirm that the rest of these properties come from the parent services by using the fully qualified FMRI, and a different value of pkg/inst_root:

```
# svcprop -p config svc:/application/pkg/server
pkg/address net_address
pkg/cfg_file astring ""
```

```
pkg/content_root astring usr/share/lib/pkg
pkg/debug astring ""
pkg/file_root astring ""
pkg/inst_root astring /var/pkgrepo
pkg/log_access astring none
pkg/log_errors astring stderr
pkg/mirror boolean false
pkg/pkg_root astring /
pkg/port count 80
pkg/proxy_base astring ""
pkg/readonly boolean true
pkg/socket_timeout count 60
pkg/sort_file_max_size astring ""
pkg/ssl_cert_file astring ""
pkg/ssl_dialog astring smf
pkg/ssl_key_file astring ""
pkg/standalone boolean true
pkg/threads count 60
pkg/writable_root astring ""
```

We can also be explicit about what property we are interested in (as opposed to the property group) by specifying this as the argument:

```
# svcprop -p pkg/inst_root application/pkg/server:default
/repositories/solaris
```

To set configuration properties, we use the svccfg command. This command provides a number of different options for setting properties—either directly at the command line, through an interactive interface, or through a text editor. Let's use the direct command line option setprop:

```
# svccfg -s pkg/server:default setprop pkg/inst_root = /tmp/repositories/solaris
# svcprop -p pkg/inst_rootpkg/server:default
/repositories/solaris
```

Having listed the property again, we notice that it hasn't been changed. This is because changes to the configuration repository aren't reflected in the running instance. This is easily seen using the composed view:

```
# svcprop-c -p pkg/inst_root pkg/server:default
/tmp/repositories/solaris
```

To reflect a change, we will need to refresh the service instance. SMF uses the concept of refreshing configuration as part of a transactional model—you may want to make several configuration changes and apply them as one transaction rather than individually.

```
# svcadm refresh pkg/server:default
# svcprop -p pkg/inst_root pkg/server:default
/tmp/repositories/solaris
```

Let's use the interactive editor to reset this property. We use the `svccfg` command line without any options to enter this interface:

```
# svccfg
svc:> select pkg/server:default
svc:/application/pkg/server:default> listproppkg/inst_root
pkg/inst_rootastring      /tmp/repositories/solaris
svc:/application/pkg/server:default> setproppkg/inst_root = /repositories/solaris
svc:/application/pkg/server:default> listproppkg/inst_root
pkg/inst_rootastring      /repositories/solaris
svc:/application/pkg/server:default> refresh
svc:/application/pkg/server:default> exit
```

`svccfg` supports a number of other useful subcommands, such as `listpg` to list property groups on a given service or service instance, `editprop` to open up a text editor to more easily allow configuration of multiple properties at the same time, and `extract` to allow administrators to easily capture service customizations as an XML profile that can be applied on other systems.

Service Bundles—Manifests and Profiles

As we hinted earlier, SMF services are described using service bundles, XML files that detail information about a service and service instance, including service dependencies, property groups, properties, and values. These service bundles are used to deliver services into Oracle Solaris, but also used to deliver custom configuration across multiple systems by the administrator.

There are two types of service bundle—a manifest and a profile. Both of these types use the same XML DTD (`/usr/share/lib/xml/dtd/service_bundle.dtd.1`) and documented in the `service_bundle(4)` main page.

Manifests

Manifests are used to describe services and service instances, including configuration, and are delivered to `/lib/svc/manifest` before being automatically imported into the SMF configuration repository. This process is handled during boot by the `svc:/system/early-manifest-import:default` service. Administrators can also deliver new services to a system by copying a manifest into `/lib/svc/manifest/site` and restarting the manifest import service instance:

```
# svcadm restart manifest-import
```

Profiles

Profiles provide customizations of a service or service instance. Customizations include whether an instance of a service should be enabled or disabled and any modifications to configuration properties. Vendor-provided profiles are located in `/etc/svc/profile`. Profile containing local customizations should be stored in `/etc/svc/profile/site`. Profiles are also automatically applied during a system reboot. Administrators can also apply new profiles by restarting the manifest import service instance as we did with manifests earlier.

Repository Layers

As we've mentioned earlier, the SMF configuration repository has four discrete layers—admin, site-profile, system-profile, and manifest. We can use the svccfg listcust subcommand to show what customizations we've made to the `svc:/network/dns/client:default` service instance:

```
# svccfg -s dns/client:default listcust -L config/nameserver
config/nameserver net_address admin                    192.168.0.1
```

Here we can see that we have a customization at the admin layer. We can remove this customization using the svccfg delcust subcommand, check again, and get an empty response from the svccfg listcust subcommand:

```
# svccfg -s dns/client:default delcust config/nameserver
# svccfg -s dns/client:default listcust -L config/nameserver
```

TIP

SMF supports a concept called masking, which enables administrators to delete properties, property groups, services, and service instances without the need to remove manifests or service profiles that may have been provided by the vendor as default configuration. This causes the entity to be "masked" across all repository layers, removing them from view. This masking ability means that administrators can make direct changes to the configuration, but also quickly return to the defaults if necessary. For example, let's delete the svc:/application/pkg/server:default *service instance. We use the* -M *option to* svccfg *to show that the service is masked. We can see that the general property group has been masked (which determines service instances) and our service instance does not show up with* svcs. *We can use* svccfgdelcust *to restore this service instance:*

```
# svccfg delete -f pkg/server:default
# svccfg listcust -M pkg/server:default
general                        admin           MASKED
general/complete astring       admin           MASKED
general/enabled boolean        admin           MASKED false
# svcs pkg/server:default
svcs: Pattern 'pkg/server:default' doesn't match any instances
STATE           STIME    FMRI
# svccfg -s pkg/server:default delcust
# svcs pkg/server:default
STATE           STIME    FMRI
disabled        8:19:52  svc:/application/pkg/server:default
```

Let's choose another example and show the config/nodename property of the svc:/system/identity:node service instance for each layer using the -l option to svcprop:

```
# svcprop -p config/nodename -l all svc:/system/identity:node
config/nodename astring manifest ""
config/nodename astring site-profile solaris
```

Here we can see more clearly that the `config/nodename` property is defined at the `manifest` layer, but empty, and set to `solaris` in the `site-profile` layer. Let's set the hostname to `myserver` with the `hostname` command and check again to see a new row printed at the `admin` layer:

```
# hostname myserver
# svcprop -p config/nodename -l all svc:/system/identity:node
config/nodename astring manifest ""
config/nodename astring site-profile solaris
config/nodename astring admin myserver
```

Creating Manifests and Profiles

At some point in time, administrators will need to get experienced with manifests and profiles. This will allow in-house applications to be integrated into SMF and thus take advantage of automatic service restarts. It will also allow site-specific system configuration to be applied at scale across many systems (and a necessary part of the Automated Installer process).

While some knowledge of XML will certainly help, a new utility introduced in Oracle Solaris 11 called `svcbundle` can automatically generate a manifest or profile for common scenarios—this can be then refined if desired afterward rather than starting from scratch. Through a series of name-value pairs specified by the `-s` option to the command line interface, different elements of the manifest or profile can be expressed, for example, whether a service instance should be enabled or disabled, property groups and properties, and start or stop methods for a given service.

Creating a New SMF Service

For example, let's suppose we wanted to integrate an in-house application with SMF. We might run the following command to first generate an SMF manifest:

```
# svcbundle -o myapp.xml -s service-name=site/myapp \
-s start-method="/opt/myapp/bin/start.sh"
# cat myapp.xml
<?xml version="1.0" ?>
<!DOCTYPE service_bundle
  SYSTEM '/usr/share/lib/xml/dtd/service_bundle.dtd.1'>
<!--
    Manifest created by svcbundle (2015-Apr-09 23:34:18+0000)
-->
<service_bundle type="manifest" name="site/myapp">
<service version="1" type="service" name="site/myapp">
```

```
<dependency restart_on="none" type="service"
name="multi_user_dependency" grouping="require_all">
<service_fmri value="svc:/milestone/multi-user"/>
</dependency>
<exec_method timeout_seconds="60" type="method" name="start"
            exec="/opt/myapp/bin/start.sh"/>
<exec_method timeout_seconds="60" type="method" name="stop"
exec=":true"/>
<exec_method timeout_seconds="60" type="method" name="refresh"
exec=":true"/>
<property_group type="framework" name="startd">
<propval type="astring" name="duration" value="transient"/>
</property_group>
<instance enabled="true" name="default"/>
<template>
<common_name>
<loctextxml:lang="C">
site/myapp
</loctext>
</common_name>
<description>
<loctextxml:lang="C">
The site/myapp service.
</loctext>
</description>
</template>
</service>
</service_bundle>
```

Once we have generated this XML file, we can simply copy it into /lib/svc/
manifest/site and restart the svc:/system/manifest-import:default
service instance to see that this new service instance is online.

NOTE

*By default svcbundle will use a transient service
model for the service instance. This means that
the master restarter does not track processes for
that service instance, and thus will only go into
maintenance with a method. By contrast, if we
specify our service instance to use a daemon
service model (also known as contract), the master
restarter will track processes associated with the
service instance. This is documented in the svc
.startd(1M) main page.*

```
# cp myapp.xml /lib/svc/manifest/site
# svcadm restart manifest-import
# svcs myapp
STATE          STIME     FMRI
online    23:38:22 svc:/site/myapp:default
```

We can also choose to install the manifest directly using the `-i` option. This will copy the manifest to `/lib/svc/manifest/site` and restart the manifest import service.

Creating a New System Profile

We can also use `svcbundle` to help us generate a new profile, by specifying properties and their values. For example, let's suppose we want to ensure at the `config/nameserver` property of the `svc:/network/dns /client:default` service instance was set to `10.0.0.1` across all systems. We could use the following:

```
# svcbundle -o nameserver-config.xml -s service-name=network/dns/client \
-s bundle-type=profile -s instance-property="config:nameserver:net_address:10.0.0.1"
# cat nameserver-config.xml
<?xml version="1.0" ?>
<!DOCTYPE service_bundle
   SYSTEM '/usr/share/lib/xml/dtd/service_bundle.dtd.1'>
<!--
     Manifest created by svcbundle (2015-Apr-09 23:44:50+0000)
-->
<service_bundle type="profile" name="network/dns/client">
<service version="1" type="service" name="network/dns/client">
<instance enabled="true" name="default">
<property_group type="application" name="config">
<propval type="net_address" name="nameserver"
                   value="10.0.0.1"/>
</property_group>
</instance>
</service>
</service_bundle>
```

In the preceding example, we need to set the `bundle-type` to `profile` (since `manifest` is default) and provide an `instance-property` as a quadruple that includes the property group, property, property type, and value. Once we have this XML file, we can either use it as part of an Automated Installer service, or apply directly by copying it into `/etc/svc/profile /site` and restarting the `svc:/system/manifest-import:default` service instance.

TIP
Administrators can use svcbundle *for many different tasks, including creating new service instances for existing services, for example, to create new instances of the Apache service that differ by document root. Administrators can also use* sysconfig *or* svccfg extract *to capture system configuration profiles. For example, we can extract customizations made at the* admin *layer for the* application/pkg/server:default *service instance:*

```
# svccfg extract -l admin application/pkg/server:default
<?xml version='1.0'?>
<!DOCTYPE service_bundle SYSTEM '/usr/share/lib/xml/dtd/service_bundle.dtd.1'>
<service_bundle type='profile' name='extract'>
<service name='application/pkg/server' type='service' version='0'>
<instance name='default' enabled='true'>
<property_group name='pkg' type='application'>
<propval name='inst_root' type='astring' value='/repositories/solaris'/>
</property_group>
</instance>
</service>
</service_bundle>
```

SMF Stencils

SMF stencils are a necessary bridge between configuration stored in files and configuration stored in the SMF configuration repository. Not all applications can easily be converted over to storing configuration in SMF, especially if they have been written to be cross platform. SMF stencils are a framework to convert configuration stored in SMF into a file that an application can read. This means that we can take advantage of all the benefits of SMF managing the application processes and configuration without having to rewrite the application.

Stencils use a combination of metadata and a template to generate and regenerate the configuration file at appropriate times. Configuring a service to use stencils requires creating a property group with a few properties that specify the stencil template located in /lib/svc/stencils and the file output path at a minimum, but can also include file ownership (user, group, permissions). The property group used must be of type configfile similar to the following:

```
<property_group type="configfile" name="myapp_stencil">
<propval type="astring" name="stencil" value="myapp.conf.stencil"/>
<propval type="astring" name="path" value="/etc/myapp.conf"/>
</property_group>
```

The service manifest should also include methods for `start`, `stop`, and `refresh` to ensure that the configuration file is generated/regenerated as required by the `svcio(1)` command. These can be dummy methods as in the following:

```
<exec_method timeout_seconds="60" type="method" name="start" exec=":true"/>
<exec_method timeout_seconds="60" type="method" name="stop" exec=":true"/>
<exec_method timeout_seconds="60" type="method" name="refresh" exec=":true"/>
```

The stencil template defines how SMF property groups and properties should be transformed into the configuration file. It closely matches how the end configuration file should look like, but identifies the property substitutions that should be made. For example, a simple stencil template might look like the following:

```
[myapp]
proxy=$%{myapp/proxy}
proxy_port =$%{myapp/port}
```

Here our template specifies two properties `myapp/proxy` and `myapp/port` that are pulled from SMF. The end result of the file could look like the following:

```
[myapp]
proxy=http://proxy.oracle.com
proxy_port=80
```

Whenever the configuration needs to change, a simple refresh of the service is enough to regenerate the configuration file. We have shown a very simple example using SMF stencils. The stencils markup language is documented in `smf_stencil(4)`.

Managing Solaris 11 Infrastructure with Puppet

Many data centers consist of a collection of different server hardware along with both proprietary and open source operating systems. Each server and OS vendor provides their own tools for managing their part of this infrastructure, optimized for their specific hardware and OS. There are commercial infrastructure management tools which support multivendor environments, for example *Oracle Enterprise Manager*. There are also widely used open source tools available, notably *OpenStack* (https://www.openstack.org) for configuring and managing cloud computing infrastructures, and *Puppet* (https://puppetlabs.com) for configuring and automating multiple server administration tasks. Several vendors, including Oracle, now include support for OpenStack and Puppet integrated with their own operating system and administration tools. In this section, we show how to install and use Puppet, now included and supported with the Oracle Solaris 11.2 operating system.

What is Puppet?

Puppet is an open source configuration management tool designed to automate system administration tasks, by defining a desired infrastructure state and enforcing and monitoring it, including for both physical and virtual servers. Puppet uses administrative *agents* on each node of the infrastructure which collect configuration and operational information and centralize control through a *master* server. The master server administrator can manually notify the agents of any required changes to each node's configuration and enforce those changes (a "push" update model), or the agent systems can periodically poll the master server to inquire and activate required configuration changes (a "pull" update model). This includes central reporting of infrastructure change history. Puppet's components are designed to integrate with vendor-specific interfaces, using a high-level administrative language. Puppet is supported on most versions of Linux including Red Hat, Ubuntu, SuSE, and Oracle Linux, as well as on Microsoft Windows Server, IBM AIX, Mac OS X, and Solaris 11, and is licensed under the Apache 2.0 Open Source License.

Using Puppet, system administrators can install and manage installation of web servers, databases, and other applications, can provision, update and enforce operating system configurations, replicate and distribute files, and can perform other common administrative tasks. Additionally, there is a growing community of Puppet module developers who create and share their tools and expertise (see https://forge.puppetlabs.com/). Puppet users and system administrators should periodically check that site for useful contributions.

Puppet works by using agents that collect configuration data and report their status to a master server. The master compiles configuration files for each of the agents and sends those files back to each agent; the agents then configure themselves according to the specified contents and report their results back to the master system. This architecture is scalable to large numbers of systems using central and distributed master systems. Puppet is a native, supported IPS package in Solaris 11.2, and is installed as a managed service using SMF.

Installing Puppet on Solaris 11.2

On Solaris 11.2, use IPS to install the Puppet group package on a master server and on any other servers that will be managed; this will include the Puppet software as well as other required tools such as Ruby:

```
# pkg install puppet
(... output truncated ...)
# pkg list puppet
NAME (PUBLISHER)                        VERSION               IFO
system/management/puppet                3.4.1-0.175.2.0.0.42.1    i--
```

In our simple example, the master server is `narya.dc.cox.net`, and the managed node where the agent will reside is `vilya.dc.cox.net`. Note that we need to reference the fully qualified system host and domain names, otherwise all system name resolution must use `/etc/host` files.

> **NOTE**
> The Puppet master and agent systems need to keep accurate time to avoid false certificate expiration problems. So, the `ntp` service should be installed and enabled on all systems being managed through Puppet:

```
# pkg install ntp
# ntpdate pool.ntp.org
# svcadm enable ntp
```

After installing Puppet, it is not yet activated:

```
root@narya:~# svcs puppet
STATE          STIME        FMRI
disabled       13:05:20     svc:/application/puppet:agent
disabled       13:05:21     svc:/application/puppet:master
```

You need to enable the appropriate Puppet service instance on the master *and* agent nodes using SMF:

```
root@narya:~# svccfg -s puppet:mastersetprop config/server=narya.dc.cox.net
root@narya:~# svcadm enable puppet:master
root@narya:~# svcs puppet:master
STATE          STIME    FMRI
online          8:31:11 svc:/application/puppet:master

root@vilya:~# svccfg -s puppet:agentsetprop config/server=narya.dc.cox.net
root@vilya:~# svcadm enable puppet:agent
root@vilya:~# svcs puppet:agent
STATE          STIME    FMRI
online          8:35:34 svc:/application/puppet:agent
```

Next, test the initial connection from the agent to the master:

```
root@vilya:~# puppet agent --test --server narya.dc.cox.net
Info: Caching certificate for ca
Info: csr_attributes file loading from /etc/puppet/csr_attributes.yaml
Info: Creating a new SSL certificate request for vilya
Info: Certificate Request fingerprint (SHA256): 53:4F:D6:27:FB:A7:32:27:ED:48:8A:CA:4D
:29:58:70:C0:BC:0C:01:61:24:E7:0D:EC:46:5D:AC:3B:E4:28:8E
Info: Caching certificate for ca
Exiting; no certificate found and waitforcert is disabled
```

We can then authorize and certify the connection from the master to the agent:

```
root@narya:~# puppet cert list
  "vilya" (SHA256) 53:4F:D6:27:FB:A7:32:27:ED:48:8A:CA:4D:29:58:70:C0:BC:0C:01:61:24:E
7:0D:EC:46:5D:AC:3B:E4:28:8E

root@narya:~# puppet cert sign vilya
Notice: Signed certificate request for vilya
Notice: Removing file Puppet::SSL::CertificateRequestvilya at '/etc/puppet/ssl/ca/
requests/vilya.pem'
```

We now have a certified connection from the master to the agent. Configuration details on the master and agent systems are recorded in the /etc/puppet directory, including the puppet.conf file used for additional customizations.

Puppet Resources

Puppet defines manageable components as *resources*. Resources are used to model system configuration. For example, a resource might declare that a package that should be installed or a service that should be running on a given system. Puppet uses a Resource Abstraction Layer (RAL) that consists of the high-level model called a *resource type* and the underlying platform-specific implementation called a *provider*. Using a combination of these, administrators can declare a consistent set of configuration to enforce across multiple different platforms regardless of the underlying configuration mechanism that is used on those platforms.

To list the resource types available on Oracle Solaris 11, we can use the puppet command as follows:

```
root@narya:~# puppet resource --types
address_object
address_properties
augeas
boot_environment
computer
(... output abbreviated ...)
zfs
zone
zpool
```

Note that some resource types, such as zfs or zone, are specific to Solaris 11. Additional details about the resource types are listed using the describe keyword:

```
root@narya:~# puppet describe --list
These are the types known to puppet:
address_object  - Manage the configuration of Oracle Solaris ad ...
address_properties - Manage Oracle Solaris address properties
augeas          - Apply a change or an array of changes to the  ...
boot_environment - Manage Oracle Solaris Boot Environments (BEs)
computer        - Computer object management using DirectorySer ...
cron            - Installs and manages cron jobs. Every cronre ...
dns             - Manage the configuration of the DNS client fo ...
etherstub       - Manage the configuration of Solaris etherstub ...
(... output truncated ...)
```

The Puppet master defines and enforces the states of the agent systems based on configuration within a *manifest*. Using a declarative language, administrators use manifests to declare an end state of a particular system. Here are a few examples of resources that can be declared:

```
package { 'gcc-45': ensure => 'present', }

service { 'svc:/network/nfs/client:default':
ensure => 'running',
```

```
enable => 'true', }

file { '/export/home/profiles.txt':
ensure => 'present',
content => $file_contents, }
```

In the preceding listing, there are three resources that are being declared. Each connecting Puppet agent will ensure that the gcc-45 compiler package is installed, that the svc:/network/nfs/client:default service instance is running, and that the file /export/home/profiles.txtis replicated across the systems.

In general, a Puppet resource can be described as follows:

```
resource_type{ 'title':
   attribute1 => 'value1',
   attribute2 => 'value2',
}
```

Each resource _ type has a title, which is an identifying string used by Puppet that must be unique per resource type. Attributes describe the desired state of the resource. Most resources have a set of required attributes, but also include a set of optional attributes. As an easy way to create these declarations, Puppet also provides a way of capturing the current state of a system using the puppet resource command as follows:

```
root@narya:~# puppet resource zone
zone { 'global':
ensure    => 'running',
brand     => 'solaris',
iptype    => 'shared',
zonepath  => '/',
}
zone { 'zone01':
ensure    => 'configured',
brand     => 'solaris',
iptype    => 'excl',
zonepath  => '/system/zones/zone01',
}
zone { 'zone02':
ensure    => 'running',
brand     => 'solaris',
iptype    => 'excl',
zonepath  => '/system/zones/zone02',
}
```

From the preceding command, we can see on the Puppet master two non-global zones on this system (along with the global zone)—zone01 is in a configured state; zone02 has been installed and booted.

Performing Configuration with Puppet

The default manifest for the Puppet master is located at /etc/puppet/manifests/site.pp and is used to declare configuration that should affect all nodes. Typically administrators will use Puppet classes to split out configuration for specific nodes.

Puppet also supports a master-less mode, allowing configuration to be applied/enforced without requiring an agent/master architecture. This is useful to test Puppet configuration and is often the first step in deploying Puppet within the data center. For example, after updates made to the site.pp file, you can enforce this configuration *locally* using the apply subcommand:

```
# puppet apply /etc/puppet/manifests/site.pp
```

You can also do a "dry run" of these changes using the noop subcommand to test the validity and check the syntax of the site.pp file:

```
# puppet apply -v -noop /etc/puppet/manifests/site.pp
```

For any agents that have been configured, they will contact the Puppet master on a regular basis (30 minutes by default) to see if there is any change in state. The agent will collect some data about itself called *facts* and send these to the master. The master will then determine what configuration should be applied and generate a *catalog* that it then passes back to the agent. The agent will then configure the node and report the results back to the master, as shown in Figure 9-1.

All Puppet configurations are *indempotent*, meaning that they can be safely run multiple times. Puppet will only make changes to the system if the system state does not match the desired configuration state.

To configure specific systems, we can use the node declaration within our manifests:

```
node vilya.dc.cox.net {
service { 'svc:/network/nfs/client:default':
            ensure => 'running',
        enable => 'true',
        }
}
```

How Does It Work?

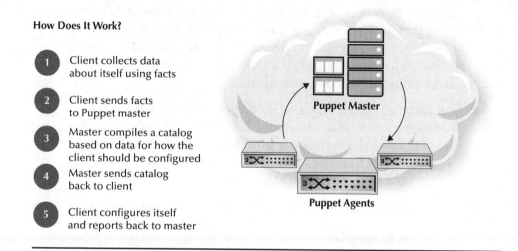

1 Client collects data about itself using facts

2 Client sends facts to Puppet master

3 Master compiles a catalog based on data for how the client should be configured

4 Master sends catalog back to client

5 Client configures itself and reports back to master

FIGURE 9-1.   *Interaction between the Puppet master and agent*

Administrators can check the contents of the `/var/log/puppet`directory to get a full log for the Puppet agent and/or master. Puppet is also integrated into the Oracle Solaris auditing framework.

Oracle thoroughly tests and integrates new versions of open source software such as Puppet to ensure stability, security, and compatibility with Solaris 11 before including it in the OS, so the supported version lag behind the currently available version. Administrators might download and install the latest releases of open source software, and although they might appear to function properly, Oracle will not support such updates.

Puppet Best Practices

Puppet is a powerful way to configure systems in the data center and administrators can quickly create a complex environment over a relatively short space of time. There are a number of best practices that can be adopted on starting out with Puppet as follows:

■   Start configuring systems on an individual basis using the Puppet "master-less" mode. Generate Puppet manifests for each node and use the Puppet `apply` subcommand to apply them. When you feel like you've got a good understanding of Puppet, then transition to an agent/master architecture.

- Store configuration in a version control system such as Mercurial, Git, or Subversion. This will make it easier to incrementally develop good Puppet manifests and quickly roll back if required. Using version control, administrators can also easily maintain different branches for different classes of systems (e.g., developer and test) and merge changes between them.

- Puppet also includes a tool called Hiera which allows you to separate configuration data from the underlying logic through variable substitution. This is a great way to focus on the logic of writing Puppet manifests and easily substitute new configuration values for different systems in your data center.

- Use an iterative approach to developing Puppet manifests. Start small and enforce configuration for a few simple things and do that well. Don't try and boil the ocean straight away and manage everything with Puppet!

- Take advantage of the Puppet Forge. Much of the ground you're trying to cover has been done already, and there is a significant set of Puppet modules that you can reuse in your own data center.

- The Puppet upstream documentation has many great tips in terms of scaling out a Puppet environment, using multiple Puppet masters and load balancing. Take advantage of Puppet environments for managing different classes of systems with different configuration— these are managed through different SMF service instances on Oracle Solaris 11.

- Puppet is just one technology that can be used for configuration management. You can also use a combination of SMF first-boot scripts and IPS packaging as described in Chapter 3 *Lifecycle Management* as a complementary technique for managing the complete software lifecycle management and compliance.

Remote Administration Daemon

The Remote Administration Daemon (RAD) provides secure and programmatic access to Oracle Solaris features through a number of different APIs and runtimes, including support for C, Java, Python, and REST. RAD is a relatively new introduction to Oracle Solaris and module support for various aspects of the platform is evolving over time.

We will not cover RAD in much detail in this chapter. RAD has been used to integrate with the OpenStack infrastructure as a Service (IaaS) cloud. OpenStack compute, network, and storage services use RAD to manage Solaris. You can read more about this in Chapter 10, *OpenStack on Oracle Solaris 11.*

As a working example to show the capabilities of RAD, we will use the Python interfaces to create a new Oracle Solaris Zone (non-global zone). We will use the interactive python interface, `ipython`, as follows:

```
# ipython
Python 2.6.8 (unknown, Jun  9 2014, 15:55:19) [C]
Type "copyright", "credits" or "license" for more information.

IPython 0.10 -- An enhanced Interactive Python.
?          -> Introduction and overview of IPython's features.
%quickref -> Quick reference.
help       -> Python's own help system.
object?    -> Details about 'object'. ?object also works, ??prints more.

In [1]:
```

The first thing we will do is to import the RAD modules that we will use `rad.connect` as the basis for connecting to RAD and the `zonemgr` RAD module for managing Oracle Solaris Zones:

```
In [1]: import rad.connect as rad

In [2]: import rad.bindings.com.oracle.solaris.rad.zonemgr as zonemgr
```

Now that we have imported these modules, we can create a local connection to RAD and hand us back a handle to the connection:

```
In [3]: rad_instance = rad.connect_unix()
```

Let's use this connection to get a handle to `ZoneManager`, for how we query and create zones on a system:

```
In [4]: zonemanager = rad_instance.get_object(zonemgr.ZoneManager())
```

Once we have this handle, we can proceed with creating a zone. In this case we will specify the creation of a zone based on the SYSsolaris-kz template, that is, a Solaris Kernel Zone:

```
In [5]: zonemanager.create("foo", None, "SYSsolaris-kz")
Out[5]: Result(code = ErrorCode(value = NONE), str = '', stdout = None, stderr = None)
```

We could have equally not provided a template name in the above statement. For example, let's create a standard non-global zone:

```
In [6]: zonemanager.create("bar", None, None)
Out[6]: Result(code = ErrorCode(value = NONE), str = '', stdout = None, stderr = None)
```

If we now exit out of the system, we can use the zoneadm list command to see what changes have been made on the system:

```
In [7]: exit()
Do you really want to exit ([y]/n)? y
# zoneadm list -cv
  ID NAME            STATUS       PATH                      BRAND      IP
   0 global          running      /                         solaris    shared
     foo             configured   /system/zones/foo         solaris-kz excl
     bar             configured   /system/zones/bar         solaris    excl
```

Support for RAD modules for other technology areas included in Oracle Solaris 11 is being added over time. Administrators or developers with a good understanding of Python, C, or Java should be able to query the system to determine what interfaces available, how they can be used and how to map those directly to core Solaris command line interfaces. It is expected that more documentation will be available in future.

Summary

In this chapter, we have covered the Service Management Facility (SMF), Puppet, and the Remote Administration Daemon (RAD) for managing system and application services on Oracle Solaris 11. These tools are the foundation for deploying system and application configuration reliably, enforcing compliance, and managing a complete lifecycle that is fault tolerant to unexpected changes. When used in combination with each other, administrators can quickly deploy applications on a very large scale that is completely secure and trusted.

References

Oracle Solaris 11 Configuration Management—How to Articles, Cheat Sheets, Screencasts, Whitepapers and Presentations,
http://www.oracle.com/technetwork/server-storage/solaris11/technologies/configuration-management-2237948.html

Managing System Services in Oracle Solaris 11,
http://docs.oracle.com/cd/E36784_01/html/E36820/index.html

Puppet Reference Manual,
http://docs.puppetlabs.com/puppet/latest/reference/

Getting Started with Puppet on Oracle Solaris 11,
http://www.oracle.com/technetwork/articles/servers-storage-admin/howto-automate-config-datacenter-2212734.html

Remote Administration Daemon Developer Guide,
http://docs.oracle.com/cd/E36784_01/html/E36869/index.html

Getting Started with the Remote Administration Daemon on Oracle Solaris 11,
https://community.oracle.com/docs/DOC-917361

Secure Remote RESTful Administration with the Remote Administration Daemon,
https://community.oracle.com/docs/DOC-918902

CHAPTER
10

Cloud and OpenStack

Oracle Solaris provides an excellent foundation for building cloud-based solutions, including Infrastructure as a Service (IaaS), Platform as a Service (PaaS), Database as a Service (DBaaS), and Software as a Service (SaaS). For years, customers have been building custom solutions based on this technology for use in their own data centers with the aim to increase resource utilization and operational agility. Oracle Solaris is, by itself, an extremely capable cloud platform with a range of technologies that provide low overhead virtualization, secure and scalable storage, and networking between virtual machines (VMs) that can be resource management—all of which are important in a typical cloud environment.

Oracle Solaris 11 now includes a complete distribution of OpenStack (also known as Oracle OpenStack for Oracle Solaris). OpenStack is a popular open source software package that administrators can use to combine compute, network, and storage resources in the data center, and centrally manage as an IaaS cloud platform through a web-based dashboard. Tenants of this cloud platform can consume these resources by creating self-service virtual environments or VMs using the same dashboard.

The National Institute of Standards and Technology (NIST) Cloud Computing definition is a broadly agreed standard for cloud computing. The NIST definition includes five characteristics: On-demand self-service, broad network access, resource pooling, rapid elasticity, and measured service. Using a combination of Oracle Solaris 11 and OpenStack, administrators can create a cloud solution that satisfies all these characteristics.

What is OpenStack?

OpenStack grew out of previous efforts by several organizations to develop a cloud platform (NASA, Nebula, etc.) and formally became an open source project in 2010. The goal of OpenStack was to create a new cloud platform that would help organizations quickly deliver cloud-based services running on standard hardware. Since then, it has gone on to be one of the fastest growing open source projects with support from all the major technology vendors and a growing OpenStack ecosystem and user base.

OpenStack is written in Python and licensed under the Apache 2.0 license. It has a very modular architecture, allowing different vendors to be easily able to integrate their own technologies across compute, network, and storage. For example, OpenStack supports a number of different hypervisor types such as Oracle Solaris Zones and kernel zones, Linux KVM and Xen,

VMware vSphere ESXi, and Microsoft Hyper-V. This modularity provides great flexibility, allowing administrators to manage a heterogeneous data center composed of different vendors and different technologies with a single pane of management.

Every six months, the OpenStack community releases a new version that follows an alphabetical naming scheme. Due to the fast-moving pace of the OpenStack community, not all of these releases are included in Oracle Solaris.

OpenStack Havana was the first release to integrate into Oracle Solaris 11, adding driver support for technologies such Oracle Solaris Zones, Elastic Virtual Switch, and the ZFS File System. We will use OpenStack Havana for the basis of this book. As newer releases get integrated into Oracle Solaris, you may experience differences in behavior (especially within the web dashboard Horizon) but the basics from an administration point of view should be similar.

Oracle has embraced the OpenStack project right across its product portfolio by integrating it with Oracle Linux and Oracle VM, Oracle ZFS Storage Appliance, Oracle Tape Storage, Oracle Virtual Networking, Oracle Database, and Oracle Enterprise Manager.

Over time, OpenStack has significantly matured offering a greater number of features and additional cloud services that have started to move up the stack toward facilitating PaaS, including DBaaS.

Core OpenStack Projects

A basic OpenStack environment comprises several core projects which, when layered together, form the basis of an IaaS solution. Each project is responsible for different tasks within the cloud. Table 10-1 lists the core projects that are central to an OpenStack environment:

An OpenStack project usually consists of a number of different services that are designed to do a specific task within a cloud environment. Each project publishes its capabilities with a RESTful Application Programming Interface (API) and these are used to communicate between different services in an OpenStack environment.

A message queue, typically RabbitMQ, also provides intraservice communication between the subcomponents of a given service. Each service stores persistent data and runtime state in an SQL database. OpenStack supports a variety of different databases, including MySQL and SQLite.

Project Name	Project Description
Cinder	Block storage
Glance	Image management
Heat	Application orchestration
Horizon	Web-based dashboard
Keystone	Authentication
Neutron	Software-defined networking (SDN)
Nova	Compute virtualization
Swift	Object storage

TABLE 10-1. *Core OpenStack Projects*

NOTE
On Oracle Solaris 11, the OpenStack services have been fully integrated into the Service Management Facility (SMF). SMF manages system and application services ensuring they run continuously, even in the event of hardware or software failure. In this chapter, we will refer to the OpenStack services on Oracle Solaris 11 using their SMF service name as opposed to the underlying process daemons they start; this may result in some services that have been created in Oracle Solaris that aren't being run on non-Solaris OpenStack environments.

Figure 10-1 summarizes the main technology integration points that have been developed for the primary OpenStack projects to ensure OpenStack can run successfully on Oracle Solaris 11.

Nova

Nova is the one of the original OpenStack projects. It provides the compute capability in a cloud environment, allowing self-service users to be able to create virtual environments from an allocated pool of resources.

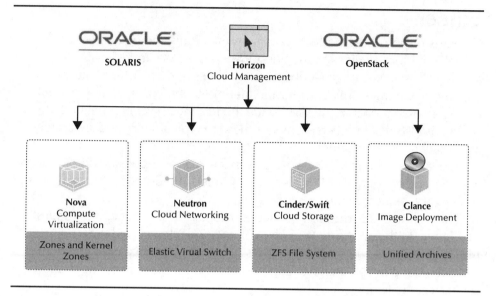

FIGURE 10-1. *The main integration points of Oracle Solaris 11 with OpenStack*

The `nova-api-osapi-compute` and `nova-api-ec2` services are responsible for accepting and responding to REST API calls—both for the OpenStack compute API and an EC2-compatible Amazon API. The API services will ensure basic authentication and then push a message to the message queue.

The `nova-scheduler` service is responsible for taking requests from the message queue and determining on which node they should be performed based on the available compute nodes, their current capacity and any requirements the self-service user may have made.

The `nova-compute` service creates, launches, and terminates VMs using the supported hypervisor types on a given compute node, and will typically call native APIs to do this. On Oracle Solaris, a Nova driver has been written to support Oracle Solaris non-global zones and Oracle Solaris kernel zones. The `nova-compute` service runs on each compute node that's allocated to the cloud environment.

The `nova-conductor` service is responsible for mediation between the `nova-compute` services and the underlying SQL, avoiding direct access to the database from each of the compute nodes.

Cinder

Cinder is responsible for block storage in the cloud and presented as virtualized block devices to the guest VMs known as Cinder volumes. There are two classes of storage—ephemeral volumes and persistent volumes. Ephemeral volumes only exist for the lifetime of the VM instance, but will persist across reboots of the VM. Once the instance has been deleted, the storage is also deleted. Persistent volumes are typically created separately and attached to an instance.

Similar to Nova, the `cinder-api` service is also responsible for accepting and responding to REST API calls for the Cinder API, doing authentication and pushing the request to the message queue.

The `cinder-scheduler` service is responsible for routing the request for volume to the appropriate cinder-volume node. It will find the best match based on some simple heuristics depending on what configuration has been done by the administrator—from round-robin scheduling to more sophisticated filtering.

The `cinder-volume` service creates and destroys volumes based on the supported storage backend. There is a wide range of supported storage platforms from just about every different storage vendor on the market. On Oracle Solaris 11, Cinder takes advantage of the ZFS file system—either creating volumes through local storage, or remote storage over iSCSI and Fibre Channel. The combination of Nova and Cinder for remote storage leads to Oracle Solaris Zones over shared storage (ZOSS). Cinder driver support has also been added to the Oracle ZFS Storage Appliance, giving administrators a comprehensive and highly reliable storage platform for their cloud environments leveraging the unique management and monitoring features of the appliance.

The `cinder-db` service creates and manages the Cinder database.

The `cinder-backup` service provides the ability for volumes to be backed up to the OpenStack Swift object store.

Neutron

Neutron manages networking within an OpenStack cloud. Neutron creates and manages virtual networks across multiple physical nodes so that self-service users can create their own subnets that VMs can connect to and communicate. Neutron uses a highly extensible plug-in architecture, allowing complex network topologies to be created to support a cloud environment. The Oracle Solaris 11 implementation of Neutron uses Elastic Virtual Switch (EVS) that provides a single point of control for creating, configuring, and monitoring a series of virtual switches that span multiple physical nodes. The supported network topology in the Oracle Solaris 11 implementation provides for multiple private networks for tenants with a shared router managed by the administrator. This means that VMs on the same private network can access each other, but require the allocation of a "floating IP" to allow the router to map public addresses from an external network to fixed IPs on a private network. Network isolation is achieved by using VLAN IDs or VXLAN.

The `neutron-server` service is responsible for accepting and responding to REST API calls for the Neutron API. It then passes these requests onto the appropriate plug-in for processing.

The `neutron-dhcp-agent` service provides DHCP services to each tenant network. This means that VMs can be automatically assigned IPs on specific subnets.

The `neutron-l3-agent` service enables L3/NAT forwarding of network traffic, allowing VMs access to the outside world. Additionally, administrators can also enable communication between VMs in different private networks of the same tenant.

Keystone

Keystone is the identity service for OpenStack. It provides a central directory of users mapped to the OpenStack projects they can access, and an authentication system between the OpenStack services. Keystone supports multiple different forms of authentication, including standard username/password and token-based authentication, and can be integrated with existing directory services such as LDAP and Active Directory.

The `keystone` service is responsible for accepting and responding to REST APIs calls for the Keystone API. It then passes these requests onto the backend identity service. The service also exposes different endpoints (in the form of web URLs) of services deployed in the form of a catalog.

Glance

Glance provides image management services within OpenStack with support for registration, discovery, and delivery of images that are used to install VMs created by Nova. Glance can use different storage backends to store these images. The primary image format that Oracle Solaris 11 uses is Unified Archives. Unified Archives have the ability to be provisioned across both bare metal and virtual systems, allowing for complete portability in an OpenStack environment.

The `glance-api` service accepts API requests made to discover what images are available, what image is to be stored or fetched.

The `glance-registry` service is responsible for storing and retrieving image metadata such as size, image type, architecture, and so on.

The `glance-db` service creates and manages the Glance database.

The `glance-scrubber` service is responsible for cleaning up images that have been deleted by the administrator. How this service cleans up will depend on the backend storage used for the images.

Horizon

Horizon is the web-based dashboard that allows administrators to manage compute, network, and storage resources in the data center and allocate those resources to multitenant users. Users can then create and destroy VMs in a self-service capacity, determine networks on which those VMs communicate, and attach storage volumes to those VMs.

Heat

Heat provides application orchestration in the cloud, allowing administrators to describe multitier applications by defining a set of resources through a template. As a result, a self-service user can execute this orchestration and have the appropriate compute, network, and storage deployed in the appropriate order.

Swift

Swift provides object- and file-based storage in OpenStack. Swift provides redundant and scalable storage, with data replicated across distributed storage clusters. If a storage node fails, Swift will quickly replicate its content to other active nodes. Additional storage nodes can be added to the cluster with full horizontal scale. Oracle Solaris 11 supports Swift being hosted in a ZFS environment.

Getting Started with Oracle OpenStack

The easiest way to get started with OpenStack on Oracle Solaris 11 is to download and deploy a preconfigured all-in-one OpenStack Unified Archive. This provides all the OpenStack services in a single node installation. In practice administrators would typically spread OpenStack services across multiple nodes but the Unified Archive is very useful for evaluation purposes.

The OpenStack Unified Archive can be downloaded from the Oracle Technology Network at the following URL:

http://www.oracle.com/technetwork/server-storage/solaris11/downloads/

Archives are available for both SPARC and x86-based systems, and also available as USB bootable images. They can be installed onto a bare-metal system using the Automated Installer (AI) or USB, or directly installed to an Oracle Solaris kernel zone.

NOTE
Alternatively, administrators can also choose to set up an OpenStack environment manually by installing packages from the IPS repository. OpenStack is a very complex set of software packages and it can take many hours to configure correctly, depending on the topology and choice of services you wish to deploy. Configuration can be a very error-prone process, so we recommend you to start with a single node instance and scale from this to multiple nodes.

Installing Using Automated Installer

To install the OpenStack Unified Archive onto bare-metal systems, you will need to have an AI server setup. Once you have this, you will need to create or modify a manifest for an appropriate install service to include the following:

```
<software type="ARCHIVE">
<source>
<fileuri="/net/aiserver/archives/sol-11_2-openstack-sparc.uar"/>
</source>
```

```
<software_data action="install">
<name>*</name>
</software_data>
</software>
```

Once this has been done and saved to the AI server, you will be able to boot your system and install from this archive. See the Automated Installer section in Chapter 3 on Oracle Solaris 11 Lifecycle Management for more details.

Installing into an Oracle Solaris Kernel Zone

To install the OpenStack Unified Archive into an Oracle Solaris kernel zones, we will use the existing `zonecfg` and `zoneadm` commands as follows:

```
# zonecfg -z openstack_zone
Use 'create' to begin configuring a new zone.
zonecfg:openstack_zone> create -t SYSsolaris-kz
zonecfg:openstack_zone> add virtual-cpu
zonecfg:openstack_zone:virtual-cpu> set ncpus=8
zonecfg:openstack_zone:virtual-cpu> end
zonecfg:openstack_zone> select capped-memory
zonecfg:openstack_zone:capped-memory> set physical=8g
zonecfg:openstack_zone:capped-memory> end
zonecfg:openstack_zone> verify
zonecfg:openstack_zone> exit
```

Here we are creating an Oracle Solaris kernel zone by using the `SYSsolaris-kz` template. We are allocating eight virtual CPUs and capping the memory at 8 GB.

Once we have successfully created the zone configuration, we can now install the kernel zone from the archive. We will use a disk size of 50 GB for this kernel zone to make sure there's enough space to create volumes for our VM instances.

```
# zoneadm -z openstack_zone install -a ./sol-11_2-openstack-sparc.uar \
-x install-size=50g
Progress being logged to /var/log/zones/zoneadm.20150325T043046Z.newzone.install
[Connected to zone 'newzone' console]
NOTICE: Entering OpenBoot.
NOTICE: Fetching Guest MD from HV.
NOTICE: Starting additional cpus.
NOTICE: Initializing LDC services.
NOTICE: Probing PCI devices.
NOTICE: Finished PCI probing.

SPARC T5-2, No Keyboard
Copyright (c) 1998, 2014, Oracle and/or its affiliates. All rights reserved.
```

```
OpenBoot 4.36.1, 8.0000 GB memory available, Serial #695619864.
Ethernet address 0:0:0:0:0:0, Host ID: 29765118.


Boot device: disk1  File and args: - install auto-shutdown aimanifest=/system/shared/
ai.xml
SunOS Release 5.11 Version 11.2 64-bit
Copyright (c) 1983, 2014, Oracle and/or its affiliates. All rights reserved.
Remounting root read/write
Probing for device nodes ...
Preparing image for use
Done mounting image
Configuring devices.
Hostname: solaris
Using specified install manifest : /system/shared/ai.xml

solaris console login:
Automated Installation started
The progress of the Automated Installation will be output to the console
Detailed logging is in the logfile at /system/volatile/install_log
Press RETURN to get a login prompt at any time.

04:32:59    Install Log: /system/volatile/install_log
04:32:59    Using XML Manifest: /system/volatile/ai.xml
04:32:59    Using profile specification: /system/volatile/profile
04:32:59    Starting installation.
04:32:59    0% Preparing for Installation
04:32:59    100% manifest-parser completed.
04:32:59    100% None
04:32:59    0% Preparing for Installation
04:33:00    1% Preparing for Installation
04:33:00    2% Preparing for Installation
04:33:00    3% Preparing for Installation
04:33:00    4% Preparing for Installation
04:33:01    5% archive-1 completed.
04:33:02    8% target-discovery completed.
04:33:05    Pre-validating manifest targets before actual target selection
04:33:05    Selected Disk(s) : c1d0
04:33:05    Pre-validation of manifest targets completed
04:33:06    Validating combined manifest and archive origin targets
04:33:06    Selected Disk(s) : c1d0
04:33:06    9% target-selection completed.
04:33:06    10% ai-configuration completed.
04:33:06    9% var-share-dataset completed.
04:33:11    10% target-instantiation completed.
04:33:11    10% Beginning archive transfer
04:33:11    Commencing transfer of stream: 40719ca5-24f4-cf45-dbfd-d7d0cd81de72-0.zfs
to rpool
04:33:21    12% Transferring contents
04:33:26    15% Transferring contents
04:33:34    19% Transferring contents
04:33:40    20% Transferring contents
04:33:46    23% Transferring contents
04:33:48    24% Transferring contents
04:33:56    28% Transferring contents
04:34:07    32% Transferring contents
04:34:11    34% Transferring contents
04:34:13    35% Transferring contents
04:34:15    36% Transferring contents
04:34:21    40% Transferring contents
04:34:36    43% Transferring contents
04:34:40    44% Transferring contents
```

```
04:34:44    46% Transferring contents
04:34:46    47% Transferring contents
04:34:50    48% Transferring contents
04:34:54    50% Transferring contents
04:35:00    52% Transferring contents
04:35:04    54% Transferring contents
04:35:11    56% Transferring contents
04:35:13    57% Transferring contents
04:35:17    58% Transferring contents
04:35:19    60% Transferring contents
04:35:25    63% Transferring contents
04:35:31    64% Transferring contents
04:35:35    66% Transferring contents
04:35:42    68% Transferring contents
04:35:46    70% Transferring contents
04:35:50    72% Transferring contents
04:35:56    74% Transferring contents
04:35:58    76% Transferring contents
04:36:06    78% Transferring contents
04:36:15    80% Transferring contents
04:36:21    82% Transferring contents
04:36:25    83% Transferring contents
04:36:29    84% Transferring contents
04:36:35    87% Transferring contents
04:36:41    88% Transferring
04:36:45    Completed transfer of stream: '40719ca5-24f4-cf45-dbfd-d7d0cd81de72-0.zfs'
from file:///system/shared/uafs/OVA
04:36:46    89% Transferring contents
04:36:48    Archive transfer completed
04:36:50    90% generated-transfer-949-1 completed.
04:36:50    90% apply-pkg-variant completed.
04:36:51    Setting boot devices in firmware
04:36:51    Setting openprom boot-device
04:36:51    91% boot-configuration completed.
04:36:51    91% update-dump-adm completed.
04:36:51    92% setup-swap completed.
04:36:52    92% device-config completed.
04:36:53    92% apply-sysconfig completed.
04:36:53    93% transfer-zpool-cache completed.
04:37:02    98% boot-archive completed.
04:37:02    98% transfer-ai-files completed.
04:37:02    98% cleanup-archive-install completed.
04:37:03    100% create-snapshot completed.
04:37:03    100% None
04:37:03    Automated Installation succeeded.
04:37:03    You may wish to reboot the system at this time.
Automated Installation finished successfully
Shutdown requested. Shutting down the system
Log files will be available in /var/log/install/ after reboot
svc.startd: The system is coming down.  Please wait.
svc.startd: 114 system services are now being stopped.
syncing file systems... done

[NOTICE: Zone halted]

[Connection to zone 'newzone' console closed]
        Done: Installation completed in 451.456 seconds
```

Once the installation is complete, we can proceed to boot the kernel zone and answer some basic configuration.

Configuring the Elastic Virtual Switch

Once the system has booted, we will need to configure the Elastic Virtual Switch (EVS). For this single node case, we can use a script to automate the configuration as follows:

```
# /usr/demo/openstack/configure_evs.py
Generating public/private rsa key pair.
Your identification has been saved in /var/user/evsuser/.ssh/id_rsa.
Your public key has been saved in /var/user/evsuser/.ssh/id_rsa.pub.
The key fingerprint is:
99:e8:e9:69:f4:7d:b0:08:f9:be:a3:c5:77:a5:c1:24 evsuser@newzone
Generating public/private rsa key pair.
Your identification has been saved in /var/lib/neutron/.ssh/id_rsa.
Your public key has been saved in /var/lib/neutron/.ssh/id_rsa.pub.
The key fingerprint is:
da:b6:7b:21:16:1f:2d:b5:2c:bc:fc:81:d6:5b:f9:cd neutron@openstack_zone
Mar 25 07:47:13 openstack_zone su: 'su root' succeeded for root on /dev/console
Oracle Corporation       SunOS 5.11      11.2     June 2014
You have new mail.
Generating public/private rsa key pair.
Your identification has been saved in /root/.ssh/id_rsa.
Your public key has been saved in /root/.ssh/id_rsa.pub.
The key fingerprint is:
56:c1:59:bd:3a:95:c6:ee:87:8e:62:1f:c9:ea:e0:1b root@openstack_zone
populating authorized_keys
configuring EVS
enabling Neutron
```

This script will set up a series of SSH keys for various users and add them to the `evsuser authorized_keys` chain used by the EVS controller for seamless authentication. It will also do the final configuration of EVS and enable the Neutron services.

NOTE
The OpenStack Unified Archive can only be installed into a kernel zone or bare-metal environment. The archive cannot be installed into a non-global zone as we cannot create nested non-global zones for self-service VMs.

Using OpenStack Horizon

Once you have successfully installed OpenStack using the Unified Archive, you can now log in to the Horizon web interface. We will use this to login. Navigate to `http://system/horizon` using a web browser and you will be greeted with a login screen as shown in Figure 10-2. The default credentials provided in the archive includes an `admin` user with password `secrete`.

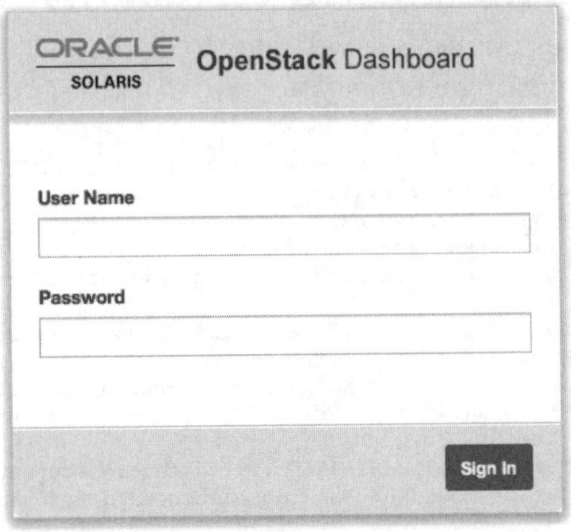

FIGURE 10-2. *The OpenStack Horizon login screen*

When we log in to the dashboard, we get an overview of the current utilization of the cloud. Unsurprisingly it's empty of details since we have only just recently installed OpenStack as shown in Figure 10-3. On the top navigation bar on the right hand side, we can see that we have logged in as the admin user, with the ability to change settings for this account. The left navigation bar will show a different view depending on access permissions and the role of the logged-in user. As we are the administrator for this cloud, we can see two tabs—the **Admin** tab and the **Projects** tab.

Adding a Self-Service User

OpenStack supports the ability to aggregate users into different projects (also known as tenants). These are essentially organizational groupings in which you can assign users. Each user has a particular role in the cloud—either a member of an administrator, and can be assigned to one or more different projects. To see this, we can navigate to the **Projects** screen under the **Identity Panel** section of the **Admin** tab as shown in Figure 10-4.

By default we have two projects—demo and `service`. The `service` project is used by the OpenStack services (Nova, Neutron, Cinder, etc.) and should not be used for any other purpose. We can make changes to this project,

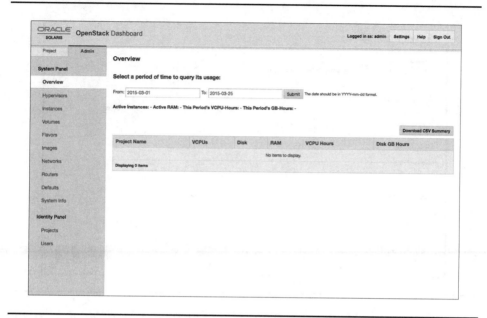

FIGURE 10-3. *An initial view of OpenStack Horizon as administrator*

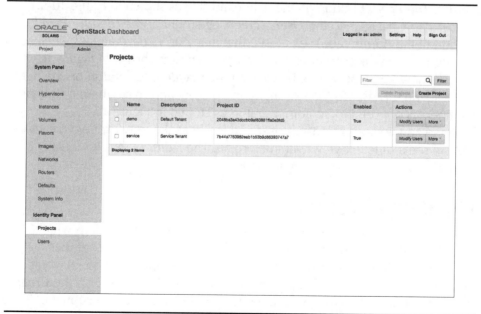

FIGURE 10-4. *Listing the projects in OpenStack Horizon*

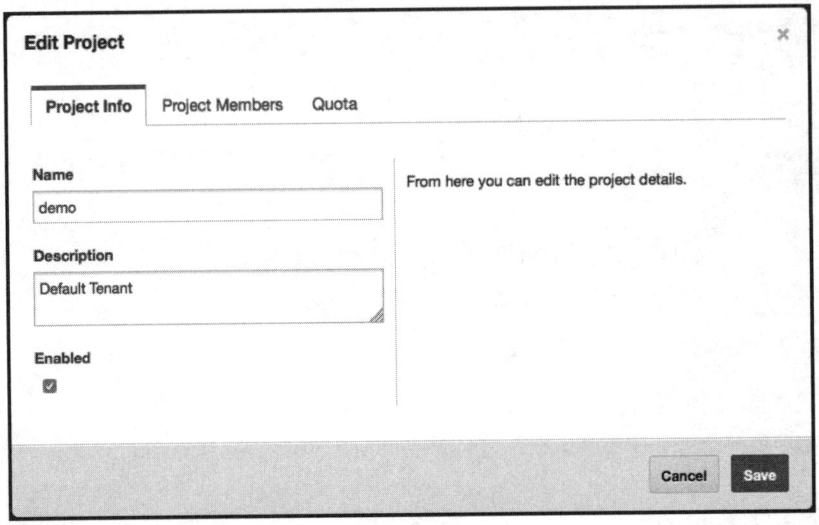

FIGURE 10-5   *Editing the demo project in OpenStack Horizon*

including adding additional members or ensuring a quota by clicking on the **More > Edit Project** button on the right hand side as shown in Figure 10-5.

Let's now navigate to the **Users** screen, again under the **Identity Panel** section of the **Admin** tab. We can see that many users have already been set up, representing the core OpenStack components, as shown in Figure 10-6.

Let's now add a new user, by clicking the **Create User** button on the right. We will add this user to the existing demo project and make them a standard member (as opposed to an administrator) as shown in Figure 10-7.

If we now log out as admin user and log in as the new user we created, we can see a different view within Horizon. The **Admin** tab is no longer available to us, as shown in Figure 10-8.

Creating a Network

The first thing we will need to do is to create a private network in which our VMs can communicate. We can go to the **Networks** screen under the **Manage Networks** section. It will be initially empty since we haven't created any networks for this project. Let's go ahead and click on the **Create Network** button. We will give it a name of mynetwork and a subnet of

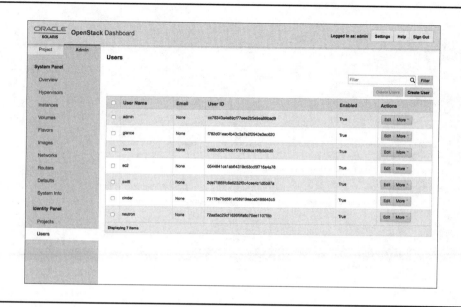

FIGURE 10-6. *Viewing existing users in OpenStack Horizon*

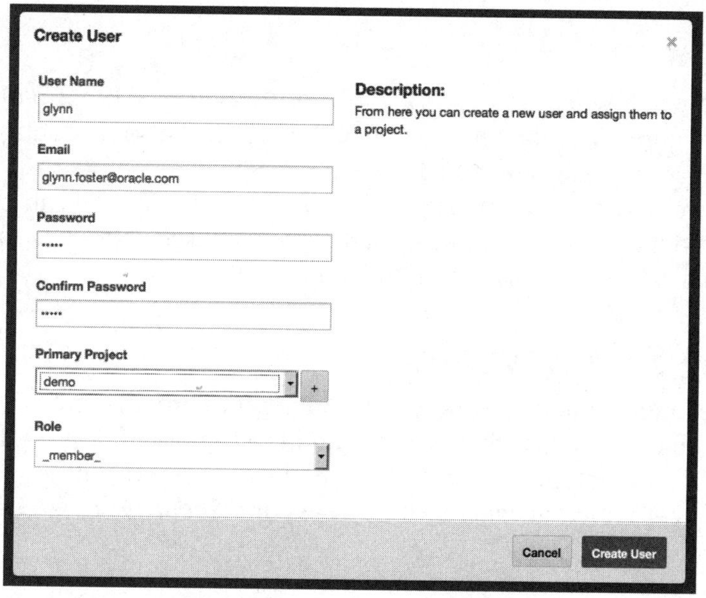

FIGURE 10-7. *Adding a new user to the demo project in OpenStack Horizon*

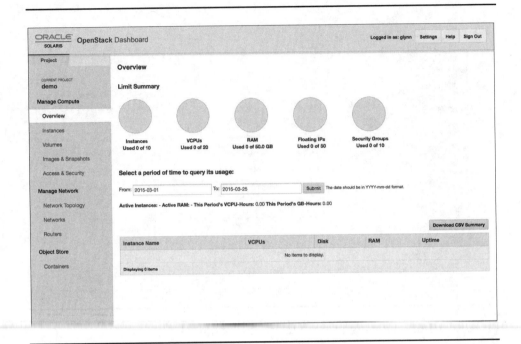

FIGURE 10-8. *The view a typical self-service user would see in OpenStack Horizon*

`mysubnetwork` with address `192.168.0.0/24` (in CIDR format) as shown in Figure 10-9. By default a DHCP server will also be configured to allocate IP addresses from `192.168.0.3` to `192.168.0.254`.

Once we have filled in the appropriate network details, we can click on the **Create** button. On the following screen, we will see that a new network is available for this project, as shown in Figure 10-10.

Adding SSH Keypair

Before we launch a new instance, it is important to provide an SSH keypair within Horizon to ensure that we can log in to the VM after it has been created—this is the only supported mechanism currently within Oracle Solaris 11. Let's now navigate to the **Access and Security** screen under the

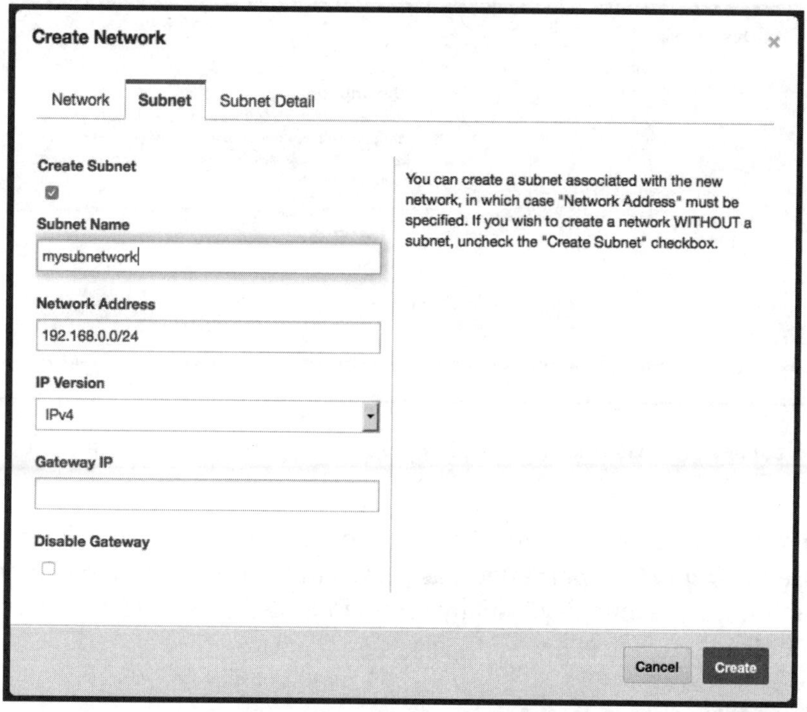

Create Network   ✕

Network   **Subnet**   Subnet Detail

Create Subnet   You can create a subnet associated with the new
☑   network, in which case "Network Address" must be
                                     specified. If you wish to create a network WITHOUT a
Subnet Name   subnet, uncheck the "Create Subnet" checkbox.

mysubnetwork

Network Address

192.168.0.0/24

IP Version

IPv4   ▾

Gateway IP

Disable Gateway
☐

Cancel   Create

FIGURE 10-9. *Creating a new network in OpenStack Horizon*

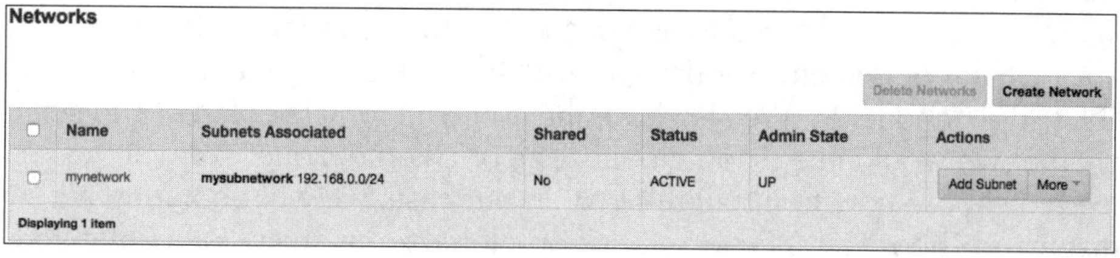

Networks

Delete Networks   Create Network

☐	Name	Subnets Associated	Shared	Status	Admin State	Actions
☐	mynetwork	**mysubnetwork** 192.168.0.0/24	No	ACTIVE	UP	Add Subnet More ▾

Displaying 1 item

FIGURE 10-10. *Network list in OpenStack Horizon*

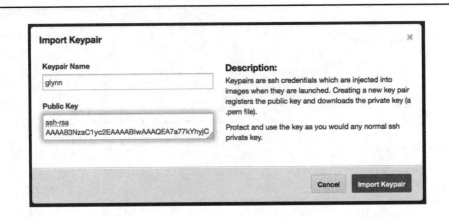

FIGURE 10-11. *Associating an SSH public keypair in OpenStack Horizon*

Manage Compute section. Since there are no keys currently associated, we will use the *Import Keypair* button as shown in Figure 10-11. We will need to copy in our SSH public key (usually found in $HOME/.ssh/id_rsa.pub) into the dialog.

Launching a VM instance

Now that we have a network and SSH keypair in place, we can start to launch a new VM. We will navigate to the *Instances* screen under the *Manage Compute* section. To launch a new instance, click on the *Launch Instance* button. The following dialog gives us an opportunity to provide a lot of details about how we would like the VM to look as shown in Figure 10-12. We will need to assign a Flavor to this instance. This tells Nova what requirements we have as a self-service user—in terms of virtual CPUs, disk, and RAM. We also have the ability in Oracle Solaris 11 to select whether we would like a non-global zone or a kernel zone. We will then need to choose how to install this VM. In our case, we will boot from an image and choose an Oracle Solaris non-global zone image (preconfigured as part of the Unified Archive).

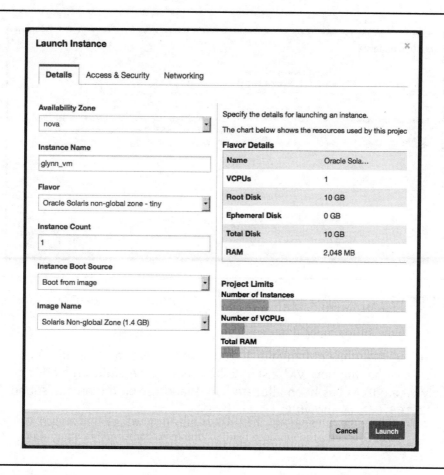

FIGURE 10-12. *Launching a new VM instance in OpenStack Horizon*

In the *Access & Security* tab, the SSH keypair that we imported will be automatically selected. In the *Networks* tab, we will need to choose the network we created as shown in Figure 10-13.

Once we are happy with this configuration, we can click on the *Launch* button. This will bring us back to the original Instances screen but we can now see the progress of our VM as Nova schedules it for creation with the appropriate Nova compute node, and the VM gets installed, as shown in Figure 10-14.

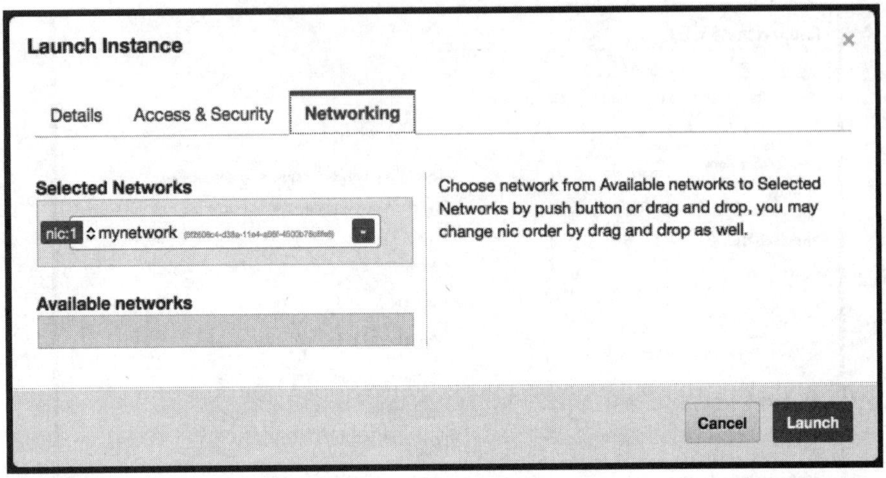

FIGURE 10-13. *Adding a network to the VM instance in OpenStack Horizon*

After a little while (it can take a little time to create and install a VM), we can see that the new VM instance has been successfully created. The newly created VM has been allocated an IP address on the private subnet of `192.168.0.3`, as shown in Figure 10-15.

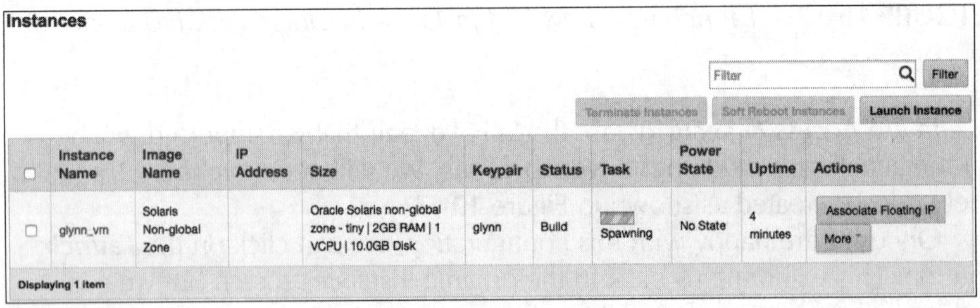

FIGURE 10-14. *VM provisioning status in OpenStack Horizon*

Instances

	Instance Name	Image Name	IP Address	Size	Keypair	Status	Task	Power State	Uptime	Actions
☐	glynn_vm	Solaris Non-global Zone	192.168.0.3	Oracle Solaris non-global zone - tiny | 2GB RAM | 1 VCPU | 10.0GB Disk	glynn	Active	None	Running	52 minutes	Create Snapshot / More ˮ

Displaying 1 item

FIGURE 10-15.   *VM successfully running in OpenStack Horizon*

Let's move to the **Network Topology** screen under the **Manage Networks** section. We can see now that we have a single instance that's plumbed into the mynetwork network, as shown in Figure 10-16.

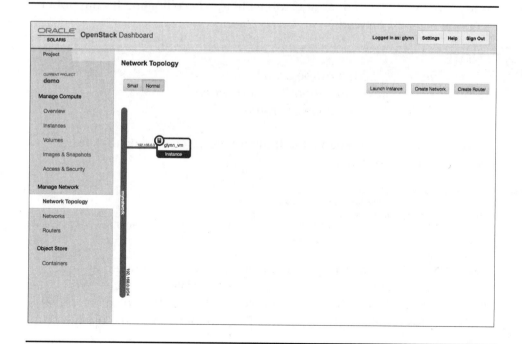

FIGURE 10-16.   *Network topology view in OpenStack Horizon*

We can now log in to this new VM using the IP address.

```
# ssh root@192.168.0.3
The authenticity of host '192.168.0.3 (192.168.0.3)' can't be established.
RSA key fingerprint is 46:f5:51:5f:ad:e8:8a:9b:8c:8e:85:06:dd:8a:77:c1.
Are you sure you want to continue connecting (yes/no)? yes
Warning: Permanently added '192.168.0.3' (RSA) to the list of known hosts.
Last login: Fri Mar 27 03:26:53 2015 from 192.168.0.2
Oracle Corporation      SunOS 5.11      11.2      February 2015
```

Access is limited to users that have already logged into the system hosting the OpenStack environment because we have not connected the OpenStack environment up to an external network. Most users will expect to have external access to these VMs from outside. We will need to use the Neutron L3 agent to achieve this.

Configuring the Neutron L3 Agent

The Neutron L3 agent provides bidirectional NAT between the router and the external network. Self-service users can then associate floating IPs as required to VMs that need outside connectivity. These floating IPs are public IPs on the external network.

NOTE
The Neutron L3 agent must be used within a global zone context and cannot be used within an Oracle Solaris kernel zone at present.

We will first need to enable the IP filtering service, and enable IP forwarding for this system as follows:

```
# svcadm enable ipfilter
# ipadm set-prop -p forwarding=on ipv4
# ipadm show-prop -p forwarding ipv4
PROTO PROPERTY          PERM CURRENT    PERSISTENT  DEFAULT   POSSIBLE
ipv4  forwardingrw  on       on         off         on,off
```

An EVS controller provides functionality for the configuration and administration of an elastic virtual switch and associated resources. We need to set properties for the EVS controller to allow us to implement virtual switching across multiple physical hosts. First, we need to set the up-link port for the controller, which tells us the port of each network that the VMs will talk over. Since we're on a single system, we will simply create an etherstub (a pseudo-Ethernet NIC) to act as the up-link port—in a multinode setup, you would typically have a VM/data network using physical NICs.

```
# dladm create-etherstub etherstub0
# dladm show-etherstub
LINK
etherstub0
# evsadm set-controlprop -p uplink-port=etherstub0
```

In this example, we are going to use VLAN, so we will also set the l2-type property to vlan and set the vlan-range property to an ID range of 1,200-300. The VLAN ID for the external network will be 1, and each tenant will be allocated an ID in the 200-300 range.

```
# evsadm set-controlprop -p l2-type=vlan
# evsadm set-controlprop -p vlan-range=1,200-300
```

Let's now review the properties for the EVS contoller.

```
# evsadm show-controlprop
PROPERTY            PERM VALUE      DEFAULT   VLAN_RANGE  VXLAN_RANGE HOST
l2-type             rw   vlan       vlan      --          --          --
uplink-port         rw   etherstub0 --        1,200-300   --          --
vlan-range          rw   1,200-300  --        --          --          --
vlan-range-avail    r-   201-300    --        --          --          --
vxlan-addr          rw   0.0.0.0    0.0.0.0   --          --          --
vxlan-ipvers        rw   v4         v4        --          --          --
vxlan-mgroup        rw   0.0.0.0    0.0.0.0   --          --          --
vxlan-range         rw   --         --        --          --          --
vxlan-range-avail   r-   --         --        --          --          --
```

Now that everything looks like it's in place, let's set up some environmental variables for Neutron. We will be making changes to the service project/tenant.

```
# export OS_AUTH_URL=http://localhost:5000/v2.0
# export OS_TENANT_NAME=service
# export OS_USERNAME=neutron
# export OS_PASSWORD=neutron
```

Let's double check these are correct by using the `neutron` command line to list configured networks:

```
# neutron net-list

+------------------------------------+-----------+-----------------------------------------------------------+
| id                                 | name      | subnets                                                   |
+------------------------------------+-----------+-----------------------------------------------------------+
| ff787c4a-d37a-11e4-990a-5d21347909e6 | mynetwork | ff8ec0e0-d37a-11e4-990b-5d21347909e6 192.168.0.0/24 |
+------------------------------------+-----------+-----------------------------------------------------------+
```

Let's now create a provider router on this system. The router will be a shared resource.

```
#neutron router-create provider_router

Created a new router:
+-----------------------+--------------------------------------+
| Field                 | Value                                |
+-----------------------+--------------------------------------+
| admin_state_up        | True                                 |
| external_gateway_info |                                      |
| id                    | 086a192f-1e20-45e0-ab9e-f66c9c8dc4d8 |
| name                  | provider_router                      |
| status                | ACTIVE                               |
| tenant_id             | 7b44a7763982eab1b53b9d86393747a7     |
+-----------------------+--------------------------------------+
```

We will need to copy the router ID 086a192f-1e20-45e0-ab9e-f66c9c8dc4d8 into the router_id key of /etc/neutron/l3_agent.ini as follows:

```
router_id = 086a192f-1e20-45e0-ab9e-f66c9c8dc4d8
```

Finally, we can enable the L3 agent with SMF:

```
# svcadm enable neutron-l3-agent
```

We now need to create the external network in OpenStack using the VLAN ID of 1 to match the external network configuration within the EVS controller:

```
# neutron net-create --provider:network_type=vlan \
--provider:segmentation_id=1 --router:external=true externalnetwork
Created a new network:
+-------------------------+---------------------------------------+
| Field                   | Value                                 |
+-------------------------+---------------------------------------+
| admin_state_up          | True                                  |
| id                      | 27104430-d41c-11e4-9931-5d21347909e6  |
| name                    | externalnetwork                       |
| provider:network_type   | vlan                                  |
| provider:segmentation_id| 1                                     |
| router:external         | True                                  |
| shared                  | False                                 |
| status                  | ACTIVE                                |
| subnets                 |                                       |
| tenant_id               | 7b44a7763982eab1b53b9d86393747a7      |
+-------------------------+---------------------------------------+
```

Let's create a new subnet within this external network and allocate an IP range of 10.134.79.230 through 10.134.79.240 as our floating IPs.

```
# neutron subnet-create --enable-dhcp=False \
--allocation-pool start=10.134.79.230,end=10.134.79.240 \
--name externalsubnetwork externalnetwork 10.134.79.0/24
Created a new subnet:
+------------------+---------------------------------------------------+
| Field            | Value                                             |
+------------------+---------------------------------------------------+
| allocation_pools | {"start": "10.134.79.230", "end": "10.134.79.240"}|
| cidr             | 10.134.79.0/24                                    |
| dns_nameservers  |                                                   |
| enable_dhcp      | False                                             |
| gateway_ip       | 10.134.79.1                                       |
| host_routes      |                                                   |
| id               | 806e998a-d41e-11e4-9932-5d21347909e6              |
| ip_version       | 4                                                 |
| name             | externalsubnetwork                                |
| network_id       | 27104430-d41c-11e4-9931-5d21347909e6              |
| tenant_id        | 7b44a7763982eab1b53b9d86393747a7                  |
+------------------+---------------------------------------------------+
```

We will now need to set the gateway to the router that we created earlier for this new external network. We will use the router ID (086a192f-1e20-45e0-ab9e-f66c9c8dc4d8) and the network ID (27104430-d41c-11e4-9931-5d21347909e6) as follows:

```
# neutron router-gateway-set 086a192f-1e20-45e0-ab9e-f66c9c8dc4d8
27104430-d41c-11e4-9931-5d21347909e6
Set gateway for router 086a192f-1e20-45e0-ab9e-f66c9c8dc4d8
```

Finally, we can add this router to the existing tenant network. We will use the keystone command to get the tenant ID to be able to list the subnetworks under the demo tenant.

```
# keystone tenant-list
+----------------------------------+---------+---------+
|                id                |  name   | enabled |
+----------------------------------+---------+---------+
| 2048ba3a43dccbb9af83881ffa0e3fd5 |  demo   |  True   |
| 7b44a7763982eab1b53b9d86393747a7 | service |  True   |
+----------------------------------+---------+---------+
# neutron net-list --tenant-id=2048ba3a43dccbb9af83881ffa0e3fd5
+--------------------------------------+-----------+-------------------------------------------------------+
| id                                   | name      | subnets                                               |
+--------------------------------------+-----------+-------------------------------------------------------+
| ff787c4a-d37a-11e4-990a-5d21347909e6 | mynetwork | ff8ec0e0-d37a-11e4-990b-5d21347909e6 192.168.0.0/24   |
+--------------------------------------+-----------+-------------------------------------------------------+
# neutron router-interface-add 086a192f-1e20-45e0-ab9e-f66c9c8dc4d8 ff8ec0e0-d37a-11e4-990b-5d21347909e6
Added interface 20b3ea98-d420-11e4-9934-5d21347909e6 to router 086a192f-1e20-45e0-ab9e-f66c9c8dc4d8.
```

Logging back in as the admin user, we can see our router has been created in the Routers screen under the System Panel section of the *Admin* tab as shown in Figure 10-17.

We can find out more details about this router by clicking on the router name, as shown in Figure 10-18. In our example, it will give us detail about what the internal interface is along with what external gateway it is connected to.

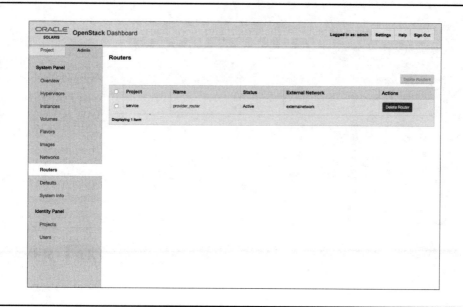

FIGURE 10-17.   *The new router shown in OpenStack Horizon*

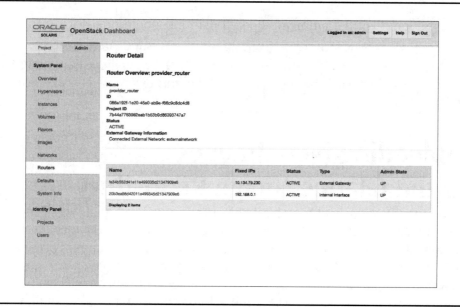

FIGURE 10-18.   *The router shows internal interface and external gateway in OpenStack Horizon*

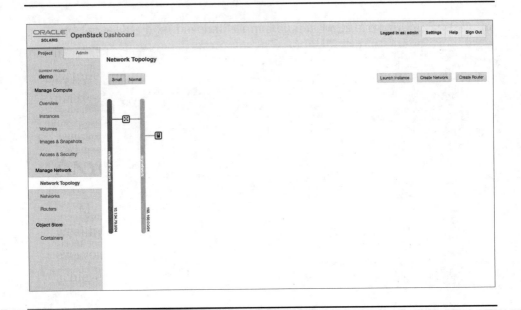

FIGURE 10-19. *Network topology view with external network in OpenStack Horizon*

If we navigate to the **Projects** tab and look at the Network Topology screen under Manage Network, we now see a different view with our external network added, as shown in Figure 10-19. We will see that the VM instance that we created has now connected to this external network via a provider router.

Uploading New Images to the Glance Image Repository

Administrators may want to upload new images to Glance that represent golden images used by their organization. Oracle Solaris 11 uses Unified Archives as the main archive type. We have already covered how to create Unified Archives in Chapter 3, Lifecycle Management. However, the most important thing is to ensure that we can authenticate using an SSH keypair, so an additional step needs to be done before capturing the clone archive.

Within the environment we wish to create an archive, edit the `/etc/ssh/sshd_config`, and change the following key-value pair:

```
PermitRootLogin without-password
```

Once this configuration has been saved, you may capture the archive as usual:

```
# archiveadm create -z appzoneappzone.uar
```

The next step is to use the glance command line to upload this image to the image repository. For convenience, we'll first set a few environmental variables that we will use to authenticate with OpenStack keystone:

```
# export OS_AUTH_URL=http://localhost:5000/v2.0
# export OS_USERNAME=admin
# export OS_PASSWORD=secrete
# export OS_TENANT_NAME=demo
```

NOTE

Many of the OpenStack command lines use a common set of environmental variables. This helps to cut down on using options when doing a lot of command line operations.

Now we use the `glance image-create` command to upload this image to the repository. We need to make sure we provide it a number of different properties so we can tag this image as only deployable on systems capable of running Oracle Solaris Zones and SPARC.

```
# glance image-create --container-format bare --disk-format raw \
--is-public true --name "App Golden Image" --property architecture=sparc64 \
--property hypervisor_type=solariszones --property vm_mode=solariszones\
< ./appzone.uar
+-------------------------------+--------------------------------------+
| Property                      | Value                                |
+-------------------------------+--------------------------------------+
| Property 'architecture'       | sparc64                              |
| Property 'hypervisor_type'    | solariszones                         |
| Property 'vm_mode'            | solariszones                         |
| checksum                      | 2ec6327a592ce4cc8b11d8c5dacab830     |
| container_format              | bare                                 |
| created_at                    | 2015-03-26T07:22:42.043649           |
| deleted                       | False                                |
| deleted_at                    | None                                 |
| disk_format                   | raw                                  |
| id                            | d8989ed9-1ad3-422d-a94a-a404af5982f2 |
| is_public                     | True                                 |
```

```
| min_disk   | 0                                       |
| min_ram    | 0                                       |
| name       | App Golden Image                        |
| owner      | 2048ba3a43dccbb9af83881ffa0e3fd5        |
| protected  | False                                   |
| size       | 1470156800                              |
| status     | active                                  |
| updated_at | 2015-03-26T07:23:18.438834              |
+------------+-----------------------------------------+
```

Table 10-2 lists the configuration options that are mandatory for uploading an Oracle Solaris-based image to Glance.

Now that the image has been uploaded, we can check the **Images & Snapshots** screen of the **Manage Compute** section as shown in Figure 10-20.

NOTE

OpenStack Flavors are managed in Nova. The nova flavor-list *command displays the list of configured Flavors. Additional zone configuration can be provided to OpenStack using the* extra_specs *property. For example, an administrator could ensure immutability by using the* zonecfg:file-mac-profile *property. Additionally, administrators can provide a default system configuration profile using the* sc_profile *property.*

Property	Value
disk_format	raw
container_format	bare
architecture	sparc64 or x86_64
hypervisor_type	solaris_zones
vm_mode	solaris_zones

TABLE 10-2.   *Essential Properties for Oracle Solaris Glance Images*

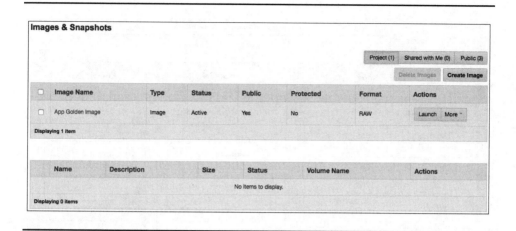

FIGURE 10-20. *Listing images for the* demo *project in OpenStack Horizon*

Setting Up a Multinode OpenStack Environment

For a production environment, administrators will need to create a multinode OpenStack architecture rather than the single node system that we have explored earlier in this chapter. A very minimal multinode setup would typically involve a controller node, a compute node, and a network node, as shown in Figure 10-21.The administrator can then choose to split this out further if desired and provide high availability capabilities to their cloud using Oracle Solaris Cluster.

In the above architecture, there are three nodes. All three nodes are synchronized with an NTP service. The controller node hosts supporting services required for OpenStack such as message queuing with RabbitMQ and a MySQL database (as opposed to SQLite that was used in our single node example). It also hosts basic OpenStack services such as Keystone, Glance, Cinder, Horizon, and Heat. The big difference is that we have split out the scheduling and management services of Nova and Neutron from the worker services. The compute node will run the `nova-compute` service. The network node will run the EVS controller and DHCP/L3 agents, as networking can often be a bottleneck to warrant running on a separate node.

When we used the OpenStack Unified Archive, everything was preconfigured. With a multinode setup, the administrator will need to manually install software and configure each node as appropriate.

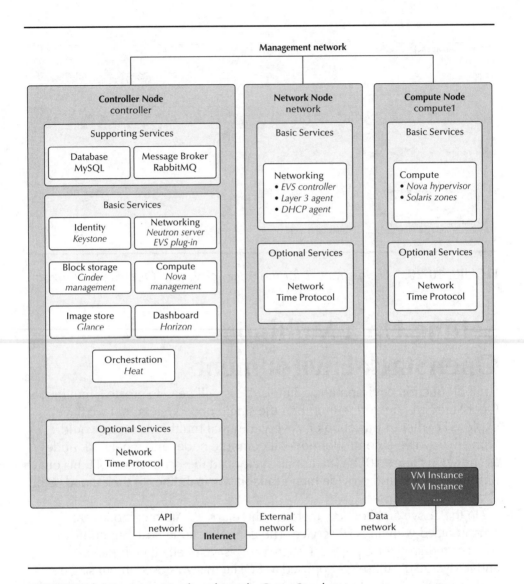

FIGURE 10-21. *A typical multinode OpenStack setup*

Depending on the environment that the administrator wishes to set up, they will need to install different IPS packages from the `pkg:/cloud/openstack` package namespace. For example, a compute node would typically install `pkg:/cloud/openstack/nova` but only enable the `nova-compute` service.

Administrators configure an OpenStack environment with files located in /etc/<project_name>. Each OpenStack project has its own separate set of configuration files for different services that are used. Each file has many different configuration options and can look overwhelming. It is best to stick to a basic set of configuration before trying to do anything more complex. For example, Nova uses the following simplified configuration across two configuration files as listed in Table 10-3.

Configuration File	Configuration Key	Typical Value
/etc/nova/api-paste.ini	auth_uri	http://CONTROLLER_HOST:5000/v2.0
	identity_uri	http://CONTROLLER_HOST:35357
	admin_tenant_name	service
	admin_user	nova
	admin_password	nova
/etc/nova/nova.conf	keystone_ec2_url	http://CONTROLLER_HOST:5000/v2.0/ec2tokens
	glance_host	CONTROLLER_HOST
	neutron_url	http://CONTROLLER_HOST:9696
	neutron_admin_username	neutron
	neutron_admin_password	neutron
	neutron_admin_tenant_name	service
	neutron_admin_auth_url	http://CONTROLLER_HOST:5000/v2.0
	rabbit_host	CONTROLLER_HOST
	connection	mysql://nova:nova@CONTROLLER_HOST/nova

TABLE 10-3.   *Common Configuration for Nova*

We will not cover further multinode OpenStack configuration in this chapter. This is covered in more detail in the Oracle Solaris 11 product documentation: *Installing and Configuring OpenStack in Oracle Solaris 11.* Administrators may also choose to implement further scaling techniques. For example, OpenStack offers the ability to segregate a cloud environment for faster access, redundancy, or legal considerations relating to data storage— techniques such as *cells, regions, availability zones,* or *host aggregates* can provide powerful ways to architect a more reliable environment. These are covered extensively in the OpenStack upstream community documentation.

Additional OpenStack Services

The OpenStack community is a large ecosystem with many different contributors from different backgrounds. As a result, the OpenStack project has grown since its initial focus on infrastructure to consider other services adding more functionality. Table 10-4 shows a list of some other services that are available.

It is likely that some of these services will be included in a future release of OpenStack on Oracle Solaris 11.

Project Name	Project Description
Barbican	Storage and management of keys
Ceilometer	Telemetry for metering and monitoring
Designate	DNS as a service
Ironic	Bare metal provisioning
Magnum	Application containers
Manila	NFS as a service
Murano	Application catalogs
Sahara	Hadoop as a service
Trove	Database as a service

TABLE 10-4. *Other Common OpenStack Services*

Summary

In this chapter, we have explored some of the cloud capabilities of Oracle Solaris 11. Oracle Solaris includes all the technologies you need to be able to create a complete cloud solution that is reliable, scalable, secure, and observable. Oracle Solaris 11.2 also includes OpenStack, a popular open source platform that administrators can use to manage compute, network, and storage resources and make them available to self-service users. OpenStack has been integrated into the enterprise grade technologies included in Oracle. Administrators can quickly extend this cloud solution into Platform as a Service (PaaS), Database as a Service (DBaaS) and Software as a Service (SaaS), and take advantage of Oracle's hardware and software optimizations for a single vendor solution.

References

Oracle Solaris 11 Cloud Management Technologies—How to Articles, Cheat Sheets, Screencasts, Whitepapers and Presentations, http://www.oracle.com/technetwork/server-storage/solaris11/technologies/openstack-2135773.html

Installing and Configuring OpenStack in Oracle Solaris 11, http://docs.oracle.com/cd/E36784_01/html/E54155/index.html

OpenStack Official Project, http://www.openstack.org

OpenStack Community Documentation, http://docs.openstack.org/

APPENDIX
A

Oracle Solaris 11.2
Cheat Sheet General
Administration

System Configuration

Common system configuration tasks have changed in Oracle Solaris 11 with the Service Management Facility (SMF) configuration repository being used to store configuration data. With the addition of configuration layers, administrators now have better control and assurance that their configuration changes will be preserved across system updates.

Configure nodename

```
# hostname myhost
```

Configure nameserver via SMF

```
# svccfg -s dns/client \
 setprop config/nameserver = net_address: 192.168.1.1
# svccfg -s dns/client \
 setprop config/domain = astring: \"myhost.org\"
# svccfg -s name-service/switch \
 setprop config/host = astring: \"files dns\"
# svcadm restart name-service/switch
# svcadm restart dns/client
```

Configure nameserver (alternate approach to editing /etc/resolv.conf **and** /etc/nsswitch.conf **and then importing these modifications into SMF)**

```
# nscfg import -f svc:/system/name-service/switch:default
# nscfg import -f svc:/network/dns/client:default
```

Unconfigure a system and start an interactive configuration tool on reboot

```
# sysconfig configure -s
```

Create a system configuration profile

```
# sysconfig create-profile -o sc-profile.xml
```

Configure a system according to a system configuration profile

```
# sysconfig configure -c sc-profile.xml
```

Locales, Timezone, and Keyboard

Install nlsadm for easier management of national language properties (Solaris 11.2)

```
# pkg install nls-administration
```

Get current configuration

```
# nlsadm get-console-keymap
# nlsadm get-system-locale
# nlsadm get-timezone
```

List available timezones
`# nlsadm list-timezone`
List available console keymaps
`# nlsadm list-console-keymap`
List available locales
`# nlsadm list-locale`
Set timezone to Europe/Berlin
`# nlsadm set-timezone Europe/Berlin`
Set locale to de_DE.UTF-8
`# nlsadm set-system-locale de_DE.UTF-8`
Set console keymap to UK-English
`# nlsadm set-console-keymap UK-English`

Import Legacy Files into SMF (`nscfg`)

The nscfg commands allow you to import the content of legacy files into the SMF. While the cheat sheet showed already two examples, the `nscfg` command isn't limited to these scenarios. When you make changes to the legacy files mentioned in the following tables (instead of doing it the SMF way), you can import them by `nscfg -fq {FMRI}`.

FRMI	Legacy files
`svc:/system/name-service/switch:default`	`/etc/nsswitch.conf`
`svc:/system/name-service/cache:default`	`/etc/nscd.conf`
`svc:/network/dns/client:default`	`/etc/resolv.conf`
`svc:/network/nis/domain:default`	`/etc/defaultdomain` `/var/yp/binding/$DOMAIN/*`
`svc:/network/nis/client:default`	`no legacy file import`
`svc:/network/ldap/client:default`	`/var/ldap/*`
`svc:/network/nis/server:default`	`no legacy file import`
`svc:/network/nis/passwd:default`	`no legacy file import`
`svc:/network/nis/xfr:default`	`no legacy file import`
`svc:/network/nis/update:default`	`no legacy file import`
`svc:/system/name-service/upgrade:default`	`no legacy file import`

Users and Roles

The traditional root account has been changed to a "root" role on Oracle Solaris 11 interactive installations that configure an initial administrator account. This is a standard part of the Role-based access control (RBAC) feature set. This change gives improved auditability across the operating system and the ability for administrators to delegate various system tasks to others in a safe way.

Revert root to a normal user account

```
# rolemod -K type=normal root
```

Configure root as a role (default)

```
# usermod -K type=role root
```

Configure root role to use the user password instead of root password

```
# rolemod -K roleauth=user root
```

Add a new user and delegate the System Adminstrator profile to the user

```
# useradd -m -P "System Administrator" joerg
```

Add a new user with a ZFS file system as the user's home directory and add an entry in auto_home

```
# useradd -m -d localhost:/export/home/joerg joerg
# grep "joerg" /etc/passwd
joerg:x:101:10::/home/joerg:/usr/bin/bash
# cat /etc/auto_home
[...]
joerg localhost:/export/home/joerg
+auto_home
# zfs list | grep joerg
rpool/export/home/joerg          35K    201G   35K  /export/home/joerg
```

Add a new user on a second server using another NFS server for the user's home directory

```
# useradd   -d nfsserver:/export/home/joerg joerg
# grep "joerg" /etc/passwd
joerg:x:103:10::/home/joerg:/usr/bin/bash
# tail -2 /etc/auto_home
joerg nfsserver::/export/home/joerg
+auto_home
```

Boot Environments

Boot environments are individual bootable instances of the operating system that take advantage of the Oracle Solaris ZFS File System snapshot and clone capability. During a system update, new boot environments are created so that system software updates can be applied in a safe environment. Should anything go awry, administrators can boot back into an older boot environment. Boot environments have low overhead and can be quickly created, giving administrators an ideal best practice for any system maintenance work.

List available boot environments
`# beadm list`
Create a boot environment
`# beadm create solaris-05032012`
Activate a boot environment
`# beadm activate solaris-05032012`
Delete an inactive boot environment
`# beadm destroy solaris-05032012`
Show boot environments from SPARC boot PROM
`ok boot -L`
Boot into a boot environment from SPARC boot PROM
`ok boot -Z rpool/ROOT/solaris-05032012`

Packaging

Oracle Solaris 11 includes Image Packaging System (IPS), a new network-centric package management framework with automatic dependency checking. IPS has integrated package and patching and can seamlessly manage system updates to Oracle Solaris Zones environments.

Install a package called `diagnostic/wireshark`
`# pkg install diagnostic/wireshark`
Install a group package to provide a desktop environment
`# pkg install solaris-desktop`
Enforce a minimized installation on an existing system
Warning! All packages that are not a dependency of this package will be removed while installing it. This is what the command is meant for.
`# pkg exact-install web/server/apache-22/module/apache-wsgi-26`
Update all possible packages to the newest version, including any zones
`# pkg update`

List available updates

```
# pkg list -a
```

Do a dry run of a system update to identify what packages might change

```
# pkg update -nv
```

Uninstall a package called `diagnostic/wireshark`

```
# pkg uninstall wireshark
```

List all packages installed on a system

```
# pkg list
```

Get more information about an installed package called `diagnostic/wireshark`

```
# pkg info wireshark
```

List the contents of an installed package called `diagnostic/wireshark`

```
# pkg contents wireshark
```

Search all packages in the configured repositories for a file called `math.h`

```
# pkg search math.h
```

Search for all packages installed on a system that have a dependency on `library/libxml2`

```
# pkg search -l -o pkg.name 'depend::library/libxml2'
```

List currently associated package publishers

```
# pkg publisher
```

Connect to the Oracle support repository and update the system

```
# pkg set-publisher -g https://pkg.oracle.com/solaris/support \
 -G http://pkg.oracle.com/solaris/release -k /path/to/ssl_key \
 -c /path/to/ssl_cert solaris
# pkg update
```

Where can I get the nescessary certificates and keys to access the support repository to get fixes?

You can get them at https://pkg-register.oracle.com given you have a valid support aggreement.

Local Package Repository

Setting up your own package repository

Download all the IPS repository files from
http://www.oracle.com/technetwork/server-storage/solaris11/downloads/

```
# zfs create -p rpool/export/repo/solaris
# ./install-repo.ksh  -d /export/repo/solaris/
# zfs snapshot rpool/export/repo/solaris@initial
```

Setting up a depot server to enable other systems to update themselves via HTTP

```
# svccfg -s application/pkg/server setprop pkg/inst_root=/export/repo/solaris/
# svccfg -s application/pkg/server setprop pkg/readonly=true
# svccfg -s application/pkg/server setprop pkg/port=8081
# svcadm refresh application/pkg/server
# svcadm enable application/pkg/server
```

Updating the repository with a SRU

Get the most current SRU for your Oracle Solaris release. For 11.2 a list is available with My Oracle Support (MOS) ID 1672221.1.

For this example we've downloaded all three files in the "IPS repository" column for SRU9 (reachable via link to 20845979 and 20845983) and loaded into /export/home/ {username}/sru9 of my repository server.

```
# cd /export/home/{username}/sru9
# unzip p20845983_1100_SOLARIS64.zip
# ./install-repo.ksh -d /export/repo/solaris
# svcadm restart application/pkg/server:default
# zfs snapshot rpool/export/repo/solaris@sru9
```

File Systems—Basic ZFS Administration

Oracle Solaris ZFS is the default root file system on Oracle Solaris 11. ZFS has integrated volume management, preserves the highest levels of data integrity, and includes a wide variety of data services such as data compression, RAID, and data encryption.

Create a ZFS pool with a single disk

```
# zpool create testpool c3t2d0
```

Create a ZFS pool with 3 disks in RAID0 configuration

```
# zpool create testpool c3t2d0 c3t3d0 c3t4d0
```

Create a ZFS pool with 3 disks in RAID1 configuration

```
# zpool create testpool mirror c3t2d0 c3t3d0 c3t4d0
```

Create a ZFS pool with 3 disks in a RAIDZ configuration (single parity)

```
# zpool create testpool raidz c2t2d0 c3t3d0 c3t4d0
```

Create a ZFS pool with 1 disk, and 1 disk as seperate ZIL (ZFS Intent Log)

```
# zpool create testpool c3t2d0 log c3t3d0
```

Create a ZFS pool with 1 disk, and 1 disk as L2ARC (Level 2 Storage Cache)

```
# zpool create testpool c3t2d0 cache c3t3d0
```

Create a ZFS file system and share it via NFS

```
# zfs create rpool/export/nfstest
# zfs set share.nfs=on rpool/export/nfstest
```

Share a file system via CIFS

```
# svcadm enable -r smb/server
# echo "other password required pam_smb_passwd.so.1 nowarn" \
 >> /etc/pam.d/other
# passwd {username}
# zfs create -o nbmand=on rpool/export/smbservertest
# zfs share -o share.smb=on rpool/export/smbservertest%smb_st
# mkdir /export/smbservertest/archiv
# chown junior2 /export/smbservertest/archiv
```

Now you can access the share via smb://junior2:password@192.168.1.200/
smb_st . You have to set a new password for each user that wants to access a SMB share
after adding the PAM module

Use shadow migration

```
# pkg install shadow-migration
# svcadm enable shadowd
# zfs set readonly=on rpool/export/shadowmigtest
# zfs create \
 -o shadow=file:///export/shadowmigtest rpool/export/shadowmigtestnew
```

Create an encrypted zfs dataset

```
# zfs create -o encryption=on rpool/export/secretproject
```

Change the wrapping key

```
# zfs key -c rpool/export/secretproject
```

Change the encryption key of a dataset

Please keep in mind that you can't set the encryption key to a user-defined value, you
just can initiate the generation of a new encryption key. The wrapping key encrypting the
encrytion key can be set to a user definable value.

```
# zfs key -K rpool/export/secretproject
```

Managing Disks in a ZFS Storage Pool

Show all disks on a system

```
# cfgadm -al
```

**Replace a faulty disk c1t1d0 from ZFS pool testpool. Only SATA disks must be
unconfigured with cfgadm before being replaced**

```
# zpool offline testpool c1t3d0
# cfgadm | grep c1t3d0
sata0/3::dsk/c1t3d0              disk         connected    configured   ok
# cfgadm -c unconfigure sata0/3
Now replace the failed disk
# cfgadm -c configure sata0/3
# zpool replace tank c1t3d0
# zpool online tank c1t3d0
```

Replace a faulty disk of a ZFS root pool (SPARC or x86/VTOC)

```
# zpool offline rpool c1t0d0s0
# cfgadm -c unconfigure c1::dsk/c1t0d0
Now replace the disk
# cfgadm -c configure c1::dsk/c1t0d0
# zpool replace rpool c1t0d0s0
# zpool online rpool c1t0d0s0
# zpool status rpool
# bootadm install-bootloader
```

Replace a faulty disk of a ZFS root pool (SPARC or x86/EFI (GPT))

```
# zpool offline rpool c1t0d0
# cfgadm -c unconfigure c1::dsk/c1t0d0
Now replace the disk
# cfgadm -c configure c1::dsk/c1t0d0
# zpool online rpool c1t0d0
# zpool replace rpool c1t0d0
# zpool status rpool
# bootadm install-bootloader
```

Checking the logical blocksize of a disk device

```
devprop -vn /dev/dsk/c3t0d0 device-blksize
```

Checking the physical blocksize of a disk device

```
devprop -vn /dev/dsk/c3t0d0 device-pblksize
```

iSCSI

Configure an iSCSI target

```
# pkg install group/feature/storage-server
# zfs create rpool/export/iscsiluns
# zfs create -V 16g rpool/export/iscsiluns/lun1
# svcadm enable stmf
# stmfadm create-lu /dev/zvol/rdsk/rpool/export/iscsiluns/lun1
Logical unit created: 600144F0BE1002000000553776B00001
# stmfadm add-view 600144F0BE1002000000553776B00001
# svcadm enable -r svc:/network/iscsi/target
# itadm create-target
Target iqn.1986-03.com.sun:02:e8e0aa2d-1011-4136-9c9a-ddebb6279801
successfully created
```

Use the iSCSI target just configured

```
# svcadm enable svc:/network/iscsi/initiator
# iscsiadm add discovery-address 192.168.1.200:3260
# iscsiadm modify discovery --sendtargets enable
# devfsadm -c iscsi
# iscsiadm list initiator-node
Initiator node name: iqn.1986-03.com.sun:01:e00000000000.55365ebd
[..]
```

Add birectional authentication between iSCSI target and initator

From the last two examples, we know that the IQN of the target is `iqn.1986-03.com.`
`sun:02-e8e0aa2d-1011-4136-9c9a-ddebb6279801` and from the initiator is `iqn.1986-`
`03.com.sun:01:e00000000000.55365ebd`. The secret that authorizes the target to the
initiator is `foobarfoobar`, the secret that authorizes the initator to the target is `snafusnafusna`

```
target# itadm modify-target -s iqn.1986-03.com.sun:02:e8e0aa2d-1011-4136-
9c9a-ddebb6279801
Enter CHAP secret: snafusnafusna
Re-enter secret: snafusnafusna
target# itadm create-initiator -s iqn.1986-03.com.
sun:01:e00000000000.55365ebd
Enter CHAP secret: foobarfoobar
Re-enter secret: foobarfoobar
initiator# iscsiadm modify initiator-node --CHAP-secret
Enter secret: foobarfoobar
Re-enter secret: foobarfoobar
initiator# iscsiadm modify initiator-node --authentication CHAP
# iscsiadm modify target-param --authentication CHAP iqn.1986-03.com.
sun:02:e8e0aa2d-1011-4136-9c9a-ddebb6279801
# iscsiadm modify target-param --CHAP-secret iqn.1986-03.com.
sun:02:e8e0aa2d-1011-4136-9c9a-ddebb6279801
Enter secret: snafusnafusna
Re-enter secret: snafusnafusna
```

Basics of Oracle Solaris Zones

Oracle Solaris Zones provide isolated and secure virtual environments running
on a single operating system instance, ideal for application deployment.
When administrators create a zone, an application execution environment is
produced in which processes are isolated from the rest of the system.

Create a zone

```
# zonecfg -z testzone
 testzone: No such zone configured
 Use 'create' to begin configuring a new zone.
 zonecfg:testzone> create
 zonecfg:testzone> set autoboot=true
 zonecfg:testzone> verify
 zonecfg:testzone> commit
 zonecfg:testzone> exit
 root@test1:~# zoneadm -z testzone install
```

Create a zone on shared storage

```
# zonecfg -z zoss-zone
Use 'create' to begin configuring a new zone.
zonecfg:zoss-zone> create
create: Using system default template 'SYSdefault'
zonecfg:zoss-zone> add rootzpool
zonecfg:zoss-zone:rootzpool> add storage iscsi://192.168.1.200/luname.naa
.600144F0BE1002000000553776B00001
zonecfg:zoss-zone:rootzpool> end
zonecfg:zoss-zone> commit
zonecfg:zoss-zone> exit
# zoneadm -z zoss-zone install
```

Create a kernel zone

```
Modify kernel tuning parameters to enforce a maximum ZFS ARC.
# echo "set zfs:zfs_arc_max=0x40000000" > /etc/sytem.d/zfs_arc
# reboot
# zonecfg -z kernelz1 create -t SYSsolaris-kz
# zoneadm -z kernelz1 install
```

List all running zones verbosely

```
# zoneadm list -v
```

List all configured zones

```
# zoneadm list -c
```

List all installed zones

```
# zoneadm list -i
```

Install a zone

```
# zoneadm -z testzone install
```

List configuration of a zone

```
# zonecfg -z testzone info
```

Login to the console of a zone

```
# zlogin -C testzone
```

Halt a zone

```
# zoneadm -z testzone halt
```

Shutdown a zone

```
# zoneadm -z testzone shutdown
```

Monitor a zone for CPU, memory, and network utilization every 10 seconds

```
# zonestat -z testzone 10
```

Immutable Oracle Solaris Zones

Making a non-global Zone immutable

```
# zonecfg -z zone1
zonecfg:zone1> set file-mac-profile=strict
```

Making a global zone immutable

```
# zonecfg -z global
zonecfg:global> set file-mac-profile=flexible-configuration
```

Profile Name	Description
none	Standard, read-write zone. Is the default.
strict	Read-only file system, no exceptions. ■ IPS packages cannot be installed. ■ Persistently enabled SMF services are fixed. ■ SMF manifests cannot be added from the default locations. ■ Logging and auditing configuration files are fixed. Data can only be logged remotely.
fixed-configuration	Permits updates to /var/* directories, with the exception of directories that contain system configuration components. ■ IPS packages, including new packages, cannot be installed. ■ Persistently enabled SMF services are fixed. ■ SMF manifests cannot be added from the default locations. ■ Logging and auditing configuration files can be local. syslog and audit configuration are fixed.
flexible-configuration	Permits modification of files in /etc/* directories, changes to root's home directory, and updates to /var/* directories. Closest configuration to a Solaris 10 sparse zone. ■ IPS packages, including new packages, cannot be installed. ■ Persistently enabled SMF services are fixed. ■ SMF manifests cannot be added from the default locations. ■ Logging and auditing configuration files can be local. syslog and audit configuration can be remote.

Log into the immutable zone to make changes via the Trusted Path

```
# zlogin -T {zonename}
```

Remove restriction rpool/zone in an otherwise immutable global zone

```
zonecfg:global> add dataset
zonecfg:global:dataset> set name=rpool/zones
zonecfg:global:dataset> end
```

Basic Networking

Show physical network interfaces

```
# dladm show-phys
```

Show state information of physical ethernet ports

```
# dladm show-ether
```

Show datalinks

```
# dladm show-link
```

Show properties of the datalink `net0`

```
# dladm show-linkprop net0
```

Show IP interfaces

```
# ipadm show-if
```

Show properties of a IP interface

```
# ipadm show-ifprop net0
```

Show IP address objects

```
# ipadm show-addr
```

Show properties of a IP address objects

```
# ipadm show-addrprop
```

Putting an IP address down and up again

```
# ipadm down-addr net0/v4
# ipadm up-addr net0/v4
```

Create interface with static IPv4 configuration

```
# ipadm create-ip net0
# ipadm create-addr -a 10.1.1.10/24 net0/addr1
```

Add an IP address to an existing IP interface

```
# ipadm create-addr -a 10.1.2.10/24 net0/addr2
```

Create interface with DHCP configuration

```
# ipadm create-ip net0
# ipadm create-addr -T dhcp  net0/addr1
```

Create interface with auto-generated IPv6 configuration

```
# ipadm create-ip net0
# ipadm create-addr -T addrconf  net0/addrv6
```

Create a virtual network interface over existing physical interface net0 **with address**
192.168.0.80

```
# dladm create-vnic -l net0 vnic0
# ipadm create-ip vnic0
# ipadm create-addr -a 192.168.0.80 vnic0/v4
```

Set the default route

```
# route -p add default 192.168.1.1
```

Create two virtual network interfaces over a virtual switch (without a physical network interface)

```
# dladm create-etherstub stub0
# dladm create-vnic -l stub0 vnic0
# dladm create-vnic -l stub0 vnic1
```

Reduce the bandwidth of the virtual network interface vnic0 to 100Mbps

```
# dladm set-linkprop -p maxbw=100 vnic0
```

Restrict the bandwidth going to IP address 192.168.0.30 **by creating a flow on virtual network interface vnic0, then restrict its bandwidth to 50 Mbps**

```
# flowadm add-flow -l vnic0 -a remote_ip=192.168.0.30 flow0
# flowadm set-flowprop -p maxbw=50 flow0
```

Restrict network traffic to TCP for local port 443 for network interface net0 to 75 Mbps

```
# flowadm add-flow -l net0 -a transport=TCP,local_port=433 flow1
# flowadm set-flowprop -p maxbw=75 flow1
```

Activating Jumbo Frames (ethernet packets greater than 1500 bytes)

```
# dladm set-linkprop -p mtu=9000 net0
```

Configure Link Aggregation

```
# dladm create-aggr -l net0 -l net1 aggr0
# ipadm create-ip aggr0
# ipadm create-addr -T static -a 10.1.1.2/24 aggr0/v4
```

Configure VLANS

```
# dladm create-vlan -l net0 -v 100 administration1
# dladm create-vlan -l net0 -v 2 production1
# ipadm create-ip administration1
# ipadm create-ip production1
# ipadm create-addr -T static -a 192.168.2.2/24 administration1/v4static
# ipadm create-addr -T static -a 192.168.1.2/24 production1/v4static
```

Configure an IPMP group

```
# ipadm create-ip net0
# ipadm create-ip net1
# ipadm create-ip net2
# ipadm create-ipmp ipmp0
# ipadm add-ipmp -i net0 -i net1 -i net2 ipmp0
# ipadm create-addr -T static -a 192.168.1.27/24 ipmp0/v4
# ipadm create-addr -T static -a 192.168.1.50/24 net0/test
# ipadm create-addr -T static -a 192.168.1.51/24 net1/test
# ipadm create-addr -T static -a 192.168.1.52/24 net2/test
```

Creating a LACP Trunk Aggregation

```
# dladm create-aggr -L active -l net0 -l net1 aggr1
```

Creating a Data Link Multi Pathing Aggregation

```
# dladm create-aggr -m dlmp -l net0 -l net1 aggr1
```

How to configure Probing for DLMP aggregates with a failure detection time of 15 sec

```
# dladm set-linkprop -p probe-ip=+ aggr1
# dladm set-linkprop -p probe-fdt=15 aggr1
```

Enable Ipv4 forwarding between two interfaces

```
# routeadm -e ipv4-forwarding
# routeadm -u
```

Disable Ipv4 forwarding between two interfaces

```
# routeadm -d ipv4-forwarding
# routeadm -u
```

How to configure an Virtual eXtensible LAN with the VNI 100 between two systems using the `10.254.1.0/24` **network**

```
node1# dladm create-vxlan -p vni=100,interface=net0 vxlan1
node1# dladm create-vnic -l vxlan1 vnic1
node1# ipadm create-ip vnic1
node1# ipadm create-addr -a 10.254.1.1/24 vnic1/vxlan1
node2# dladm create-vxlan -p vni=100,interface=net0 vxlan1
node2# dladm create-vnic -l vxlan1 vnic1
node2# ipadm create-ip vnic1
node2# ipadm create-addr -a 10.254.1.2/24 vnic1/vxlan1
```

Advanced Networking—Highly Available Load Balancer

In this example, the Virtual Router Redundancy Protocol and the Integrated Load Balancer (ILB) features of Solaris are used to create an highly available Load Balancer. This longer example thus shows how to configure VRRP as well as the ILB feature, which could both used without the other.

Shorthand	System	Use	IP
ilb1	Loadbalancer 1	Outside interface	10.0.1.10/24
ilb2	Loadbalancer 2	Outside interface	10.0.1.20/24
ilb1/2	Loadbalancer	Virtual IP	10.0.1.100/24
ilb1	Loadbalancer 1	Inside interface	10.0.10.10/24
ilb2	Loadbalancer 2	Inside Interface	10.0.10.20/24
ilb1/2	Loadbalancer	Virtual Default Gateway	10.0.10.100/24
rs1	Real Server 1	Single Interface	10.0.10.200/24
rs2	Real Server 2	Single Interface	10.0.10.210/24

Preparing Webserver 1

```
ws1# ipadm create-ip -T static -a 10.0.10.200 net0/v4
ws1# route -p add default 10.0.10.100
ws1# svcadm enable apache22
```

Preparing Webserver 2

```
ws2# ipadm create-ip -T static -a 10.0.10.210 net0/v4
ws2# route -p add default 10.0.10.100
ws2# svcadm enable apache22
```

Installing prerequisites on both loadbalancers

```
ilb1/ilb2# pkg install vrrp
ilb1/ilb2# pkg install ilb
```

Configuring VRRP on the first loadbalancer

```
ilb1# dladm create-aggr -m dlmp -l net0 -l net2 outside0
ilb1# dladm create-aggr -m dlmp -l net1 -l net3 inside1
ilb1# ipadm create-ip outside0
ilb1# ipadm create-ip inside1
ilb1# ipadm create-addr -T static -a 10.0.1.10/24 outside0/v4
ilb1# ipadm create-addr -T static -a 10.0.10.10/24 inside1/v4
ilb1# dladm create-vnic -m vrrp -V 2 -A inet -l inside1 vnic2
ilb1# dladm create-vnic -m vrrp -V 1 -A inet -l outside0 vnic1
ilb1# ipadm create-ip vnic1
ilb1# ipadm create-addr -T static -d -a 10.0.1.100/24 vnic1/lb1
ilb1# vrrpadm create-router -V 1 -A inet -l outside0 -p 255 vrrp1
ilb1# ipadm create-ip vnic2
ilb1# ipadm create-addr -T static -d -a 10.0.10.100/24 vnic2/lb1
ilb1# vrrpadm create-router -V 2 -A inet -l inside1 -p 255 vrrp2
```

Configuring VRRP on the second loadbalancer

```
ilb2# dladm create-aggr -m dlmp -l net0 -l net2 outside0
ilb2# dladm create-aggr -m dlmp -l net1 -l net3 inside1
ilb2# ipadm create-ip outside0
ilb2# ipadm create-ip inside1
ilb2# ipadm create-addr -T static -a 10.0.1.20/24 outside0/v4
ilb2# ipadm create-addr -T static -a 10.0.10.20/24 inside1/v4
ilb2# dladm create-vnic -m vrrp -V 2 -A inet -l inside1 vnic2
ilb2# dladm create-vnic -m vrrp -V 1 -A inet -l outside0 vnic1
ilb2# ipadm create-ip vnic1
ilb2# ipadm create-addr -T static -d -a 10.0.1.100/24 vnic1/lb1
ilb2# vrrpadm create-router -V 1 -A inet -l outside0 -p 100 vrrp1
ilb2# ipadm create-ip vnic2
ilb2# ipadm create-addr -T static -d -a 10.0.10.100/24 vnic2/lb1
ilb2# vrrpadm create-router -V 2 -A inet -l inside1 -p 100 vrrp2
```

Configuring ILB on the first loadbalancer

```
ilb1# routeadm -u -e ipv4-forwarding
ilb1# svcadm enable ilb
ilb1# ilbadm create-servergroup -s server=10.0.10.200,10.0.10.210
servergroup1
ilb1# ilbadm create-rule -ep -i vip=10.0.1.100,port=80,protocol=tcp -m
lbalg=roundrobin,type=HALF-NAT,pmask=32 -o servergroup=servergroup1 rule1
```

Configuring ILB on the second loadbalancer

```
ilb2# routeadm -u -e ipv4-forwarding
ilb2# svcadm enable ilb
ilb2# ilbadm create-servergroup -s server=10.0.10.200,10.0.10.210
servergroup1
ilb2# ilbadm create-rule -ep -i vip=10.0.1.100,port=80,protocol=tcp -m
lbalg=roundrobin,type=HALF-NAT,pmask=32 -o servergroup=servergroup1 rule1
```

Compliance

List all compliance benchmarks available on the system

```
# compliance list -b -v
```

List all compliance benchmarks available on the system and their profiles

```
# compliance list -b -p -v
```

Run a compliance assessment with the PCI-DSS benchmark

```
# compliance  assess -b pci-dss
```

Run a compliance assessment with the "Oracle Solaris Security Policy" benchmark in the "Recommended" profile

```
# compliance  assess -b solaris -p Recommended
```

Show all assessment results available on the system
`# compliance list -a`
Create a compliance report from an assessment
`# compliance report -a pci-dss.Solaris_PCI-DSS.2015-04-03,11:01`

Security

Per-file authorized edit of administrative files

<pre>As root user:
# profiles -p "httpd.conf configure" 	
profiles: syslog Configure> set auths=solaris.admin.edit/etc/apache2/2.2/
httpd.conf
profiles: syslog Configure> set desc="Edit http configuration"
profiles: syslog Configure> exit
# usermod -P +"httpd.conf configure" <username> 	
As normal user {username}:
$ pfedit /etc/httpd.conf</pre>

Enabling logging of changes via pfedit in the audit log

<pre># profiles -p "httpd.conf configure" 	
profiles:httpd configure> add always_audit=as
profiles:httpd configure> exit</pre>

Viewing the audit trail of the pfedit invocations
`# auditreduce -c as	praudit`
Check in which packages a given CVE-ID has been fixed
`# pkg search :CVE-2015-0397:`
Check what CVE-ID has been fixed in a Critical Patch Update (2015.4 in this example)
`# pkg search -r info.cve:	grep "2015.4"|tr -s " "	cut -d " " -f 3`
Check if a fix for a given CVE-ID has been installed
`# pkg search -l CVE-2015-0397`
How make a port above 1023 a privileged port?
`# ipadm set-prop -p extra_priv_ports+=10025 tcp`

How to lock down a service with Oracle Solaris Extended Policies?

Lets assume that you have a service listening to port 10025, you just made this port a privileged one to prevent a normal user from starting a fake service on 10025. The FRMI of the service is `svc:/application/crcaserv`. It's started via `/lib/svc/method/creditcardservice`. You know that it just writes in `/var/CrCaServ/data` and `/var/CrCaServ/tmp`. It runs as user ccserv and group ccserv.

```
# ipadm set-prop -p extra_priv_ports+=10025 tcp
# profiles -p "CrCaServ Profile"
CrCaServ Profile> set desc="Jailing in creditcardservice"
CrCaServ Profile> add cmd=/lib/svc/method/creditcardservice
CrCaServ Profile:creditcardservice> set privs=basic
CrCaServ Profile:creditcardservice> add privs={net_privaddr}:10025/tcp
CrCaServ Profile:creditcardservice> add privs={file_write}:/var/CrCaServ/
data/*
CrCaServ Profile:creditcardservice> add privs={file_write}:/var/CrCaServy/
tmp/*
CrCaServ Profile:creditcardservice> end
CrCaServ Profile> set uid=ccserv
CrCaServ Profile> set gid=mysql
# svccfg -s svc:/application/crcaserv:default
svc:/application/crcaserv:default> setprop method_context/
profile="CrCaServ Profile"
svc:/application/crcaserv:default> setprop method_context/use_profile=true
svc:/application/crcaserv:default> refresh
svc:/application/crcaserv:default> exit
```

How to enable packet filtering?

```
# svcadm enable network/ipfilter
```

How to configure the IP filter?

```
# svccfg -s ipfilter:default setprop firewall_config_default/policy =
astring: "custom"
# svccfg -s ipfilter:default setprop firewall_config_default/custom_
policy_file = astring: "/etc/ipf/c0t0d0s0.ipf.conf"
# cat < EOT >> /etc/ipf/c0t0d0s0.ipf.conf
block in log all head 100
block out log all head 101
pass in quick on lo0
pass out quick on lo0
pass in quick on net0 proto tcp from any to 192.168.1.202 port = 22 keep
state group 100
pass in quick on net0 proto tcp from any to 192.168.1.202 port = 80 keep
state group 100
pass out quick proto tcp all flags S/SA keep state group 101
pass out quick proto udp all keep state group 101
pass out quick proto icmp all keep state group 101
EOT
# svcadm refresh ipfilter
```

How to disable packet filtering?

```
# svcadm disable network/ipfilter
```

How to enable IPsec?

This example assumes that server1 is 192.168.1.200 and server2 is 192.168.1.202. We will use IKEv2 in the shared-secret mode.

```
On server1 configure:
server1# cat << EOT > /etc/inet/ike/ikev2.config
ikesa_lifetime_secs 3600
ikesa_xform { encr_alg aes(256..256) auth_alg sha384 dh_group 20 }
ikesa_xform { encr_alg aes(128..128) auth_alg sha256 dh_group 19 }
{ label "server1-server2"
  auth_method preshared
  local_addr  192.168.1.200
  remote_addr 192.168.1.202
}
EOT
server1# /usr/lib/inet/in.ikev2d -c # to check your file is correct
server1# cat << EOT > /etc/inet/ike/ikev2.preshared
{ label "server1-server2"
   key "an obviously rather weak password. Choose wiser"
}
EOT
server1# svcadm enable ipsec/ike:ikev2
server1# /usr/sbin/ipsecconf -c /etc/inet/ipsecinit.conf
server1# svcadm refresh ipsec/policy:default
On server2 configure:
server2# echo "{laddr server2 raddr server1} ipsec {encr_algs aes encr_
auth_algs sha512 sa shared}" > /etc/inet/ipsecinit.conf
server2# cat << EOT > /etc/inet/ike/ikev2.config
ikesa_lifetime_secs 3600
ikesa_xform { encr_alg aes(256..256) auth_alg sha384 dh_group 20 }
ikesa_xform { encr_alg aes(128..128) auth_alg sha256 dh_group 19 }
{ label "server2-server1"
  auth_method preshared
  local_addr  192.168.1.202
  remote_addr 192.168.1.200
}
EOT
server2# /usr/lib/inet/in.ikev2d -c
server2# cat << EOT > /etc/inet/ike/ikev2.preshared
{ label "server2-server1"
   key "an obviously rather weak password. Choose wiser"
}
EOT
server2# svcadm enable ipsec/ike:ikev2
server2# /usr/sbin/ipsecconf -c /etc/inet/ipsecinit.conf
server2# svcadm refresh ipsec/policy:default
```

Did You Know?

Just because a binary is setuid root in Solaris 11, it doesn't mean that it is run as root. Solaris 11 has a feature called Forced Privileges. Most of the setuid root binaries of Solaris just add the nescessary privileges when executed to allow the proper run of the application without switching to user id root at all. For information, read https://blogs.oracle.com/darren/entry/when_setuid_root_no_longer.

Tasks and Projects

Workloads seldom consist of a single process; thus a convenient way to label all processes of workloads is really useful. With such a label, you could address all processes of workloads in one step instead of repeating this step for each process. Tasks and projects are such facilities to label workloads. The predominant uses of task and projects are accounting and (probably more important) a way to group processes for resource control.

Facility	Description
`task`	Collects a group of processes into a set of of processes, to give you an entity that you can manage or monitor as a whole. A new task is started, when you ■ Login ■ cron ■ newtask ■ setproject ■ su
`project`	Projects are network-wide identifiers of workloads that are assigned by administrators. A user and group can be part of one or more projects. A user can start tasks and thus processes in any project he or she is a member.

Show all projects on your system
`# projects -l`
Create a project with the name "`testproj`" and the project id `4711` and assign the user `jmoekamp` to it
`# projadd -U jmoekamp -p 4711 testproj`
Create a project `user.oracle` that is the default project for the user `oracle`
`# projadd user.oracle`

Delete a project

```
# projdel testproj
```

Check the project you are currently running in

```
# id -p
```

Start a task in a different project

```
# newtask -p testproj
```

Assign process 5431 to a different project

```
# newtask -p testproj -c 5431
```

What are the default projects of a user

The default project of a user is determined and assigned in the following order. First fullfilled condition exits the mechanism.

- The user has a project attribute in /etc/user_attr. The value of this attribute is used as the default project
- If there is a project with the name user.{username} it's the default project of the user
- If theres is a project with the name group.{groupname} it's the default project of the user
- If there is a project default, it's simply used as the default project

Assign a project to a user (as in the first condition above)

```
# usermod -K project=testproj jmoekamp
```

Check the task id and the project of a running process

```
# ps -ef -o pid,user,zone,project,taskid,args
```

Processors, Processor Sets, and Pools

Show processors in the system

```
# psrinfo -v
```

Free processors from interrupt processing

```
# psradm -i 1-7
```

Put processors offline

```
# psradm -f 1-7
```

Put processors online again and reactivate interrupt processing

```
# psradm -n 1-7
```

Create two processor pools and assign two zones to them

```
# cat << EOT >> pools.configfile
create pool testzone1pool
create pset testzone1pset (uint pset.min = 2 ; uint pset.max = 2 )
associate pool testzone1pool (pset testzone1pset)
transfer to pset testzone1pset ( cpu 4 ; cpu 5 )
create pool testzone2pool
create pset testzone2pset (uint pset.min = 2 ; uint pset.max = 2 )
associate pool testzone2pool (pset testzone2pset)
transfer to pset testzone2pset (  cpu 6 ; cpu 7)
EOT
# poolcfg -d -f pools.configfile
# zonecfg -z testzone1
zonecfg:testzone1> set pool=testzone1pool
# zonecfg -z testzone2
zonecfg:testzone2> set pool=testzone2pool
```

Scheduling

List the currently configured scheduling classes

```
# dispadmin -l
```

Check which scheduling classes are in use by currently running processes

```
# ps -ef -o pid,class,pri,args
```

Move a process into the realtime scheduling class

```
# priocntl -c RT -s 1349
```

Move a process into the scheduling class FX with a priority of 10 and a user priority limit of 20

```
# priocntl -c FX -m 10 -p 20 -s 1349
```

Resource Management

Using the Fair Share Scheduler without processes

In this example we want to ensure that one process is getting 75% of the compute power and another one is getting 25% in case CPU resources are a contended resource. The FSS scheduler is based on the concept of shares: Let's assume I cut the total compute power to 200 shares, we have to assign 150 shares to the first process and 50 to the second.

```
# dispadmin -d FSS
# reboot
# projmod -K "project.cpu-shares=(privileged,150,none)" importantproject
# projmod -K "project.cpu-shares=(privileged,50,none)" unimportantproject
# newtask -p importantproject /opt/bomb/cpuhog1.pl &
# newtask -p unimportantproject /opt/bomb/cpuhog1.pl &
```

How to create two zones using FSS to limit CPU consumption in case of resource contention?

```
zonecfg:tz1> create
create: Using system default template 'SYSdefault'
zonecfg:tz1> set autoboot=true
zonecfg:tz1> set cpu-shares=150
zonecfg:tz1> verify
zonecfg:tz1> commit
zonecfg:tz1> exit
root@aramaki:~# zonecfg -z tz2
Use 'create' to begin configuring a new zone.
zonecfg:tz2> create
create: Using system default template 'SYSdefault'
zonecfg:tz2> set autoboot=true
zonecfg:tz2> set cpu-shares=50
zonecfg:tz2> verify
zonecfg:tz2> commit
zonecfg:tz2> exit
```

Setting a number of resource controls for the project user.oracle

```
# projmod -sK "project.max-shm-memory=(privileged,64G,deny)" user.oracle
# projmod -sK "process.max-sem-nsems=(priv,4096,deny)" user.oracle
# projmod -sK "project.max-shm-ids=(priv,1024,deny)" user.oracle
# projmod -sK "project.max-sem-ids=(priv,1024,deny)" user.oracle
```

Allow 10 processes per task in project class2005

```
# projmod -K "task.max-lwps=(privileged,10,deny)" class2005
```

What are the available resource controls?

```
# man resource_controls
```

Assign the processes of a SMF service to a project

```
# svccfg -s ssh setprop start/project = astring: testproj
```

Observability

How to install top on a Solaris 11.2 system?

```
# pkg install diagnostics/top
```

What should you use instead of top?

```
# prstat -mL
```

| **What is the content of the environment variables of a process?** |
| `# pargs -e {pid}` |
| **Which arguments were used to start a process?** |
| `# pargs {pid}` |
| **Print the command that started a process ready to paste into a shell** |
| `# pargs -l {pid}` |
| **Get per-partition IO statistics** |
| `# iostat -mxPzn 1` |
| **Report TCP statistics** |
| `# tcpstat -T tcp -c 1` |
| **Report UDP statistics** |
| `# tcpstat -T udp -c 1` |
| **What user and process is using a port?** |
| `# netstat -aun` |

Unified Archives

| **Creating an Unified Archive** |
| `# archiveadm create /archivepool/aramaki.uar` |
| **Creating an Unified Archive for recovery purposes** |
| `# archiveadm create -r /archivepool/aramaki.uar` |
| **Creating an Unified Archive from a single zone of the source system** |
| `# archiveadm create -z togusa /archivepool/togusa.uar` |
| **Looking what's inside an Unified Archive** |
| `# archiveadm info /archivepool/aramaki.uar` |
| **Installing a single zone from a Unified Archive** |
| `# zonecfg -z ishikawa create -a /archivepool/aramaki.uar -z batou`
`# zoneadm -z ishikawa install -a /archivepool/aramaki.uar -z batou` |

How to use an Unified Archive in a AI manifest

Using the following AI manifest fragment,   `/root/uar_ai.manifest`

```
<!DOCTYPE auto_install SYSTEM "file:///usr/share/install/ai.dtd.1">
<auto_install>
  <ai_instance name="archive0">
    <target name="desired">
      <logical>
        <zpool name="rpool" is_root="true">
        </zpool>
      </logical>
    </target>
    <software type="ARCHIVE">
      <source>
        <file uri="http://example-ai.example.com/recovery.uar">
        </file>
      </source>
      <software_data action="install">
        <name>*</name>
      </software_data>
    </software>
  </ai_instance>
</auto_install>
```

```
# installadm create-manifest -f /root/uar_ai.manifest -m uar_manifest -n
service_092910
```

Service Management Facility

The Oracle Solaris SMF is responsible for managing system and application services, replacing the legacy init scripting start-up mechanism common to other UNIX operating systems. SMF helps improves the availability of a system by ensuring that essential services run continuously even in the event of any software or hardware failures with an automatic restart capability. SMF is a part of the wider predictive self-healing capability in Oracle Solaris. Another crucial component of this is the Fault Management Architecture (FMA), responsible for reporting and isolating failed hardware components.

Understanding the SMF Fault Managed Resource Indicator

Each SMF-managed service instance is unique described by a Fault Managed Resource Indicator (FMRI), that an administrator can use to enable or disable the service, find out information about or modify configuration properties related to that service. For example, the file system automounter service described by `svc:/system/filesystem/autofs:default`

FMRI segment	Description
`svc:/`	FMRI scheme
`system/filesystem`	Service category
`Autofs`	Service name
`default`	Service instance

Many SMF commands allow FMRI abbreviations by specifying the instance name, or any of the trailing portion of the service name, assuming it is unique on the system. For example, administrators could also refer to the above service as `filesystem/autofs:default`, `autofs:default` and `autofs`. We will deliberately use multiple abbreviations in this cheat sheet.

Enabling, Disabling, and Restarting Services

Enable service `svc:/network/smtp:sendmail`
`# svcadm enable smtp:sendmail`
Disable service `svc:/network/telnet:default`
`# svcadm disable telnet`
Restart service `svc:/network/httpd:apache22`
`# svcadm apache22 restart`

Listing Information About Services

Show all enabled services (including temporarily disabled services)
`# svcs`
Show all enabled and disabled services
`# svcs -a`

List detailed information about `svc:/system/zones:default`	
`# svcs -l zones:default`	
List processes associated with `svc:/network/netcfg:default`	
`# svcs -p network/netcfg`	
Show why services that are enabled but are not running (or preventing other services from running)	
`# svcs -xv`	
Display all services which depend on the `svc:/network/ssh:default` **service**	
`# svcs -D network/ssh`	
List all services `svc:/network/ssh:default` **depends on**	
`# svcs -d network/ssh`	
Show the location of the SMF logfile of `network/ssh`	
`# svcs -L network/ssh`	
Show the content of the SMF logfile of `network/ssh`	
`# svcs -Lv network/ssh`	

Configuration Layers in the SMF Repository

Service configuration is defined in a number of layers within the SMF configuration repository that helps preserve any local administrative customizations during system upgrade, particularly when the underlying vendor provided default configuration changes. A service property could have different values at different layers of the repository. A simple priority mechanism is used to determine which value is used by the service.

Configuration Layer	Description
`manifest`	Values provided as part of SMF manifests located in `/lib/svc/manifest/`
`system-profile`	Values provided as part of SMF profiles located in `/etc/svc/profile/` `generic.xml`
`site-profile`	Values provided as part of SMF profile located in `/etc/svc/profile/` `site/`
`admin`	Values provided by interactive use of SMF commands or libraries

Listing Service Property Configuration

Service configuration can be listed using two different commands, svcprop and svccfg, and can be used interchangeably.

List all properties (including inherited properties) of the service instance `svc:/network/ssh:default`
`# svcprop ssh:default`
List properties specific to the service instance `svc:/network/ssh:default`
`# svcprop -c ssh:default`
List `firewall_context/ipf_method` **property of the service instance**
`# svcprop -p firewall_context/ipf_method ssh:default`
List all properties within the `firewall_context` **property group of the service instance** `svc:/network/ssh:default`
`# svcprop -p firewall_context svc:/network/ssh:default`
Interactively display the `general/enabled` **property for the service** `svc:/network/ssh:default`

`# svccfg`
`svc:> select ssh:default`
`svc:/network/ssh:default> listprop general/enabled`
`svc:/network/ssh:default> exit`

Setting Service Property Configuration

Configure the `config/nodename` **property on the** `svc:/system/identity:node` **service instance**

`# svccfg`
`svc:> select identity:node`
`svc:/system/identity:node> setprop config/nodename = "myhost"`
`svc:/system/identity:node> refresh`
`svc:/system/identity:node> exit`

Configure the `config/nameserver` **property on the** `svc:/network/dns/client` **service with two IP addresses**

`# svccfg -s dns/client`
`svc:/network/dns/client> setprop config/nameserver = ("192.168.0.1"`
`"10.0.0.4")`
`svc:/network/dns/client> refresh`

List all configuration changes (on all layers) to `svc:/system/nameservice/switch:default`	
`# svccfg -s switch:default listcust -L`	
Delete an administrative customization to the `config/nameserver` **property in the** `svc:/network/dns/client` **service**	

`# svccfg -s dns/client`
`svc:/network/dns/client> delcust config/nameserver`
`svc:/network/dns/client> refresh`	

Delete the `config/nameserver` **property from the** `svc:/network/dns/client` **service (and thus masking it)**	
`# svccfg -s dns/client` `# svc:/network/dns/client> delprop config/nameserver`	
Extract an SMF system profile in order to apply configuration to other systems	
`# svccfg extract -a > system-profile.xml`	
Apply an SMF system profile to a system	
`# cp system-profile.xml /etc/svc/profile/site` `# svcadm restart manifest-import`	

Notifications

Configure email notifications for all services that drop from online to maintenance state
`# svccfg setnotify -g from-online,to-maintenance mailto:junior`
Show all service state notifications, that are configured on a system
`# svcs -n`

Service Models

FRMI	Legacy file
`contract`	The processes are monitored by the contract file system. As soon as a certain contract event is reported, the SMF restarts the service.
`daemon`	Synonym for contract
`child`	As soon as the method script terminates, it's restarted by SMF.
`wait`	Synonym for child
`transient`	The method script is executed once. After this it's not longer monitored by SMF. Optimal for tuning scripts.

Using svcbundle

Creating and installing a service for a transient service

```
# svcbundle -i -s service-name=site/networktuning \
-s start-method=/lib/svc/method/networktuning
```

Creating and installing a manifest for a daemon service

```
# svcbundle -i -s service-name=site/ccprocessingdaemon \
-s start-method=/lib/svc/method/ccprocessingdaemon \
-s model=daemon
```

Using svcbundle to Create an SMF System Profile

```
# svcbundle -o nameserver-config.xml -s service \
 -name=network/dns/client -s bundle-type=profile \
 -s service-property="config:nameserver:net_address:192.168.0.1"
```

Using an SMF manifest created by `svcbundle`

```
# cp ccproccessingdaemon.xml /etc/svc/profile/site
# svcadm restart manifest-import
```

Using the SMF System Profile

```
# cp nameserver-config.xml /etc/svc/profile/site
# svcadm restart manifest-import
```

Converting a rc-script running in run level 2 into an SMF script

```
# svcbundle -s service-name=narf -s rc-script=/etc/init.d/narf:2
```

SMF Stencils

Basic configuration for an SMF stencil

```
# svccfg -s /network/http:apache22
svc:/network/http:apache22> addpg virtualhosts_stencil configfile
svc:/network/http:apache22> setprop virtualhosts_stencil/path = astring:
"/etc/apache2/2.2/conf.d/vhost_smf.conf"
svc:/network/http:apache22> setprop virtualhosts_stencil/stencil = astring:
"vhost_smf.conf"
svc:/network/http:apache22> setprop virtualhosts_stencil/mode = astring:
"0444"
svc:/network/http:apache22> setprop virtualhosts_stencil/user = astring:
"root"
svc:/network/http:apache22> setprop virtualhosts_stencil/group = astring:
"sys"
svc:/network/http:apache22> refresh
```

Basic configuration for an SMF stencil with static content

```
# cat << EOT > /lib/svc/stencils/vhost_smf.conf
> # Automatically generated ... do not edit
> EOT
# svcadm refresh svc:/network/http:apache22
```

SMF stencil with variables

```
# svccfg -s svc:/network/http:apache22 \
addpg vhost_config application
# svccfg -s svc:/network/http:apache22 \
setprop vhost_config/namevirtualhost = astring: "*:80"
# cat << EOT > /lib/svc/stencils/vhost_smf.conf
# Do not edit
NameVirtualHost $%{vhost_config/namevirtualhost}
# Do not edit
EOT
# svcadm refresh svc:/network/http:apache22
```

SMF stencils with repeating structures

```
root@master:~# cat << EOT > /lib/svc/stencils/vhost_smf.conf
# Do not edit
NameVirtualHost $%{vhost_config/namevirtualhost}

$%/vhosts_([0-9]*)/ {
<VirtualHost $%{vhost_config/namevirtualhost}>
ServerName $%{vhosts_$%1/servername}
ServerAlias $%{vhosts_$%1/serveralias}
DocumentRoot $%{vhosts_$%1/documentroot}
</VirtualHost>
}
# Do not edit
EOT
# svccfg -s apache22 addpg vhosts_1 application
# svccfg -s apache22 \
setprop vhosts_1/serveralias = astring: 'c0t0d0s0.org'
# svccfg -s apache22 \
setprop vhosts_1/servername = astring: 'www.c0t0d0s0.org'
# svccfg -s apache22 \
 setprop vhosts_1/documentroot = astring: '/var/www/c0t0d0s0.org'
# svccfg -s apache22 addpg vhosts_2 application
# svccfg -s apache22 \
setprop vhosts_2/serveralias = astring: 'moellenkamp.org'
# svccfg -s apache22 \
setprop vhosts_2/servername = astring: 'www.moellenkamp.org'
# svccfg -s apache22 \
setprop vhosts_2/documentroot = astring: '/var/www/moellenkamp.org'
# svcadm refresh svc:/network/http:apache22
```

Installation and Deployment

Automated Installer (AI) is the new network-based multi-client provisioning system in Oracle Solaris 11. AI provides hands-free installation of both SPARC and x86 systems by using an installation service that installs systems by leveraging software package repositories on the network.

Automated Installation

Creating an AI zone on an existing server specifying an x86 based DHCP client starting at address `192.168.3.100` **with a total count of 20 addresses**

```
global# zonecfg -z instserv
zonecfg:instserv> create
zonecfg:instserv> set autoboot=true
zonecfg:instserv> select anet linkname=net0
zonecfg:instserv:anet> set lower-link=net0
zonecfg:instserv:anet> end
zonecfg:instserv> add dataset
zonecfg:instserv:dataset> name=rpool/ai/install
zonecfg:instserv:dataset> set name=rpool/export/install
zonecfg:instserv:dataset> set alias=install
zonecfg:instserv:dataset> end
zonecfg:instserv> verify
zonecfg:instserv> commit
zonecfg:instserv> quit
global# zoneadm -z installserver install
global# zoneadm -z installserver boot

Log in to the newly created zone:
instserv# ipadm create-ip -a 192.168.3.200 net0/v4
instserv# pkg install install/installadm
instserv# mkdir /install/ai
instserv# installadm create-service -n s11-i386 -d /install/ai
instserv# installadm set-server -i 192.168.3.100 -c 20 -m
```

List all enabled services

```
# installadm list
```

List any installation manifests associated with the install services

```
# installadm list -m
```

List any installation manifests associated with the install services

```
# installadm export -n s11-i386 -m orig_default -o  manifest.xml
```

Import a manifest to be associated with the s11x86 service
`# installadm update-manifest -n s11-i386 -m orig_default -f ./manifest.xml`
Apply a criteria that all clients must have 4096 MB memory or greater to the manifest `manimaxi` **of** `s11x86` **service**
`# installadm create-manifest -n s11-i386 -f ./bigmanifest.xml -m manimaxi -c mem="4096-unbounded"`
AI integration with ISC DHCP server configured via
`/etc/inet/dhcpd4.conf`
Zones can be installed thru the AI manifest, when system is installed (method 1)
`<configuration type="zone" name="zone1" source="http://xyz/zone1/config.txt" />`
Zones can be installed thru the AI manifest, when system is installed (method 2)
`<configuration type="zone" name="zone1" source="file:///net/server/zone2/config.txt" />`
Specify an AI manifest for the Zone installation, to apply to either `zone1` **or** `zone2`
`# installadm create-manifest -n s11 -f /tmp/zmanifest.xml -c zonename="zone1 zone2"`
Define a system configuration profile for zone1
`# installadm create-profile -n s11 -f /tmp/zprofile1.xml -c zonename="zone1"`
Install a Zone after system has been built, while leveraging AI manifest and profile
`# zoneadm -z zone2 install -m /tmp/my_zone_AI_manifest -c /tmp/my_zone_SC_profile`

Installation Troubleshooting

For Open Boot Prom (OBP) on SPARC via install_debug boot argument
`boot net:dhcp - install install_debug`
For x86 via GRUB, to kernel line boot entry add the following
`install_debug=enable`
Default root password on AI clients during installation is
`solaris`

Installation log file during installation
`/system/volatile/install_log`
AI client manifest downloaded from the AI server during installation
`/system/volatile/ai.xml`
AI client derived manifest (if a derived manifest script is used)
`/system/volatile/manifest.xml`
System configuration profiles downloaded from the AI server during installation
`/system/volatile/profile/*`
List of AI services located
`/system/volatile/service_list`
AI client SMF service log for manifest/profile locator, during installation
`/var/svc/log/application-manifest-locator:default.log`
AI client SMF service log for Automated Installer installation service
`/var/svc/log/application-auto-installer:default.log`
AI server log file for access requests from AI clients
`/var/ai/image-server/logs/access_log`
AI server log file for errors encountered from AI clients
`/var/ai/image-server/logs/error_log`
AI server SMF service log
`/var/svc/log/system-install-server:default.log`
AI server boot configuration files
`/etc/netboot`
Specify location of AI imagepath, default is `/export/auto_install/{servicename}`
`# installadm create-service -d`
Boot without starting an installation on SPARC
`ok> boot net:dhcp`
Boot without starting an installation on x86
`From GRUB menu, select first entry (Text)`

System Configuration Profiles

System Configuration Profiles are used to provide system configuration information profiles as used by AI.

Interactively create a system configuration profile and save it to a file, to be subsequently used for deployments
`# sysconfig create-profile -o sc-profile.xml`
Specify a system configuration profile to use when installing a system with a specific MAC criteria
`# installadm create-profile -n s11service -f sc_profile.xml -c` `MAC=00:11:22:33:44:55`
List what system configuration profiles are associated with a service, and for which criteria (if any)
`# installadm list -n s11service -p`
List all non-default system configuration profiles associated with any of the install services
`# installadm list -p`
Validate a system configuration profile against the default x86 install service
`# installadm validate -n default-i386 -P profile.xml`
Associate a system configuration profile with the default x86 install service and give it a name `sc-profile`
`# installadm create-profile -n default-i386 -f profile.xml -p sc-profile`
Default system configuration profile and AI manifest used for zone installs are
`/usr/share/auto_install/sc_profile/enable_sci.xml /usr/share/auto_install/` `manifest/zone_default.xml`

Used with permission of Joerg Mollenkamp; with contributions from Glynn Foster, Isaac Rozenfeld, Glenn Faden, Cindy Swearingen, and Jeff Taylor.

APPENDIX
B

Oracle Solaris 11.3
Beta Release

Oracle Solaris 11.3

Oracle released a public beta version of Solaris 11.3 in July 2015. This release is targeted at system administrators, developers, and IT architects who need to evaluate the next version of Solaris for performance and scalability, for security and compliance, and for ease of management. This release emphasizes built-in security enhancements, new virtualization capabilities, easier software lifecycle management, and significant performance improvements for Oracle Database software. Solaris 11.3 extends and enhances the cloud computing features of the OS, providing an advanced, enterprise-class foundation for today's rapidly evolving IT infrastructure.

In this Appendix, we briefly review some key features of the 11.3 release. The final, "Generally Available (GA)" release of Oracle Solaris 11.3 is scheduled for later in 2015.

Obtaining Oracle Solaris 11.3 Beta

Download the Solaris 11.3 Beta release for Intel or SPARC from http://www.oracle.com/technetwork/server-storage/solaris11/downloads/index.html. Note that you must accept the *Oracle Technology Network Early Adopter Development License Agreement*. Create DVD or USB install media, or use one of the Oracle VM templates or Unified Archive files, as we described in Chapter 8. Installation procedures are the same as for Solaris 11.2. You will need to update system firmware on certain SPARC systems in order to test live migration for kernel zones. Additionally, there are instructions for downloading and configuring a local IPS repository for this release, as we described in Chapter 3.

As with Solaris 11.2, you will need a system (or VM) of 2 GB or more of DRAM, at least 6 GB of storage for the `solaris-minimal-server` package group, at least 9 GB for the `solaris-large-server` package group, and 13 GB or more if you are installing the `solaris-desktop` package group. See http://www.oracle.com/technetwork/server-storage/solaris11/documentation/solaris11-3-sys-reqs-2489267.pdf for additional details on installation requirements for non-Oracle hardware.

Major New Features of Oracle Solaris 11.3

Solaris 11.3 includes new security and compliance features that prevent new threats through anti-malware protection and enable security administrators to meet strict compliance obligations. These features are outlined below.

Security

Solaris 11.3 includes new security and compliance features that prevent new threats through anti-malware protection and enable security administrators to meet strict compliance obligations. These features are outlined below.

SPARC M7 Application Data Integrity   Oracle's new SPARC M7 processor, in addition to providing hardware acceleration for encryption, SQL, Java, and decompression, includes the Application Data Integrity (ADI) feature for detecting and preventing memory access errors such as buffer overflows which are commonly exploited by system intruders. ADI can be used during application development as well as during production activity to address potential memory corruption issues; new DTrace extensions for ADI are now included with Solaris 11.3. See http://www.oracle.com/technetwork/server-storage/softwareinsilicon/index.html for additional details on the SPARC M7's "Software in Silicon" features.

Compliance Tailoring   The Solaris 11.2 `compliance` (see Chapter 7) tool has been enhanced to support interactive customization of system security profiles. This feature helps security administrators create rule sets specific to their organizations' security policies. For example, to add a rule requiring at least one numeric digit in user passwords, create a custom compliance rule set (called a "tailoring"), like this:

```
# compliance tailor -t newtailor
tailoring: No existing tailoring: newtailor, initializing
tailoring:newtailor> set benchmark=solaris
tailoring:newtailor> set profile=Baseline
tailoring:newtailor> include rule=OSC-47501
tailoring:newtailor> export
set tailoring=newtailor
set benchmark=solaris
set profile=Baseline
# Passwords require at least one digit include OSC-47501
tailoring:newtailor> exit
```

Then any new password change will require the new rule, and the `compliance` program will check and report for adherence to that new rule in addition to those rules required by the `solaris` benchmark profile.

OpenBSD Packet Filter Firewall   Solaris 11.3 now includes an implementation of the OpenBSD Packet Filter (OPF) firewall software as an alternative to the Solaris IP Filter (IPF) firewall. OPF includes bandwidth management and packet prioritization, and is installed and configured as an SMF service:

```
# pkg install pkg:/network/firewall
# svcadm enable svc:/network/firewall:default
```

Verified Boot for Kernel Zones   Kernel zones, first introduced in Solaris 11.2, now supports Verified Boot, which checks the digital signatures of the system's firmware, boot software, and OS kernel to ensure secure startup. New `verified-boot` options to the `zonecfg` program are supported, including "ignore," "warn and continue," and "refuse to load."

Virtualization

The Solaris 11.2 release introduced a new type of zone—kernel zones— that allowed for independent kernels (see Chapter 4). The 11.3 release enhances that feature by adding support for secure live migration of kernel zones. Live migration relocates a running OS instance from a source server to a destination server of the same hardware type. VMware's VMotion is a common example of this type of feature. Solaris 11.3 enables movement of active kernel zones without processing interruption, for load-balancing or other administrative purposes.

Kernel Zone Live Migration   Kernel zone live migration is supported on both SPARC and Intel versions of Solaris 11.3, and is implemented using both encryption and compression in order to speed the transfer and to ensure security of the migrating OS image. Kernel zone live migration is simple to initiate using the familiar `zoneadm` command, for example:

```
# zoneadm -z kzone01 migrate ssh://newhost/
```

The zone on the source system will continue to run until the memory pages and OS image are fully migrated; login sessions are terminated, but network connections to the zone remain. This migration process assumes shared storage access by the zone from both the source and destination servers.

Kernel Zone Live Reconfiguration   Another virtualization enhancement in Solaris 11.3 is support for reconfiguring kernel zones' network and attached devices without rebooting the zone, ensuring uninterrupted operation. This feature also uses the familiar `zoneadm` and `zonecfg` commands, for example:

```
# zonecfg -z kzone01 "set cpu-shares=4"
# zoneadm -z kzone01 apply
```

Zones on Shared Storage over NFS   Solaris 11.3 now supports zones on shared storage (ZOSS) over a Fiber-Channel SAN, iSCSI device, or NFS-mounted device. Again, this feature is implemented using the zonecfg program, for example:

```
# zonecfg -z kzone01
zonecfg:kzone01> add device
zonecfg:kzone01:device> set storage=nfs://host01:/export/zones/kzone01
zonecfg:kzone01:device> set create-size=8g
zonecfg:kzone01:device> end
zonecfg:kzone01> exit
```

OpenStack

A new version of OpenStack has been included with Oracle Solaris 11.3, synced with the upstream OpenStack *Juno* release. This new version includes many new enhancements and bug fixes as part of the standard community release.

Additionally, new features have been added to the driver integrations that have been made to support Oracle Solaris in an OpenStack Environment as listed below:

1. Administrators can now configure their compute environments to support access to them through Horizon with VM consoles. This enhancement introduces two new SMF services, `nova-novncproxy` and `nova-consoleauth`, that can be configured to provide a VNC server connection to VMs.

2. The Elastic Virtual Switch (EVS) feature now supports several new capabilities, including Source Network Address Translation (SNAT) to provide external access to VMs through a shared gateway, flat networks to provide administrators the ability to plumb into an existing fixed network, full IPv6 support, and support for multiple uplink ports.

3. Several new OpenStack services are being added, including Ironic providing bare metal provisioning of systems, Heat providing orchestration of applications and cloud resources, and Murano providing an application catalog service through Horizon.

4. Administrators can seamlessly update from an OpenStack environment running Havana to one running Juno with the Image Packaging System (IPS) and first boot services using the Service Management Facility (SMF).

Oracle Database Acceleration

Oracle Solaris 11.2 introduced a new memory interface with Optimized Shared Memory (OSM). This provides a new way to manage shared memory, bringing together the benefits of Intimate Shared Memory (ISM) and Dynamic Intimate Shared Memory (DISM). One early consume of this was the Oracle Database 12c, allowing administrators to bring up the System Global Area (SGA) of an Oracle Database 12c instance 2× faster for a small SGA, and 6.5× faster for a large (28 TB) SGA. Oracle Database shutdown times have also improved to nearly twice as fast for a small SGA and six times faster for large SGA. Oracle Solaris 11.3 introduces a new public API to allow other consumers to take advantage of OSM.

Lifecycle and Configuration Management

Oracle Solaris 11.3 includes new features to enhance the overall lifecycle management of the platform; to ensure it's easy to manage at cloud scale. New system management features include periodic and scheduled SMF services, and remote administration APIs for managing ZFS, IPS, and other services. We highlight two of these features below.

Periodic Services with the Service Management Facility The Service Management Facility (SMF) now provides the ability to define and configure services to run on a scheduled basis, similar to the functionality already provided by the cron daemon. This allows all the benefits of cron, but also taking advantage of automatic service dependencies and a simplified lifecycle.

For example, administrators and developers can use the following fragment in their SMF service manifests to define a periodic service:

```
<periodic_method
                period='30'
                delay='15'
                jitter='5'
                exec='/usr/bin/periodic_service_method'
                timeout_seconds='0'>
            <method_context>
                <method_credential user='root' group='root' />
            </method_context>
        </periodic_method>
```

This defines the service to run every 30–35 seconds (using a jitter value of 5) with a 15-second delay after the service has transitioned to the online state.

Programmatic REST API interfaces with the Remote Administration Daemon   The Remote Administration Daemon (RAD) has been a feature of Oracle Solaris for some time, providing programmatic interfaces for administrators and developers to manage Oracle Solaris 11 subsystems, including Oracle Solaris Zones, the ZFS File System, SMF, and more using Python, Java, and C. With Oracle Solaris 11.3, we add a REST-based API, popular with a new trend in remote management.

As an example, administrators can now use the following HTTP requests to create a RAD connection session and query the list of Oracle Solaris Zones configured on a system:

```
# curl -H "Content-type: application/json" -X POST --data-binary @body.json \
localhost/api/com.oracle.solaris.rad.authentication/1.0/Session \
--unix-socket /system/volatile/rad/radsocket-http -v -c cookie.txt -b cookie.txt
```

where body.json provides the access credentials of the host:

```
{
        "username": "root",
        "password": "solaris11",
        "scheme": "pam",
        "preserve": true,
        "timeout": -1
}
```

Once the connection has been established and we store the connection token in a file called `cookie.txt`, we can then query for zones:

```
# curl -H "Content-type: application/json" -X GET \
localhost/api/com.oracle.solaris.rad.zonemgr/1.0/Zone \
--unix-socket /system/volatile/rad/radsocket-http -b cookie.txt
{
        "status": "success",
        "payload": [
                {
                        "href": "api/com.oracle.solaris.rad.zonemgr/1.2/Zone/zone1"
                },
                {
                        "href": "api/com.oracle.solaris.rad.zonemgr/1.2/Zone/zone2"
                },
                {
                        "href": "api/com.oracle.solaris.rad.zonemgr/1.2/Zone/zone3"
                }
        ]
}
```

References

What's New in Oracle Solaris 11.3,
http://docs.oracle.com/cd/E53394_01/html/E54847/index.html

Oracle Solaris 11.3 Beta Frequently Asked Questions (FAQ),
http://www.oracle.com/technetwork/server-storage/solaris11/documentation/
solaris-11-3-faqs-2489291.pdf

Oracle Solaris Optimizations for the Oracle Stack,
http://www.oracle.com/us/products/servers-storage/solaris/solaris-oracle-
stack-optimizations-1871633.pdf

Getting Started with the Remote Administration Daemon on Oracle Solaris 11,
https://community.oracle.com/docs/DOC-917361

Index

Join the Largest Tech Community in the World

 Download the latest software, tools, and developer templates

 Get exclusive access to hands-on trainings and workshops

 Grow your professional network through the Oracle ACE Program

 Publish your technical articles – and get paid to share your expertise

Join the Oracle Technology Network
Membership is free. Visit oracle.com/technetwork

@OracleOTN   facebook.com/OracleTechnologyNetwork

Hardware and Software
Engineered to Work Together

ORACLE®
ACE PROGRAM

Need help? Need consultation?
Need an informed opinion?

Stay Connected

oracle.com/technetwork/oracleace

 oracleaces

 @oracleace

 blogs.oracle.com/oracleace

You Need an Oracle ACE

Oracle partners, developers, and customers look to
Oracle ACEs and Oracle ACE Directors for focused
product expertise, systems and solutions discussion,
and informed opinions on a wide range of data center
implementations.

Their credentials are strong as Oracle product and
technology experts, community enthusiasts, and
solutions advocates.

And now is a great time to learn more about this
elite group—or nominate a worthy colleague.

For more information about the
Oracle ACE program, go to:
oracle.com/technetwork/oracleace

ORACLE®

Reach More than 700,000 Oracle Customers with Oracle Publishing Group

Connect with the Audience that Matters Most to Your Business

Oracle Magazine
The Largest IT Publication in the World
Circulation: 550,000
Audience: IT Managers, DBAs, Programmers, and Developers

Profit
Business Insight for Enterprise-Class Business Leaders to Help Them Build a Better Business Using Oracle Technology
Circulation: 100,000
Audience: Top Executives and Line of Business Managers

Java Magazine
The Essential Source on Java Technology, the Java Programming Language, and Java-Based Applications
Circulation: 125,000 and Growing Steady
Audience: Corporate and Independent Java Developers, Programmers, and Architects

For more information or to sign up for a FREE subscription:
Scan the QR code to visit Oracle Publishing online.

Beta Test Oracle Software

Get a first look at our newest products—and help perfect them. You must meet the following criteria:

✓ **Licensed Oracle customer or Oracle PartnerNetwork member**

✓ **Oracle software expert**

✓ **Early adopter of Oracle products**

Please apply at: pdpm.oracle.com/BPO/userprofile

If your interests match upcoming activities, we'll contact you. Profiles are kept on file for 12 months.